DATE DUE

DENISE LEVERTOV

Denise Levertov. (David Geier Photography, courtesy of New Directions Publishing Corporation.)

DENISE LEVERTOV

The Poetry of Engagement

Audrey T. Rodgers

Rutherford ● Madison ● Teaneck
Fairleigh Dickinson University Press
London and Toronto: Associated University Presses

Associated University Presses
440 Forsgate Drive
Cranbury, NJ 08512

Associated University Presses
25 Sicilian Avenue
London WC1A 2QH, England

Associated University Presses
P.O. Box 338, Port Credit
Mississauga, Ontario
Canada L5G 4L8

The paper used in this publication meets the requirements of the American National Standard for Permanence of Paper for Printed Library Materials Z39.48-1984.

Library of Congress Cataloging-in-Publication Data

Rodgers, Audrey T.
    Denise Levertov : the poetry of engagement / Audrey T. Rodgers.
        p.   cm.
    Includes bibliographical references and index.
    ISBN 0-8386-3494-X (alk. paper)
    1. Levertov, Denise, 1923–   —Criticism and interpretation.
I. Title.
PS3562.E8876Z86   1992
811'.54—dc20   92-53065
                                                                              CIP

For
Beverly and Bart

One of the obligations of the writer, and perhaps especially of the poet, is to say or sing *all* that he or she can, to deal with as much of the world as becomes possible to him or her in language.
—*The Poet in the World*

Contents

Foreword

John Balaban

In Book II of his *De Vulgari Eloquentia*, Dante writes that "the proper subjects for poetry are love, virtue, and war." Writing when military means for mass destruction were less genocidal, the poet-wanderer in the "dark wood" could, perhaps, more easily see the battlefield as a stage where love and virtue might be illuminated and humanity thereby defined. Whatever the causes of Dante's linking of these "proper subjects," their parity may seem odd to inhabitants of our century.

Our modern sense of war's good uses—at least in literature—started dwindling sharply with the poetry of Walt Whitman and the fiction of Stephen Crane, as these writers dramatized the particularities of the mass destruction of hundreds of thousands of men in the American Civil War. Yet, as wanton and enormous as that was, it was still the destruction of individual *soldiers* fighting for causes they seemed to appreciate. A poet like Whitman might decry their loss, but suffer it as a necessary sacrifice. With World War I—and its concomitant mustard gas, Hotchkiss rifles, long-range artillery, aerial strafing, and so on—we find in the poetry of Rupert Brooke, Robert Graves, Wilfred Owen, Siegfried Sassoon, Edmund Blunden, et al., a raging at the vast carnage of the fallen transmogrified into slaughtered livestock. With World War II and the wholesale destruction of *civilian* populations by artillery and aerial bombardments and, finally, by nuclear incineration, modern poets seemed to flee the battlefield altogether, as if the whole topic were too polluted for poetry to make sense of it, as if the modern battlefield were too obscene a setting for any revelations—at least within the confines of poetry—much less revelations about love and virtue.

By the time of the Vietnam War, poetry about warfare seemed entirely off limits, as the lyric poem in English, in America especially, generally eschewed any topic that was not personal and domestic. Poetry about public things, about politics, or the politics of war was an oxymoron. The disaffection with war poetry became so general that for many critics, maybe for *most* critics, a poem written about the war in Vietnam could only be polemic—probably sincere and right-minded, but almost certainly marred by shrill yapping from the soapbox.

By the time of the Vietnam War, the duties of the poem to "teach and delight" were performed on mostly small stages before private audiences. Even fiction writers were having a hard time, as Philip Roth put it, in "making credible much of the American reality." Thus, while exquisite lyric poetry of the self was given us by such poets as Roethke, Berryman, Williams, Plath, Sexton, Merwin, Bly, Levertov, and others, political, social, and international issues were present in poetry usually by inference.* This retreat by poets from public things is extravagantly described (along with some psychic side effects) by Saul Bellow in his *Humboldt's Gift:*

> For after all Humboldt did what poets in crass America are supposed to do. He chased ruin and death even harder than he chased women. He blew his talent and his health and reached home, the grave, in a dusty slide. He plowed himself under. Okay. So did Edgar Allan Poe, picked out of the Baltimore gutter. And Hart Crane over the side of a ship. And Jarrell falling in front of a car. And poor John Berryman jumping from a bridge. For some reason this awfulness is peculiarly appreciated by business and technological America. The country is proud of its dead poets. It takes terrific satisfaction in the poets' testimony that the USA is too tough, too big, too rugged, that American reality is overpowering.

Enter Denise Levertov and, with her, a long-standing controversy about the responsibilities of the poet. Critics had long praised her earlier lyric poems, such as her much-anthologized "The Jacob's Ladder" from the collection of the same title. What they did not notice was the other poems in that *1961* collection, the political poems that look back on the Nazi horrors. And when her later volumes directly took on contemporary events in America and Vietnam, the critics' responses were often sharply dismissive, as Professor Rodgers notes in her examination of this debate:

> The critics who chose to attack the turn in Levertov's journey from the subjects of nature, women, marriage, children, and myth to the more immediate problems of the '60's labored under a double misapprehension. First, they had completely failed to recognize the social awareness

---

*There are powerful exceptions, of course, both among the work of these poets and in the lifelong interests of a few "raw and cooked" poets like Ginsberg, Larkin, and Lowell, whose poems seldom drifted far from the "res publicam."

that was the underpinning of many of her earlier poems; and, secondly, they dismissed her poems on Vietnam and the evils perpetrated by that war as unfit subjects for poetry (from a poet with 'Orphic' gifts). Moreover, they felt her aesthetic and "polemical" objectives were antithetical, and they censured her for lowering her sights to become "preachy," emotional, and bathetic. They saw in many of the Vietnam volumes a schism between the private poet and the public dissident. She had, they agreed, sacrificed her poetic gifts on the altars of social conscience or "obligation."

As Professor Rodgers argues, there never was a separation between social and orphic consciousness in Levertov's poetry. Her first published poem was about World War II. As a child, she was sent out of London during the Blitz; as a young woman she served as a nurse in no less than five hospitals, including one in Paris just after the war. And she came from a family of political activists whose Welsh, Jewish, and Christian backgrounds merged in her in a highly tuned social and spiritual conscience that—whatever the immediate topic— searched in her poems for the whole, the human, and the healthy. Although her form is the lyric and not the narrative poem, she is Dantean in her sense that each poem is a means of discovery of a divine or spiritual order, in her sense of the poet as a wanderer in a "selva oscura."

For a poet tuned to finding the love and virtue still accessible in our twentieth-century selves, the war in Vietnam would become an inevitable topic, just as it became the singlemost threat to love and virtue. Only she and Muriel Rukeyser, of all the critically acknowledged poets of the sixties, actually went to Vietnam to see for themselves. Levertov's poems are filled with images of a real Vietnam, not a hypothetical soap-box Vietnam. In poems like "The Altars in the Streets" those poems achieve a great beauty that should be instructive still to poets who would entertain their larger worlds.

These war poems and the debate around them are ably described by Professor Rodgers, who spent a decade on a work that included interviews with Denise Levertov as well as revealing correspondence with other poets, some of which appears here for the first time. *Denise Levertov: The Poetry of Engagement* should help American critics and poets view the naïve dichotomy we have set up between the poetic and the political. Finally, it gives due credit to the accomplishment of one poet who took pains to write a poetry that could face war and its human implications, including the extinguishing of love and virtue, as well as their rising up.

Acknowledgments

I am deeply grateful to Denise Levertov for all of her support in the writing of this book: several interviews and her openness in discussing poetic theory with me. In addition, I am indebted to the fine annotated bibliography of Levertov's work by Liana Sakelliou-Schulz. To John Balaban, I owe a special thanks for his reading the manuscript and for his Foreword, which reveals his knowledge of Vietnam poetry in general and the work of Denise Levertov in particular. I thank the Liberal Arts College at Penn State for a grant to support my research. To Professor Evan Carton of the University of Texas, I am indebted for his help in my research. Lastly, I wish to thank my husband, Allan Rodgers, whose confidence in me has been the bulwark of my professional life.

DENISE LEVERTOV

Introduction: "make truth real to us"

Make truth real to us,
flame on our lips.

Lift us to seize the present,
wrench it
out of its downspin.
    —"Two Threnodies and a Psalm"

In "The Poet," Emerson noted, more incisively than most writers, the enormous resistance creative artists must summon in confronting both their critics and their inner doubts.

> Doubt not, O poet, but persist. Say "It is me and shall out." Stand there, balked and dumb, stuttering and stammering, hissed and hooted, stand and strive, until, at last, rage draw out of thee that *dream*-power which every night shows thee is thine own; a power transcending all limit and privacy, and by virtue of which man is the conductor of the whole river of electricity.[1]

The poets of the twentieth century have not escaped the censure of critics who too often feel it incumbent upon them to dictate subject, theme, style, and tone. Yet, with remarkable tensile strength, the best modern poets have pursued their poetic goals with spirit and persistence, echoing Emerson: "It is me and shall out."

Such a poet is Denise Levertov. For a very long period of her poetic career, Levertov was highly praised as a lyric poet of considerable sensitivity and talent whose poems were succinct, at times mystical, at times sensuous; whose technical gifts were impeccable; whose music was precisely scored; whose emotional range swept from ecstacy to somberness. All of her experience, it was observed, became the raw material for poetry: a woman awakening to the world of men, the act of being and staying alive, burgeoning nature, the city and its people, even "illustrious ancestors." But too many critics forget that Denise Levertov's social consciousness was hinted in her poetry

17

from the very beginning. We have only to recall that her first published poem "Listening to Distant Guns," in *Poetry Quarterly* in 1940, revealed Levertov's sensitivity to the encroachment of war even in remote Buckinghamshire.

Among her many concerns as a poet, Denise Levertov mirrored her "experience" with war and violence, but only upon her emergence as a political dissident in the 1960s did a handful of critics initiate their "undeclared war." Alas, the Orphic poet had metamorphosed into the inartistic polemicist! Although never "balked or dumb, stuttering or stammering," Levertov has nonetheless stood and strived.

This study, in one respect, is an account of one poet's attempt to follow Emerson's declaration of independence: "We will walk on our own feet; we will work with our own hands; we will speak our own minds."[2] History tells us that art need never justify itself. It will endure on its own merits or will pass into the dust of obscurity.

In the case of Denise Levertov's poetry of conscience, the controversy necessitates a defense of the assumption that aesthetics and politics are not incompatible. This can be accomplished *only* by assessing the aesthetic quality of her "poems of engagement," for finally it is the poem, perfectly harmonizing theme and form, that endures.

Denise Levertov was born in 1923 in the hiatus between two world wars: the first, the "war to end all wars"; the second, a holocaust whose fires burned round the globe leaving death and devastation and radioactivity that would claim countless lives over the succeeding decades. Ten million people died in the first "great war," and death figures including civilian populations in World War II hover at fifty-five million. For the writers born in the twentieth century, there were greater threats to come.

The young Denise Levertov wakened to her world aware of the devastation and tragedy wrought by war and violence. Perhaps the fact of war led to her decision to make a career in nursing before the end of hostilities, although as Levertov points out, her nursing was civilian because, she says, ". . . I don't recall bombing casualties, which seems strange but I guess I just happened to be on medical wards."[3] But, as a young woman, she did know the bomb shelters and walked through the rubble of London. She worked at St. Luke's Hospital in London as well as five other hospitals, including one in Paris after the cessation of the war. These experiences increased her sensitivity to human pain and suffering.

Later, in Switzerland, she would meet her future husband, Mitchell Goodman, who brought her to the United States where her Welsh-Jewish-Christian heritage would become fused with her new American identity. She would become not only a "poet in the world" but a "citizen of the world," alert and alive to its triumphs as well as what she perceived to be its "failings." She came to the United States in 1948, an event, as she told me, that was the single most important one of her literary journey. In America, she said, she found much to admire and deplore.[4] Most significantly, she found her place as a poet.

It is Denise Levertov's social consciousness with which I am largely concerned—her activist stance against war, violence, inhumanity, the nuclear threat, and the environmental crisis, as it became an integral part of her poetry—although it is impossible to gloss over that other side of Levertov: her celebration of life "amidst ruins," her witty saga of Sylvia in "Pig Dreams," her inner conflict with religious faith that ebbed and flowed as her despair and hope for man to save himself alternated in her mind and heart. Emerson's words in "The Poet" seem especially fitted to Levertov's lifelong "pilgrimage":

> The poet has a new thought; he has a whole experience to unfold; he will tell us *how* it was *with him* (emphasis mine), and all men will be richer in his fortune. For the experience of each new age requires a confession, and the world seems always waiting for its poet.[5]

"How it was with [her]" takes us a long way toward an understanding of Denise Levertov's poetry. William Carlos Williams remarked in 1960 that he felt closer to Denise Levertov than to any other modern poet.[6] He joined with Flossie Williams in speculating that Levertov would be America's poet of the future. Now, more than thirty years later, I feel the time has come to explode some myths, reveal the trajectory of Levertov's poetic career from the sixties to the present, assess her much-criticized war and protest poetry, and judge Williams's gift for prophecy.

The assumption of many poets and fiction writers of the twentieth century was that art and politics were not incompatible, although much controversy among critics focuses on this very matter. Many literary critics feel that politics in poetry leads to polemics, preaching, and a loss of aesthetic concern, the intrinsic justification for poetry. Thus, the question of aesthetics and polemics has assailed many writers in the past, but most notably in the twentieth century when poets cast aside the posture of distancing themselves from the realities of the modern world and transmuted their experiences of war, violence, holocaust, and nuclear annihilation into literature.

We stand breathless before Picasso's *Guernica*, experience its greatness as a *work of art*, yet conscious for a moment that horror, terror,

tragedy, and pity have been encapsuled for all time. Future generations may not know of the impulse that stirred the artist's creative
imagination: the brutal destruction of Guernica, Spain, in 1937 by
the Germans during the Spanish Civil War. The event (such that
inspired Manet to create the "Execution of Maximillian"), even the
artist, may mingle in the dust of history; but the masterpiece remains,
and we acknowledge its greatness because art transcends the event.
But literature, as we know, recreates the event through the perspective of the writer, and often *both* the event and the poem, novel, or
play remain with us. In an essay praising the power of John Balaban's
war poems, critic Jeffrey Walsh writes about "Along the Mekong":
"The objective cast of the analysis here strengthens the poem's air
of factual veracity. The war is encapsulated as an ecological disaster:
drinking water is polluted, the food chain poisoned, the Vietnamese
river contaminated by American science."[7]

In the case of Denise Levertov, she has been censured on the basis
that art and politics don't mix—that this basic "incompatibility" flaws
the poetry of the sixties and the seventies. While it would seem that
the *choice of subject* needs no defense, some of the criticism levelled
against her is that she sacrificed her aesthetic standards for the immediacy of her political concerns. This criticism must be addressed since
it raises a larger issue: What is the role of the artist as a political
dissident? One of my tasks here is to examine Levertov's poetic
theory and the "poems of engagement" to determine whether, in
fact, her critics' judgments were well taken.

At the outset, I will try to set the stage for a whole century of
artists who responded to the crises of their contemporary world. The
debate on the "conflict" between art and dissent is ongoing, though
it has been a subject for writers and critics for hundreds of years. It
is essential to remind ourselves that many of America's most distinguished artists, musicians, novelists, and poets of the twentieth century have committed their talents to the creation of an art of dissent.
The cataclysmic events of this century have mandated that attention
be paid to a world at times repellent in its inhumanity to man, lacking
in hope, too "quick to arm,"[8] as Pound noted, unresponsive to the
burden it bears for future generations.

Thus, in order to explode the notion, as some of her critics believed, that Denise Levertov was a singular "off-key" poetic voice
raised in the sixties, the record needs to be set straight. This would
include a brief view of other important Americans who spoke out—
and indeed, still speak out—against the immorality of the Vietnamese
War, the inhumanity of man to man, and the nuclear threat.

At this point, I shall tackle the problem of the poet and the poem.

The criteria by which we judge poetry must be juxtaposed to Denise Levertov's own conception of "what makes a good poem." Levertov has been generous in her prose discussions of her view of "organic poetry," and this has contributed to the conclusion that her poetry is a *continuity* that sometimes *appears* to be fragmented but in essence defines a pattern.

But it should be emphasized that Levertov's *poetry*, not her prose, is the subject of this study. Although her prose writings are strong works of *protest* and may cast light on the poet's convictions expressed in the poetry, I do not feel it incumbent upon me to either confirm or refute the positions she takes in her prose writings.

In an interview in 1982, Levertov spoke of an order, a coherence, in her poetry that in itself is a kind of faith. Her poems, she feels

> . . . are little bits of a hidden pattern that is there—the little bits don't make any particular sense any more than a fragment, you know, a very small fragment of a pattern from a piece of china or a fabric, but you've got just enough in that fragment to see that it *is* part of a pattern.[9]

It is this pattern that I shall trace, focusing upon Levertov's lifelong preoccupation with the world which "lies at hand." This would necessarily include her poetry on war, if one accepts the thesis that the artist and her art are indivisible.

At this point we must hear from her *critics:* while some critics are harsh—sincerely believing that poets should avoid writing political poetry—several responsible critics build their assessment of her "decline" on a set of assumptions about the art of poetry. Such criticism focused on Levertov's work that appeared during the sixties and early seventies. It is important to note, however, that with her most recent volumes of poetry, such as *Oblique Prayers, Breathing the Water,* and *A Door in the Hive,* the tide of criticism had shifted. Levertov's defense, largely in prose essays, of what she terms "engaged poetry" has been both spirited and carefully reasoned; and a part of this study will be devoted to her view of her art. But even Levertov needed to know that her task was risky.

Neruda's qualified observation of the demanding and dangerous, yet challenging, task of writing political poetry that is *good poetry* as well, was one she knew well!

> Political poetry should emanate from profound emotion and convictions. . . . And a political poet must be ready to take all the blame heaped on him for "betraying poetry and literature by serving a definite cause." Therefore political poetry must arm itself internally with enough sub-

stance and content and emotional and intellectual richness to defy anything of the sort. It seldom succeeds.[10]

The fact is that Levertov took up that challenge, and in her most
successful poems of "engagement" combines "substance and content
and emotional and intellectual richness," for she wrote in *Light Up
the Cave*, "The didactic has a place in poetry, but only when it is
inseparable from the intuitive . . . the poetry of political anguish is
its best both didactic and lyrical."[11]

From this point I examine *briefly* the poetic journey Levertov em-
barked upon that began with her early lyric impulses, inspired by
Keats and the whole tradition of English Romantics. Such a backward
glance may offer clues to the direction Levertov would take in the
sixties and documents the continuity of her work. Then, I follow her
into the milieu that brought her finally to her role as a "poet in the
world."

The remainder of the study concentrates upon the poetry written
after the sixties and traces Levertov's poetic journey into the seventies and eighties with special emphasis on the poems on Vietnam,
though earlier poems will be noted as a key to the direction Levertov
was moving toward from the very beginning. Of special importance,
however, is the "poetry of engagement"—a term Levertov prefers
over "protest": her stance against the Vietnam War is expressed
strongly in *Relearning the Alphabet* and *To Stay Alive*. Most crucially, it
is important to examine Levertov's activist poetry to judge where it
meets the test and where, on the basis of her critics' assessment, it
falls short. There is no question that a poet's work does not always
maintain the high standards he or she aspires toward. The study of
Levertov's poems that grew from her social conscience will focus on
both their themes and their artistic merit: where did she succeed?
and where did she cease to maintain a balance between theme and
poetic value? I avoid blanket generalizations as unproductive. Yet I
feel that a greater number of Levertov's war poems than critics have
been willing to allow are, indeed, successful, and that they will long
remain in our canon of significant modern American poetry, while
others are not as controlled and aesthetically satisfying.

Following Levertov's poetic journey into the middle seventies and
eighties, I try to show that although her concerns for peace and
human rights would never be abandoned, the road takes another
turn. The last volumes, from *Candles in Babylon* to *A Door in the Hive*,
develop a theme that is a constant *presence* in Levertov's poetry but
never so explicitly expressed before: her inner religious life. The
final volumes are both "worldly"—for Levertov never loses sight of

events and "happenings"—but they also reveal her deep faith, her spiritual values, and her belief that modern man can—with resolution—bring order to his life.

Finally, I assess Levertov's poetry as an artist "in the world." I would hope that a clearer understanding of her poetry of social consciousness and her poetry of faith will result in placing them as an integral part in the *whole* body of her work—not the aberration of a militant activist who lost hold of her "Orphic" gift—but a coherent part of the poet's view of poetry and the role of the poet in society. Denise Levertov's words that serve as touchstones for her art are pattern, order, continuity, and the organic nature of art that joins the imagination of the poet to the world. It is a recognition of such a pattern that inspired this study.

Levertov believes with Ezra Pound that poetry "must teach, or move, or delight . . ."[12] citing Neruda as combining all three. I would amend this statement to suggest that while poetry can and often does teach,* it must *always move and delight*. If not, the aesthetic value of a writer's art is diminished. Denise Levertov knows this, and it is the purpose of this study to determine how faithfully she was able to achieve this goal. But her poetic journey is not completed. There is no evidence that her "saying" and "singing" have ceased.

---

*Levertov emended this passage in *Light Up The Cave* from Ezra Pound's *ABC of Reading*. The original passage reads, "Rodolpho Agricola in an edition dating from fifteen hundred and something says one writes: ut doceat, ut moveat ut delectet, to teach, to move or to delight."

1

A Portrait of the Artist in the Twentieth Century: "as never before"

Who can utter
the poignance of all that is constantly
threatened, invaded, expended

and constantly
nevertheless
persists in beauty.
—"In California: Morning, Evening, Late January"

The year 1914 raised the curtain on a century of war. But even earlier the rumblings of chaos and upheaval were portentous and awesome. Although the world of the opening decades of the twentieth century must have *seemed* tranquil, uncomplicated, and laden with hope to the large, struggling, unreflective mass of people ("I lift my lamp beside the golden door,"[1] as Emma Lazarus had promised), the writers, artists, musicians, and thinkers—self-appointed seers of the age—had a more disquieting vision.

Yeats had warned: "Things fall apart; the centre cannot hold; / Mere anarchy is loosed upon the world."[2] In America, the spiritual crisis, the sense that modern man was a god in ruins, the vacuum bred of a discontinuity with a meaningful past, and the constant economic, social, and moral flux—all left the sensitive artist bewildered, rebellious, and continually in search of the means to express his angst. By 1922, T. S. Eliot had encapsuled the mood of the artist in *The Waste-Land*.

The brave new world ushered in by a turn-of-the-century optimism engendered by "progress," wealth, and the seemingly unlimited opportunity offered to millions of immigrants would suffer a sea-change, as the writers saw it, into something inhuman and strange. The poets would find the words to define it: arid, indifferent, godless, loveless, mechanistic—its people inert, alienated, uncommitted, anonymous, unable or unwilling to save themselves. In Williams's words there was

> No one
> to witness
> and adjust, no one to drive the car[3]

The black vision of writers held hostage by Naturalism that hovered over the western world by the first decade of the new century had not yet included the spectre of war; but the artists, poets, and thinkers were already darkly pessimistic about the future. Like Cassandra, they prophesied doom, while at the same time they searched for enduring values. It is no wonder, as M. L. Rosenthal notes, "Poetry and perhaps modern poetry especially, is saturated with political consciousness, the power of the state is so great, the problems of war and peace and of human need and human freedom so pressing, that only the utterly innocent can believe themselves unaffected by political matters."[4] Among such writers were Edwin Arlington Robinson, Edgar Lee Masters, T. S. Eliot, Ezra Pound, Theodore Dreiser, Ernest Hemingway, and other novelists. It was no coincidence that the "Harlem Renaissance" during the twenties brought forth the protest literature of such black poets as Langston Hughes, Claude McKay, Countee Cullen, and the commanding voices of black writers like James Weldon Johnson, Richard Wright, James Baldwin, and Ralph Ellison.

In another part of America, other voices were to be heard. In a letter to F. Scott Fitzgerald in 1936, John Dos Passos wrote of the "murderous forces of history."[5] As Andrew Hook has written, "For Dos Passos the duty of the writer is not to look inward, to the exploration of the individual consciousness, but *outward to society at large*, to the broader forces and movement which mould and control man's destiny. . . . *Commitment . . . the acceptance by the writer of an extra-artistic, usually political, programme of action and belief . . . lies behind his creative endeavors*"[6] (Emphasis mine).

It was inevitable that the poet, artist, philosopher, sculptor, painter, and musician—as prophets—would take up the revolutionary causes of their times and, whether coldly analytical or fiercely passionate, would transmute them into works of lasting significance. Too soon, the twentieth century provided artists with *war* as the raw material from which to shape not only protest but art. As the nineteenth century neared an end, the artist had already risen in protest to repression and tyranny.

The crucial problem posed to the creative imagination was how to maintain the highest levels of "art." How to guard against poetry or painting or music that was mere "polemic." How to strike the delicate balance between one's commitment to a cause and one's commitment to craft so that *finally* the artist would be judged *as* artist as well as activist. Often, it was difficult to maintain this integrity.

To "speak out" implies language, but music is a language as are painting and sculpture. One of the most courageous expressions of protest was *Finlandia*, written by Sibelius when the forces of Finnish nationalism were severely threatened by Russian domination at the end of the nineteenth century. This commanding work, as well as his Symphony #2, was a response to the "February Manifesto" of 1899 which curtailed freedom of speech and assembly.

In the literature at the close of the nineteenth century, Stephen Crane's *The Red Badge of Courage* was the first American novel in modern times that protested a romantic view of war. America's last great love affair with "Heroes" and "Causes"—the Civil War—was over. It left in its wake the images of the South's romantic idealism like hundreds of dead magnolia blossoms scattered across the broken landscape: courage, bravery, manliness in combat, and heroic death. This was America's *rite de passage*—never again would war be revered as an arena where wide-eyed boys grew into brave men. What they learned was that war was a holocaust: wasteful, ugly, degrading, and gratuitous to the process of maturity. What they learned was that dreams of heroism had little to do with the stark realities of war. The Civil War, apart from a few monuments to the South's "heroic" stance, tore the blinders from the eyes of an innocent America. The fragmented and ruined South bore testimony to the demands of war. The barren ground was the high price the country paid to maintain union, but no longer would Americans take a romantic view of war.

The Red Badge of Courage, therefore, was a novel that would provide a realistic model for the new century. The novel was an honest view of modern war that had an impact on young, romantic would-be "heroes." Of course, there were differences. Some wars had to be fought; as in the Civil War, the Union had to be preserved. But many questioned war as a solution for any problem, and possibly the defeat of Adolf Hitler's insane plan for the domination of the western world, spelled out with much precision in *Mein Kampf,* was the last crisis that *demanded* solution by war. Nonetheless, the idealism that war bred, from the time of the Crusades, died on the battlefields of Antietam, Gettysburg, and in the shards of burning Atlanta.

It was no surprise that with the advent of World War I, Ernest

Hemingway—long an admirer of Crane—would make modern war his own battleground against a faintly prevailing romanticism about the hero and the cause. In *The Sun Also Rises, A Farewell to Arms,* and *For Whom the Bell Tolls,* as well as countless short stories, Hemingway reveals his debt to Crane and to the new realism of war in the twentieth century. Another novel that caught the popular imagination was Elliot Paul's terse and dramatic account of political events in Spain between 1931 and 1936 and the outbreak of the Spanish Civil War: *Life and Death of a Spanish Town.* Countless other American novels were written about the "war to end all wars." Among the most well known were F. Scott Fitzgerald's *Tender Is The Night,* Dalton Trumbo's *Johnny Got His Gun,* and John Dos Passos' pacifistic novel based on his own experience in war: *Three Soldiers.*

During World War I, there were other voices raised round the world. The French writer, Henri Barbusse (1873–1935), long remaining in oblivion to American writers, wrote an early novel, almost forgotten, about World War I, *Le Feu (Under Fire,* 1917). It graphically portrays life in the trenches during World War I in France and deals with the simple but very human feelings of the "poilu"—the French foot-soldier—in the heat of battle. The "enemy," as well, had suffered a similar awakening, and both Erich Remarque's novel, *All Quiet On The Western Front*—presenting the individual as victim—and the classic Italian film (suppressed during the Mussolini years) *Tutti A Casa* [*Everyone Is Going Home*]—a moving account of the massive desertions by Italian soldiers to save their homes and families—bear witness to the revulsion against war.

The bitterness was often expressed in some of the finest American poetry to emerge in the twenties. At the end of the first part of his portrait of the artist in the modern world, "Hugh Selwyn Mauberly," Ezra Pound's invective against war reflected the country's mood.

> There died a myriad,
> And of the best, among them,
> For an old bitch gone in the teeth,
> For a botched civilization,
>
> Charm, smiling at the good mouth,
> Quick eyes gone under earth's lid,
>
> For two gross of broken statues,
> For a few thousand battered books.[7]

M. L. Rosenthal's observation seems particularly relevant to the spirit of protest literature at this time: "The political poetry that counts may at times be polemical, but the main point about it is that like other real poetry it is rooted in personal awareness."[8]

Among other artists who declared themselves against the war, Ben Shahn, Vasily Kandinsky, and Jacob Lawrence would reflect Pablo Picasso's *Guernica* in their depiction of the horrors evoked by such futile destruction and inhumanity. Thus protest did not end with World War I but continued in the work of activists against violence around the globe. Man's inhumanity toward man would become a major preoccupation of the artist from that time forward—as in the suffering of countless individuals in the Spanish Civil War and in the shooting of Federico Lorca in 1936.

It has been observed that the "Great Depression of the 1930s and the rise of fascism . . . gave rise to a literature of social concern or social protest of another kind. For many artists, the economic and political upheaval taking place in Europe and America in the years between the wars seemed to call for an art that . . . would speak to issues of social concern. . . . The artists working in the 1930's . . . wished their art to speak for the poor and oppressed, for liberty in opposition to fascism . . ."[9] Pablo Neruda expressed it this way. "Political poetry should emanate from profound emotion and convictions . . ."[10] The artists touched upon here lacked neither, nor did they lack the creative talent needed to transform those emotions and convictions in works of lasting significance.

By the advent of World War II, writers, painters, poets, and musicians were familiar with the concept of criticism and protest as an integral part of modern art. The difference lay in the conviction—reluctantly expressed—that war was the final option in ridding the world of the Hitlerian blight. The story needed to be told, but without heroic stances or romantic notions.

Among a proliferation of novels that revealed both the writers' portrayal and disenchantment with war, I mention only a few: James Jones's *From Here to Eternity;* Joseph Heller's *Catch-22;* Norman Mailer's *The Naked and the Dead;* Irwin Shaw's *The Young Lions;* Herman Wouk's *The Caine Mutiny;* and John Hersey's *Hiroshima.* When a stunned world began to understand the enormity of dropping atomic bombs on Japanese civilian populations, John Hersey's small volume found its place forever as a testament of that infamy.

The story of the annihilation of European Jewry, of civilian populations in Russia, England, Poland, Japan, and Eastern Europe was to be recorded in history and art. The recently released *Sho'ah* (Holocaust), an oral history recounted by scores of Poles, Germans, and Jewish survivors of the death camps, is a staggering reminder of that tragedy. It was felt by writers and all humanitarians that the world must never be permitted to forget. This was a spirit completely in keeping with the artist-prophet's sense of responsibility—the burden of becoming a voice of protest, the need to engage in activism, the need to "remind," and the need to awaken the sleepers. Abundant documentation can be found; such poems as Randall Jarrell's "The Death of the Ball Turret Gunner" and Robert Lowell's "The Dead in Europe" convey the spirit of such protest.

The "reports" were legion: poems, plays, novels, motion pictures, paintings, sculpture. They are our heritage in the art of Bertolt Brecht, Allen Ginsberg, Robert Bly, Galway Kinnell, Robert Graves, Siegfried Sassoon, Aleksandr Solzhenitsyn, Federico Lorca, Octavio Paz, Nadine Gordimer, Denise Levertov, and countless others. They have confronted not only war but repression, inhumanity, the exploitation of innocent populations, and the darkest threat of all—the omens of nuclear disaster.

Vietnam

The greatest American tragedy of recent times was this country's pursuit of a war that, before its close, divided her people more profoundly than any national conflict since the Civil War. While the poets, fiction writers, academics, specialists, and other intellectuals who make it their business to closely follow American involvement abroad tended to become impatient with what they perceived as apathy among the great mass of Americans, the fact is that it is necessary to understand how the Vietnam war protest evolved.

While poets like Denise Levertov, John Balaban, William Eberhart, and countless others were raising their voices against the happenings in Vietnam, the great American public—the Silent Majority, as they thought of themselves—was solidly behind America's commitment to the conflict in Vietnam. Until the war entered American living rooms on TV, the *average* American was ill-informed. Believing that America could never lose a war and unable to comprehend, while accepting, the theory of the domino effect, many Americans were stunned by the rising protests of the young. It was not clear to many Americans what Vietnam was all about—hence their increasing preoccupation with the events that occurred more than thirty years ago. To this day, Americans are first hearing about the effects of agent orange on both humans and the environment. "Waking sleepers" was a goal for those who voiced their protest against destruction and death halfway across the globe, and names like Vietnam, Cambodia, and Viet Cong fell strangely on most American ears.

As noted earlier, this country did finally awaken to the fact that America *could* lose a war, and the impatience of such poets like Levertov needed to be tempered by an understanding of the optimistic, good-news perspective of citizens who understood only "kill ratios." But slow as it was in coming, Americans did begin to understand many of the implications of its country's involvement in the war.

As a beleaguered President Nixon capitulated to the mounting pressure that had gradually—almost unconsciously—accelerated over several years, Americans rose to the reality of the issues dividing the country: intellectual, emotional, psychological, political. Some fathers and sons were pitted against each other as many refused to serve; sincere confusion arose about why we were fighting in southeast Asia and whether we could ever win such a war. Indeed, true ignorance existed of what each "side" represented, and a mounting awareness that America had made a terrible mistake heightened the emotional quality of the debate until it ended in violence at home—at Kent State, Berkeley, and numerous other universities. America was on its feet in protest, as the war entered our living rooms on the 7 o'clock news with all the starkness of "You are there!" Even today, more than twenty years after the beginning of America's excursion into the Vietnam conflict, a huge outpouring of literature is examining the many profound facets of that experience.

Americans flock to see such films as *Platoon, Full Metal Jacket, The Deer Hunter,* and, most recently, *Born on the Fourth of July.* For many the enigma increases instead of disappearing with time, and it was not until *Born on the Fourth of July* that Americans began to understand the plight of the returned veteran—alone in his alienation from society, haunted by his memories, and courageously trying to put the war behind him even as he had to confront his lingering physical and psychic wounds.

Since the mid-sixties, sensitive thinkers from every profession, every age group, every level of American society have ruminated on the complex phenomenon that was the Vietnam War. This would include statesmen, historians, journalists with firsthand knowledge, creative writers and artists, scientists, and academicians. Thus, an enormous number of books, essays, poems, novels, films—first appearing in the mid-sixties and continuing into the present—has flooded the world with often-conflicting, often-confusing, often-questioning reactions to the war. The issues themselves were multiple: as one would expect, the question of the loss of American lives; the question of American involvement; the loss of American prestige abroad. It should be made clear that there was not agreement on these matters; frequently, Americans defended U.S. involvement in the Vietnam War, and just as emphatically these same voices—while abhorring the loss of American lives—believed the sacrifice was necessary and a source of national pride.

But in the sixties the major groundswell of protest, demonstration, and activism in various forms came from two distinct voices in America, conscious of a multitude of concerns: the student community and the artistic community. While they cried out against the huge investment of men and materiel, the confusion about American objectives, and the "business-as-usual" attitude at home, the major dissenters were opposed to the inhumanity of man against man on both sides of the conflict. They inveighed against the break-up of Vietnamese villages and dispersal of native populations, the grim reports of atrocities, the defoliation of the land through the use of chemical agents, and the uncompassionate statistical reports of kill ratios, village plundering, and "battle wins" delivered in newspapers and on evening TV. While many did not exculpate the "enemy" for its share in this tragedy, the major thrust was toward a government that would listen. They sang the insurrectional songs *softly* intoned by Peter, Paul and Mary and Joan Baez, and they carried banners, marched on Washington, and forced administrators to remove Americans from Vietnam—resulting (a few mourned) in "our losing our first war."

It would be a monumental task to note the vast amount of literature that came out of the Vietnam War, but I will touch on two distinct sources; those by public figures, largely in essay form, and those that emanated from the creative imaginations of concerned artists. Most of the writing coming out of Vietnam grew, first, from purely journalistic reports during the sixties to editorials and essays and finally to extensive book-length, detailed accounts of the "story" behind the headlines. Among these were Marguerite Higgins' *Our Vietnam Nightmare* (1965), David Schoenbrun's *Vietnam: How We Got In, How to Get Out* (1968), and Mary McCarthy's "Vietnam" (1967) included in her larger work *The Seventeenth Degree: 1967–1974*. Other nonfiction works that are worthy of mention are Arthur Schlesinger Jr.'s *The Bitter Heritage* (1967); Vance Hartke's *The American Crisis in Vietnam* (1968); *Vietnam: The Unheard Voices*, edited by Don Luce and John Sommer (1969); Seymour Hersh's *My Lai 4: A Report on the Massacre and Its Aftermath* (1970); Noam Chomsky's *At War with Asia* (1970); Hannah Arendt's *Cries of a Republic* (1972); Marvin Kalb and Elie Abel's *Roots of Involvement: The U.S. in Asia* (1971); Robert J. Lifton's *America and the Asian Revolution* (1971); Frank Browning and Dorothy Forman's *The Wasted Nations* (1972); Frances Fitzgerald's *Fire in the Lake* (1972); and William R. Corson's *Conquerors of Failure* (1973).

Fitzgerald's work, which contains more than 200 bibliographical entries of works on the Vietnam War, concluded that "The Vietnam War in itself was an over-whelming atrocity," that resulted in the destruction of an entire society. I should like to cite just one passage of this exhaustive study that sums up so much of the sentiment of the works mentioned here:

> To the traditional Vietnamese, the nation consisted of a landscape, "our mountains and our rivers" and the past of the family, "our ancestors." The land and the family were the two sources of national as well as personal identity. The Americans have destroyed these sources for many Vietnamese, not merely by killing people but by forcibly separating them, by removing the people from the land, and depositing them in vast camp-cities.[11]

It would be impossible to include here all the works and words of those who protested American involvement in the Vietnam War, but hundreds of entries are listed in such compilations as "Vietnam War Literature, 1958–1979; A Checklist," in the *Bulletin of Bibliography* for January–March, 1981, regarded as the "largest published enumerative bibliography" compiled by Tom Colonnese and Jerry Hogan. Among the key bibliographies of imaginative literature are Peter Leonard Stromberg's *The Long War's Writing: American Novels About the Fighting in Vietnam Written While Americans Fought* (1974) and John Newman's *Vietnam War Literature* (1982). This annotated bibliography contains 244 entries and does not even cover all of the literature on this subject, such as films and artistic work after 1980.

Among the short stories, only a few can be noted here: Asa Baber's "The French Lesson," Charles A. Belanger's "Once Upon a Time When it was Night," Merritt Clifton's "In the Field," Walter McDonald's "Lebowitz," and Len Deighton's "First Base." These stories chronicle life in Vietnam for the ordinary soldier: a life of violence, death, fear, hatred of the anti-war movement at home, the killing of peasants, the loss of "buddies," and the despair experienced by pilots who knew the destruction they were reaping with their bombs.

Most of the novels deal with the same experiences, and in such works as Richard E. Baker's *Feast of Epiphany* (1981), Corinne Brown's *Body Shop* (1973), William Eastlake's *The Bamboo Bed* (1969), David Halberstam's *One Very Hot Day* (1969), and John Del Vecchio's *The Thirteenth Valley* (1982), there is greater depth and character development and a more profound study of such problems as the confusion about tactics among enlisted men, the tragic experiences of Vietnamese families, the pain of "coming home," and the hopelessness of winning the war. These and other novels are replete with descriptions of life as a foot soldier in Vietnam, the inhumanity with which native villages were burned and the inhabitants dispersed, the friendships and the antagonisms generated by the conditions facing Americans in combat, and the drug trade as it flourished in Vietnam. Not all of these novels are well written and some are highly suspicious as bona fide reports of what actually took place, but what is apparent immediately is the recurrence of issues and problems and factual testimony in too many accounts to dismiss them all as purely "fictional."

Naturally, my major interest lies with the body of poetry that came out of the Vietnam conflict, for it is something of a misnomer to call Denise Levertov the "Voice of the Sixties." Quite conversely, hers was one voice raised among many other creative and sensitive poets who felt the obligation to express their experiences during this critical time in American history.

Richard E. Baker's *Shell Burst Pond* (1980) contains a group of poems describing the poet's experiences as an infantryman in Vietnam. What is interesting here are the first-hand experiences in this and other poetry that came before and after its publication. *Demilitarized Zones* (1976), edited by Jan Barry and W. D. Ehrhart, is considered to be one of the finest selections of poetry written directly about the war—more than half of which is the result of the poet's experiences in Vietnam. W. D. Ehrhart, considered by critics to be a major figure in Vietnamese literature, published *The Awkward Silence* in 1980; it contains many of Ehrhart's poems dealing with his experience as a sergeant in the Marines in Vietnam. In *Where is Vietnam?* edited by Walter Lowenfels (1967), eighty-seven poets are represented, among them James Dickey, Hayden Carruth, Lawrence Ferlinghetti, and Denise Levertov. Several of the poems date back to the early sixties and represent the voices of some of America's most prestigious avant-garde poets. A new collection of anti-war poems was published in January 1988. Titled *Peace or Perish: A Crisis Anthology*, edited by Herman Berlandt and Neeli Cherkovski, the volume contains poems by Robert Bly, Diane di Prima, William Everson, Lawrence Ferlinghetti, Susan Griffin, Allen Ginsberg, Denise Levertov, Bob Kaufman, and many others. The aim of the collection is to state the poets' case against a nuclear holocaust.

I should like to note the contribution of only one contemporary poet who counts among the most accomplished modern artists in our time: John Balaban. Balaban did not fight in Vietnam. He spent two years in Vietnam (1967–1969) as a conscientious objector, and at the age of twenty-four served as an instructor at the University of Can Tho in the Mekong Delta. After the destruction of the university, he was a field representative for the Committee of Responsibility to Save War-Injured Children. Balaban speaks Vietnamese and has translated a great deal of Vietnamese poetry. He has taped conversations with native people, returned to Vietnam since the war, and produced some of his finest work in presenting the spirit of the country itself. His poetry is not blatantly polemical, but it would be difficult to read Balaban and not feel the deep-seated tragedy that beset the dignified and courageous people who inhabit his verse. His "protest" is so frequently "whispered" that an insensitive reader could easily miss the pathos, the irony, the empathy that lies beneath the stark reality. Such a poem is "The Guard at the Binh Thuy Bridge," in which danger is an immanent reality in the threat to the innocent.

Our most distinguished critics and thinkers have accepted the belief that if artists are to "live" in the modern world, they are likely to commit themselves to protest and activism. Albert Camus wrote, "Considered as artists, we perhaps have no need to interfere in the affairs of the world. But considered as men, we do." And no artist today separates the experiences of the man or woman from the creative imagination. Camus warned against "preaching" but hastened to add "we must simultaneously serve suffering and beauty. . . . This undertaking cannot be accomplished without danger and bitterness. We must accept the dangers: the era of the chairbound artists is over. . . ."[12] Rosenthal also warns that "Emotion and mental power must work together perfectly."[13]

Thus, whatever the challenge to committed artists in their fight for whatever cause they choose—inhumanity and exploitation, war, or the threat of nuclear holocaust—they must always be aware that they are first of all artists and their work must achieve that delicate balance between "statement" and artistic expression.

For Denise Levertov, who believed firmly that "It is given to the seer to see, but it is then his responsibility to communicate what he sees, that they who cannot see may see, since we are 'members one of another',"[14] making her experience the subject matter of her poetry—in one case war and activism—required no shift in her aesthetic ideas or "prostitution" of her art. She had written emphatically: "Insofar as poetry has a social function, it is to awaken sleepers by other means than shock."[15] It is this social consciousness that illuminates much of her best poetry, whether the subject be Vietnam, the tragedy of Karen Silkwood, the threat of the nuclear age, or the inhumanity in South Africa.

She expressed the hope in the "Author's Preface" to her work *To Stay Alive* that the poems would have historical as well as aesthetic value "in being a record of one person's inner/outer experience in

America during the 60's and the beginning of the '70's, an experience which is shared by so many."[16] Levertov was doing what so many twentieth-century artists before her had done already—responding artistically to an age whose violence, destruction, disillusion, and stubborn hope have never been felt so intimately.

Even as I write in 1991, several events document our tragic awareness that the Vietnam War is still within us. Films, television documentaries, anniversaries, the Wall of Names in Washington, D.C. serve to dissipate twenty-five years of *seeming* indifference on a large part of the American public, but writers and other artists have revealed that Vietnam will not be dismissed easily by the American conscience. On 12 January 1990, John Balaban and Bruce Weigl, a poet who had been a soldier in Vietnam, read from their Vietnam works at the Folger Library in Washington, D.C. Commenting upon their joint reading, Balaban noted, "Vietnam was something that happened to both of us. It was overwhelming and it changed our lives, so it's something we'll be thinking about for a long time . . ."[17]

Denise Levertov shares with writers from Stephen Crane to the poets and novelists of the twentieth century, including these recent reminders by Balaban and others, both the horrors of war and the wonder of human acts and aspirations. Thus, she does not stand alone. Perhaps when we understand her view of the poet and the poem, so lucidly expressed by Levertov herself, we will understand as well how her inner and outer worlds converge in her poetry.

2

The Poet and the Poem: ". . . what lies at hand"

> . . . *the artist as explorer in language of the experiences of his or her*
> *life is*—willy-nilly—weaving a fabric, building a whole in which
> each discrete work is a part that functions in some way in relation
> to all the others.
>
> —"Author's Preface," *To Stay Alive*

I

To begin to understand the relationship between the world of Denise Levertov's experience and her body of poetry—which, I would emphasize, reveals a remarkable consistency—it would be useful to examine her concept of poetry as she has articulated it throughout her career. Of greatest importance is her concept of "organic poetry":

> For me, back of the idea of organic form is the concept that there is a
> form in all things (and in our experience) which the poet can discover
> and reveal. . . . A partial definition of organic poetry might be that it is
> a method of apperception, i.e., of recognizing what we perceive, and is
> based upon an intuition of an order, a form beyond forms, in which forms
> partake, and of which man's creative works are analogies, resemblances,
> natural allegories. Such poetry is exploratory.[1]

A bit later in the same vein, she wrote, "There is a poetry that in thought and in feeling and in perception seeks the forms peculiar to these experiences."[2]

Denise Levertov has often said, "I believe in writing about what lies at hand. . . . poetry arises out of a *need*, out of really having something to say about something that we—that the poet—that I— have actually felt or experienced."[3] An interesting illustration of Levertov's theory of poetry at work is her brief tribute, "Illustrious An-

36

cestors" in which the indivisible nature of inner reflection and practical action is revealed:

> The Rav
> of Northern White Russia declined,
> in his youth, to learn the
> language of birds, because
> the extraneous did not interest him; nevertheless
> when he grew old it was found
> he understood them anyway, having
> listened well, and as it is said, 'prayed
> with the bench and the floor.' He used
> what was at hand—as did
> Angel Jones of Mold whose meditations
> were sewn into coats and britches.
>
> Well, I would like to make,
> thinking some line still taut between me and them,
> poems direct as what the birds said,
> hard as a floor, sound as a bench,
> mysterious as the silence when the tailor
> would pause with his needle in the air.

Such is Denise Levertov's poetic definition of her artistry. The harmony, as it were, came through the genes—from the Rabbi of the Levertoffs and the Welsh great-grandfather, Angel Jones. Like the Rav, she *listened* like Angel Jones of Mold, *wove*. She noted that both she and her sister, Olga, felt they shared a "definite and peculiar destiny" with their forebears; indeed, the two men shared a kinship that "would be somehow unified and redeemed in us."[4] Those worlds of meditation and dream, here combining "sewing," and the language of birds, reappear in most of her poetry. One discovers qualities of sameness with difference; of the general with the concrete; the idea with the image. Like her ancestors, Levertov would use "what was at hand," and the humor of the poem, especially in the succinct portraits of the Rav and Angel Jones, does not divert us from the central theme of the poem: the writing of poetry. For Levertov, working, thinking, and listening are integral to the creation of art. The joy, humor, and wonder as well as thoughtfulness, worldliness, and wit suffuse this brief poem. Levertov inherited the twin worlds of her ancestors; for most of her poetry, these worlds would intermingle.

For more than forty years, the hallmark of Denise Levertov's poetry has been her absorption with achieving harmony of language with the "form in all things and in our experience which the poet can discover and reveal."[5] Levertov would agree that her poetry has been a lifetime exploration to unite the inner with the outer experience. It is her intuition of order, a form beyond forms, that elevates her poetry to a high level of art and indeed accounts for much of the continuity in her work. Although the pattern she discerns is often incomplete, there lies beneath the surface reality an acceptance of a pattern, an order, a coherence that in itself is a kind of faith. She had always recognized that experience is not chaos but order—order which has to be discovered by the attentive artist. Her credo expressed in 1960—"I believe content determines form, and yet that content is discovered only *in* form"—was the natural outcome of the new poetry that had been created in the twentieth century. But she added, "Like everything living, it [the poem] is a mystery . . ."[6] This is a clue to Levertov's belief in the inexplicable—the mystical, the dreamlike—that special reality which has a role in poetry. To Levertov, balance and wholeness were the harmonizing forces in a poem: strength of feeling, reverence for mystery, and clarity of intellect must be kept in perfect balance. She emphasized that "Writing poetry is a process of discovery, revealing *inherent* music, the music of correspondences . . ."[7] and the poets' commitment, she believed, was to devote their energy to seeing their surroundings. It is understandable that this commitment would culminate in a poet whose social consciousness would not be denied, that *a schism between poetry as art and poetry as a vehicle for moral conscience must not occur.* In acknowledging that "need" to express what poets actually "felt or experienced," Denise Levertov has guided us to the signposts of her aesthetic pilgrimage: at times, her poetry is reflective, at times ecstatic, or despairing, or hopeful, or angry, or awestruck. Her sensitivity to nature—consistent in all her poetry—her mysticism, her impish sensuality, her eagerness to write what was "at hand," her sense of mission, her poetic career as a journey have their sources in both her inner and outer experiences. The continuity in her work has rested upon an unfaltering aim to unite her two worlds. The importance of the "pilgrimage" cannot be overstated. She would write in *The Poet In the World* of "the theme of a journey that would lead from one state of being to another that later I find defined in many poems as the sense of *life as a pilgrimage.*"[8] Such a pilgrimage would fuse dream, fantasy, and myth with reality so that a poem might begin in dream or in events, both recognized by the poet as "experience" that, as William Carlos Williams had observed, must be transmuted into the materials of art—a structure.* Levertov's first printed poem, "Listening to Distant Guns," combines the awakening horror of war with the bucolic beauty of Buckinghamshire. The war invades the first world as "the low pulsation in the east"—the sound of Dunkirk's distant guns in early summer, 1940, or perhaps the rumble of artillery on the coast—impinges upon the still and dreamy evening.

Thus in many early poems, the outer reality was often the more threatening, though many of Levertov's poems, which will not be discussed here in detail, *welcome* the city, the singing birds, the city's inhabitants, other poets, marriage, and motherhood into her inner world as consummate gifts. Denise Levertov is no ascetic, but it is clear that as her political conscience developed, she saw much ugliness, inhumanity, and violence in that other dimension of reality. In some ways, she reflects the reactions of William Carlos Williams, but her bitterness is not as acrid and her hope is more firmly rooted in humanity, as it is today in her faith.

* * *

We might ask: What were the beginnings of Levertov's exposure to the events that would finally enlarge her vision and lead to her expressions of indignation against Vietnam in the sixties? This too was a journey of awareness, at first hardly noticed by her critics but gradually and surely gathering momentum even as the storms of the sixties led the nation to its first military disaster.

From her earliest memories, Denise Levertov recalls her own family's sense of "awareness" and involvement in the world at large, yet at the same time those close to her were thinkers who sought to harmonize their private and public worlds. In 1985, in a rare moment of nostalgia, Levertov wrote the following:

> Humanitarian politics came into my life early—seeing my father on a soapbox protesting Mussolini's invasion of Abyssinia; my father and sister both on soap-boxes protesting Britain's lack of support for Spain; my mother canvassing long before those events for the League of Nations Union; and all three of them working on behalf of German and Austrian refugees from 1933 onwards. When I was 11 and 12, unknown to my parents . . . I used to sell the *Daily Worker* house-to-house in the working-class streets off Ilford Lane, down toward Barking, on Saturday mornings. . . . All that has taken place in my life since—all, that is, that has any bearing on my life as a poet—was in some way foreshadowed then.[10]

---

*Levertov quoted Williams's "Against the Weather," in *Cave*, 127.[9]

Levertov's family was most unusual in its commitment to the world it lived in and in its commitment to a life of artistic awareness, reflection, scholarship, and the inner needs of conscience. Her father, a Russian-Jewish intellectual, had converted to Christianity in 1898 and was ordained into the Anglican Church in 1922 (before she was born). His scholarly studies enlarged his understanding of religion and faith and enabled him to "reconcile Jews and Christians."[11]

The effect upon Levertov can be traced in her own preoccupation with the harmony of the world and the spirit. As R. Howard has noted: "[Levertov's] longing for rituals, the need to 'transform our flesh, our deaths' is the subject of all her later poetry. . . . [Her] undertaking to convert: to connect as by a kind of magic . . . the eternal consciousness of disparities into a momentary unity of association,"[12] moved her poetic imagination to vibrate between the data of the real world and the intuition of the soul. That Levertov describes the poem as a "sacramental transaction" is a clue to the intensity of her purpose.[13] And the roots were there from her beginnings. They are always recognizable in her poems in which myth, fairytale, rite, dream, and, more recently, prayer provide the tone and often the substance.

In her tribute to her mother, Beatrice Levertoff, she emphasized her mother's commitment to the world as a teacher in her youth, and later, perhaps because of her own house arrest during World War I in Leipzig with her husband, as a tireless worker not only rescuing refugees from Hitler's Germany, as Levertov recalls, but bringing them to England and finding homes and work there.[14] Beatrice Levertoff's love for travel, her curiosity about the world outside England, harmonized with her sense of social responsibility and the awareness of misery in the lives of others. Levertov acknowledges the verbal gifts and the poetic sensitivity that she inherited from these two unusual parents, as well as her gratitude, as we have seen, for the legacy of the Rav of Russia and Angel Jones of Mold.

No less important was the early influence of her older sister, Olga, who introduced her to modern art and modern poetry. Contrary to some belief, a friend encouraged her interest in drama, a discovery that furthered Levertov's already enthusiastic interest in ballet. Moreover, it is understandable that Olga's political activism would make a lasting impression on a sister nine years younger who as a mature poet would write a series of her finest poems, the "Olga Poems." They are a "kind of elegy" Levertov tells us, written after the death of Olga in 1967. "It could be described as a fragmentary account of her life—fragmentary because I knew her only in a fragmentary way, our lives having completely separated us for years at a time."[15] Yet the importance of Olga's commitment, her sense of social justice, can be overstated, because it is difficult to measure the extent of Olga's influence on the mature Denise. Nine years' difference in age and many years of separation with little personal contact clearly affected the distancing between the two sisters. Yet, in her long poem, "Staying Alive," the image of Olga emerges twice, and Olga is evoked subtly throughout this poem of the ebb and flow of anti-war activity on the eve of the famous "trials" of the protestors. In part III, she recalls the lamps of Oxford St.:

> Olga rushed back and forth
> for years beneath them, working
> in her way for Revolution
> and I too in my youth
> knew then and was lonely, an ignorant girl.

Later in part IV, she writes:

> Those are the same lamps
> of my dream of Olga—the eel or cockle stand
> she in the flare caught, a moment, her face
> painted, clownishly, whorishly. Suffering.

Olga appears and reappears in the Vietnam poems as a kind of spectral presence. Olga's activism as an influence on the young Levertov has been argued, but it must be remembered that she came from an entire family that concerned itself with social issues. Thus many of her early poems that we shall look at briefly concern the subject of war, and the deadening impact of war upon both nature and human beings. But, as early as 1946, in *The Double Image*, Levertov possessed a strong social consciousness and already showed indications of a direction she would take in the future. Yet it was not until the sixties when she strongly protested the Vietnam War that the private activist and the public poet fused. As Levertov declared, her own commitment led her husband, Mitchell Goodman, into political activism.[16] In 1965 her name appeared in the New York *Times* ad: "Writers and Artists Protest Against the War in Vietnam." During this same period, together with Robert Bly, Allen Ginsberg, David Ray, and many others, Levertov became part of American Writers Against the Vietnam War in 1966, but she did not participate in the group readings sponsored by Bly and others.

At the same time, however, Levertov herself had awakened to the whole enigma of the role of "politics" in poetry. Her personal crisis is revealed and transcended in a striking, unpublished letter written to fellow poet Bill Burford on Boxing Day, 1965:

> Months ago you said, "It would really be a new breath for poetry if some of us were able to deal with the *actual* world—that is, the world of things that are happening outside, but inside, of course, at the same time. One simply cannot go on in the New England pastoral style . . . any longer."
>
> Hayden Carruth in a *Nation* piece about 3 years ago expressed the same hope of a poetry. In your poems and in these recent 'Passages' of Duncan's and in some of the best of Paul Goodman . . . this poetry does exist. But tho' I myself feel a frustrated longing at this point to write some poems or at least a poem of political significance, overtly political, that is, and tho' I welcome its being when it does happen in other poets (the 'topical theme'), I remain very dubious about its importance. Yes, poetry, if it is in a healthy state, *should* be able to encompass anything, and must at all times "deal with" essentials. But when in a certain period of crisis we consciously *demand* of it that it speak of that crisis, overtly, are we not in danger of treating Poetry as our servant instead of remembering we are servants of Poetry? And won't the secondary (but fatal) danger ensue, of forcing ourselves to the act of making that overt poetry of crisis? And doesn't the demand perhaps result from an improper reading of the poetry we *are* writing, the poems that, not overtly political or social, perhaps speak persistently, intensely, deeply, of analogues in *other parts of the forest?* The anguished demand a poet makes on himself in a period of history like this one, to speak directly to his anguish, to use his relation with the Muse for the arousal of the conscience of others, can paralyze him so that he either writes nothing at all or writes bad 'public' poetry. I don't know. I am in a quandary about it. Or, I think maybe I do know: that *if it happens*, if a poet is *brought to speech* of a political poem, it is a *good* thing socially for his contemporaries. And he will feel better for it . . .

Levertov then alludes to Rilke who was comparably concerned with World War I and who was sickened, disillusioned, and ultimately *opposed* to it; but he never wrote about the war—in fact—wrote little. He did not "fail," Levertov points out:

> It comes down, then, to one's obligation—being now as at *all* times, to hold oneself open and ready for whatever poems may come—not fret oneself into silence with the guilty sense of failure at *not* writing some *willed* poem. You will know I am talking rather to myself (who have been silent, but for a single 'personal' poem) since the end of October.[17]

The letter is extremely revealing from several aspects. Levertov had, at this point, already reconciled her personal involvement in the opposition to the Vietnam War, but she was still ambivalent about making her feelings *overtly* a part of her poetry. Moreover, she thought very deeply of the dangers the true poet faced: in risking art for polemics, so that the poem might be lessened in aesthetic value; in giving in to a "popular" trend by writing a "willed" poem, instead of one that sincerely grew from her own inner response to her external experience; and finally, in compromising her obligation to herself as a poet. Here in this letter, the problem is worked out. Her renewed confidence in her poetic gift and her rational faculty would enable her to write successful "engaged poetry." Throughout the prose written from this period forward, and then reflected in the poetry, her voice was sure and unflagging. "The *didactic* in poetry," she wrote "had a place in poetry, but only when it is inseparable from the intuitive. . . . In our time, a political poetry untinged with anguish, even when it evokes and salutes moments of hope, is unimaginable."[18] (Emphasis mine.)

As we shall see, it was not always easy to achieve that union. At times, the didactic voice outreaches the "anguish" and the intuitive, and moments of hope are held hostage by the urgency to inform and teach.

When we examine modern poetry, despite enormous ranges of subject, tone, and image, we are struck by the consistency of Coleridge's concept of organic unity that underlies the individual poem. Most modern poets would agree that the relationship in the poem between the "inner" and the "outer" experience; the form and the content; the idea and the emotion; the language and the "music"; the reality and the dream; the mysterious and the mundane is one of inextricable wholeness. Whatever the poets' guiding esthetics at a given stage of their poetic journey, their aim is to record as faithfully and sincerely as they can their progress in the confrontation of their inner and outer worlds. Their poems will combine all the "tools" at hand: the language of their utterance in clearly etched images; the rhythms, music, and cadences of their voices as they articulate their themes; and the magical, impenetrable gift for leaving upon the reader's memory a lasting imprint of a poem's "poetry."

Levertov had written, "I long for poems of an inner harmony in utter contrast to the chaos in which they exist. Insofar as poetry has a social function it is to awaken sleepers by other means than shock. . . . Our period in history was (is) violent and filled with horrors, and I never for a moment considered it was 'not poetic,' not the concern of poetry, to speak of them."[19]

Yet it would be a mistake to assume that the tone of Levertov's poetry, even in the sixties, was without hope and the confidence that man, as man, could find his way. "Poems," she wrote, "bear witness to the manness of man, which . . . is an exiled spark. Only by the light and heat of these divine sparks can we see, can we feel, the extent of the human range. They bear witness to the *possibility* of disinterest, freedom, and intensity."[20]

Reinforcement came from fellow poets Galway Kinnell and Hayden Carruth who, Levertov believed, were convinced that "poetry and politics need not, indeed cannot, be kept apart."[21] Both men were political activists. She also knew that contemporary poets like Allen Ginsberg, Robert Duncan, Gary Snyder, and Robert Bly believed that "poetry can only be deeply and truly revolutionary, only *be* poetry, song that suffices our need, by being in its very substance of sound and vision an ecstacy and a giving of life."[22] Never losing sight of herself as poet, Levertov said in a television program on Vietnam, taped but never aired:

> Poets differ from other people only in having a specially intimate relation to words. When I say I speak as a poet, it is the same as to say I speak as a human being.[23]

Levertov refers to the "highly emotive power" of poetry; it "affects our senses and engages our aesthetic response." She added, pointing to Paul Valery's *The Art of Poetry:* "For political poetry, as for any other kind, the *sine qua non* is that it elicit 'the poetic emotion.'"[24]

The private person of intense social commitment was united forever with the poet whose artistic matter would come from her worldly, as well as inner, experience. Denise Levertov had come to terms by the mid-sixties with the dilemma posed by the daily presence of the Vietnam conflict and the role artists needed to play in it.

She believed the "poetry of protest, indignation, anger . . . had helped to 'awaken' many people. . . . And the anti-war movement . . . has grown . . . into a revolutionary movement in which people no longer see stopping the war as a single issue which can be divorced from racism, imperialism, capitalism, male supremacy."[25]

Levertov's ideas about "engaged poetry" did not spring full-grown like Topsy. They were the result of a personal pilgrimage, of a social sensitivity ingrained in youth, of a despair with events that led human beings to the nadir of inhumanity, of her need to fuse that despair with her natural hope and faith. Those around her—at first her parents and her sister Olga, later her fellow poets and friends like Rukeyser, and surely her husband and the students who voiced their indignation loudly in the sixties—all contributed to a commitment which her heart told her was "true." Her deeply felt conviction gave an honesty and validity to her poetry that elevated it far beyond the literature of mere propaganda and polemics.

In 1965, in the "Author's Preface" in *To Stay Alive*, Denise Levertov wrote the following:

> The justification . . . of including in a new volume poems which are available in other collections, is aesthetic—it assembles separate parts of a whole. And I am given courage to do so by the hope of that whole being seen as having some value not as mere 'confessional' autobiography, but as a document of some historical value, a record of one person's inner/ outer experience in America during the '60's and the beginning of the '70's, an experience which is shared by so many and transcends the peculiar details of each life, though it can only be expressed in and through such details.[26]

More than any of her prose expressions, here Levertov reveals her faith in the organic nature of art, speaking as a poet and a human being with one voice. The corpus of her poetry, to this day, is a *continuity* that rests on that single voice—one that encompasses *all* of her experience into a unified whole. This is her goal, yet there are isolated instances when Levertov leans too much on "saying" and too little on "singing." This does not occur often, but it has, in the past, given critics ammunition for casting aside her Vietnam poetry as a sacrifice of her aesthetics.

II

> . . . the vision was given me: to know and share.
> —"The Many Mansions"

Contemporary critics of the literature written by women have tended to regard their work as "honest" accounts of the experience of being a woman. Although this would appear to be complimentary, critics often dismiss much of the work as being too subjective, emotional, confessional. They would point to modernist theories of the "impersonal poet," arguing that distancing oneself from one's experience gives objectivity and validity to a work of art. As is often the case with part truths, there *is* some merit in this argument, but Ezra Pound in "Hugh Selwyn Mauberly" clearly demonstrates the fate of the artist who escapes his world for either the higher realm of pure aesthetics or personal outpouring. As Levertov wrote, she would be "the poet *in* the world." (Emphasis mine.) Charles Olson, who played an early role in Levertov's poetic development in America, had insisted the poet's role is "to celebrate man's reconciliation with his immediate experience."[27]

The critics who chose to attack the turn in Levertov's journey from the subjects of nature, women, marriage, children, and myth to the more immediate problem of the sixties labored under a double misapprehension. First, they had completely failed to recognize the social awareness that was the underpinning of many of her earlier poems; and second, they dismissed her poems on Vietnam and the evils perpetrated by that war as unfit subjects for poetry (from a poet with "Orphic" gifts). Moreover, they felt her aesthetic and "polemical" objectives were antithetical, and they censured her for lowering her sights to become "preachy," emotional, and bathetic. They saw in many of the Vietnam volumes a schism between the private poet and the public dissident. She had, they agreed, sacrificed her poetic gifts on the altars of social conscience or "obligation."

Levertov has disdained answering her critics; as with most poets, she believes her poetry justifies its existence and will stand or fall on its individual merits.

Nevertheless, many other critics noted that artists never stand still: they grow and deepen and experiment with new forms, new subjects. Over a lifetime, the tone of their poems will vary with their perception of experience. Thus, in the poetic journey of any poet, despite the thread of continuity that runs through the work of our best poets, there is the ebb and flow of change. There is the growth of the poet from youth to maturity—often from the romantic to the sometimes painful reality of the world and its complexity. I know of no poets whose "pilgrimages" did not take them through a series of emotional, aesthetic, and intellectual crises. Any worthy artistic journey leads poets to question, doubt, suffer, and reaffirm their faith in fellow human beings or an immanent presence. The road—as Frost noted—was too often "like a pathless wood / Where your face burns and tickles with the cobwebs / Broken across it . . . ."[28] No one understood this better than Levertov herself.

> Poets owe to Poetry itself a loyalty which may at times be in conflict with the demands of domestic or other aspects of life. Out of these conflicts, sometimes, poetry itself re-emerges. For example, the impulse to reconcile what one believes to be necessary to one's human integrity, such as forms of political action, with the necessities of one's inner life, including its formal, aesthetic dynamic, motivates the attempt to write engaged or "political" poetry that is truly poetry, magnetic and sensuous. . . . One is in despair over the current manifestations of malevolent imbecility and the seemingly invincible power of rapacity, yet one finds oneself writing a poem about the trout lilies in the spring woods. . . . If

one is conscientious, the only solution is to attempt to weigh conflicting claims at each crucial moment, and in general, try to juggle well and keep all the oranges dancing in the air at once.[29]

Denise Levertov's own journey can be charted by her ever-widening involvement with the world at large, a series of experiences that, given her view of poetry, was bound to be reflected in volume after volume of her work.

It would be impossible to present all of the attacks upon her poetry of the sixties and early seventies, but it is helpful, before examining individual poems, to summarize the main arguments. In addition, critics who believed Levertov's poetry of the war years was a high point in her "pilgrimage" also need to be heard.

III. The Critics

Many of those who censured Levertov most loudly were the critics who had lauded her early "romantic" poetry written until the sixties as well within the tradition of England's Romantic poets of the nineteenth century. As we will see when we examine some of these early poems, they did *seem* Wordsworthian in their concern with nature, the poet's awe at the beauties of the world, the "portraits" of ordinary life, and the mystical experiences of the dream world. In a word, some of her critics were disappointed when her vision expanded. They had totally missed in the earlier poetry a social consciousness— present if not overt.

In 1982, William Beidler reflected the generally hostile attitude of some critics toward poets who saw the war as "their cause." In a sweeping statement, he indicted those poets who, he believed, saw Vietnam as the material for polemics. He mentioned Levertov just in passing, but agreed with Robert Shaw that the poets of the sixties "were caught between 'diatribe and documentary' producing static, predictable, ritual poetry."[30]

Paul Breslin is one of numerous critics who admired Levertov's earlier work: "[She] writes fine poetry of sensuous immediacy but poor political poetry of ideas."[31] Apart from the Olga poems, Breslin felt the anti-war poetry was not successful, mainly because of its sentimentalism.

Cary Nelson has made a more damaging judgment of Levertov's political poetry. Her poetry, he asserted, is problematic, because her mysticism is in conflict with her real world. He referred particularly to the volume most criticized, *To Stay Alive*, and believed that "She

avoided encountering the larger myths of our history and kept her
poetic territory elsewhere and self-enclosed."[32] He admired the earlier evanescent, fragile poems, but when she made a moral commitment to practical action, as it "enters the poetry itself," she failed.
He charged her war poetry with clichés of violent war and felt that
her language was flat and unconvincing. He saw no anger, only a
numb acceptance of self-extinction and personal defeat. A sense of
futility, Nelson felt, permeates the poetic enterprise. "The appro-
priate images of pain are not achievable." Later, in reviewing *The
Freeing of the Dust*, Nelson wrote that Levertov produced her first
successful Vietnam poetry based on direct experience. "The flat narration establishes Levertov's respect for suffering that is, finally, not
her own."

James F. Mersmann had written an extensive essay, "Denise Levertov: Piercing In," in his work *Out of the Vietnam Vortex: A Study of
Poets Against the War.*[33] He admired her "balanced and whole work"
which he felt came to an end in the late sixties. He wrote, "Her
[earlier] poems seek the middle way. . . . There are no excesses of
ecstasy or despair, celebration or denigration, naivete or cynicism;
there is instead an acute ability to find simple beauties in the heart
of squalor and something to relish even in negative experiences." He
praised her qualities of feeling, mystery, and intellect and viewed her
vision as one that "sees into experience" and discovers the order and
significance behind the surface chaos. With her movement into the
poetry of the Vietnam period, her work suffered "the loss and contradiction of vision that makes the war horrible to Levertov, and this
may be said without any denigration of her compassion or humanity."
Thus, Mersmann concluded, with the loss of vision came the loss of
poetic power. He accused her of hysteria, a loss of form. He felt
Levertov was not "at ease" with the movement since the needs of
the revolution ran counter to her "strong need for poetic integrity."
Although he believed the open forms she chose were less perfect than
her earlier poetry, he was drawn to many of the poems in *Relearning the
Alphabet*. But Mersmann was convinced that Levertov's "bitterness"
and anger resulted in flawed poetry, disturbing to the poet herself.
Mersmann finally believed that "Both revolution and anger are still
essentially foreign to her nature, and she would almost prefer death
rather than immersion in the intransigent and aggressive acts of revolution. . . ."

Other critics, like Robert Shaw and Alfred H. Rosenfeld, who took
this same theme—that the later Levertov betrayed the esthetics, the
forms, the harmony, and order of the earlier Levertov—need only
be mentioned in passing. Since Charles Altieri has devoted much

speculation on the shift in Denise Levertov's poetry, I have chosen to trace his argument here briefly. In *Contemporary Literature* (later expanding his argument in *Enlarging the Temple*),[34] Altieri at first recognized Levertov as a "major voice" in American poetry. He then attacked Levertov and other poets of the sixties like Bly and Ginsberg for an "irresponsible commitment to public responsibility." He called Levertov to account in abandoning her poetic objectives. He abhorred her "retreat" from "lyric intensity and speculative poetic meditation" to her new presentation of experience. Altieri saw esthetics and social conscience as an unresolvable "dichotomy."

Altieri devoted chapter 6 in *Enlarging the Temple* to "Denise Levertov and the Limits of the Aesthetics of Presence." Once again he cited the poets of the sixties as "miserable in handling social and ethical issues," convinced that they have been unable to tailor their aesthetics to the horrors of a war they sincerely opposed. Altieri noted Levertov's "lack of poetic power and authority in trying to adapt the principles that shaped her former work to social questions." The confident assertion that characterized her earlier work is missing in *To Stay Alive* and is replaced by profound doubt and questioning. Altieri believed Levertov failed to "reconcile 'the spirit of Here and Now' with the 'spirit of quest, of longing to wander toward other worlds' inherited from her father's interest in traditions of mystical thought." He believed that she herself was aware not only of the discordance between the poetry of "presence" and the poetry of "immanence," but could not reconcile an aesthetic of presence (plenitude) with the tragedy of the contemporary world. Altieri accepted only the poetry in the meditative mode, convinced that the poetry of "politics" is incompatible with the poet's objectives.

More seriously, Altieri felt that Levertov's "failure" resulted from her "inability to transform the sufferings of war into a traditionally satisfying mythic framework of heroic perfection, and her failure to align her consciousness with principles inherent in the language and in the prereflexive aspects of human culture." In other words, in "rejecting humanism" Levertov had rejected the traditions of the literature of the western world. The alternative—the aesthetics of "immanence"—is an unfit mode for a confrontation with political realities. In essence, Altieri emphasizes that "History shows that man's efforts to build temples have little effect on the specific practices characterizing life in the city." Thus, Altieri concludes, "One must recognize the fact that no poetry is likely to have much impact on the social order."

If one can accept Altieri's basic assumption that poetry, whose main mode is meditative, cannot co-exist with poetry of social conscience, one would have to reject Levertov's "poetry of engagement" outright. Yet she had written, "In our time, a political poetry untinged with anguish, even when it evokes and salutes moments of hope, is unimaginable."[35] This appears to indicate that Levertov herself was aware of the necessary conjunction of aesthetics and politics. There would appear to be no meeting of minds between poet and critic, this added to the assessment of Levertov's poetry as lacking any aesthetic merit! It is hoped that when we examine Denise Levertov's individual poems in closer detail, we will recognize the *importance of language* as a moral touchstone in all her poetry, for, from the very beginning of her life as a poet, it has been the "words" that she has returned to constantly in her search for "a door in the hive."

As an extensive critique of Denise Levertov's shift in subject and poetic theory, and her departure from the kind of poetry she had committed herself to until 1971, Peter Middleton's study, *Revelation and Revolution in the Poetry of Denise Levertov* (1981),[36] merits examination. Middleton's analysis was neither approving nor hostile; most importantly it interpreted Levertov's early work in the traditional way critics had approached her poetry: an Orphic voice in the mode of nineteenth century English Romanticism. Middleton made the charge that Levertov's war poetry was written as an "obligation" and that her poetics propelled her in the direction of that motive, making poetic response difficult.

Middleton praised the poetry that appeared before 1960; with great technical insight he gave Levertov her "rightful" place in the modernist movement. He analyzed several poems in this period and united her best efforts with the poetic giants: Eliot, Pound, H. D. and others. But then, he revealed her almost "mercurial" shift away from "expressionist" art. He referred to her statement in *Poet* as "the music of poetry comes into being when thought and feeling remain unexpressed until they become Word, become Flesh."[37]

What appeared to have troubled Middleton the most was Levertov's statement in *Poet* that "the obligation of the poet . . . is not necessarily to write 'political' poems . . . the obligation of the writer is: *to take personal and active responsibility for his words, whatever they are, and to acknowledge their potential influence on the lives of others.*"[38] Focusing on the word "obligation," Middleton assumed that Levertov raised social responsibility above artistic responsibility with dire consequences. In making an extensive study of Levertov's earlier poetry, he concluded that her achievements have been in form, in narrative power, in "her close attention to the attributes of the sentence when spoken aloud." He applauded her "simple" early poetry, and criticized not only her later "open" forms but the ambiguity, complexity, and "disruption" of her later poetry, notably "Life at War." He admired her poems of dream and fable, and only those war poems that follow a narrative line. He was distressed that much of her war poetry was unable to unite joy and agony. Thus, he believed: "The unity is gone."[39]

As we have seen in a partial summary of Levertov's most vocal critics, the argument is that the poet must recognize the "gulf, in both society and in the self, between the imagination and the empirical reality." Thus Middleton seems to be saying that the early Orphic poet who so successfully followed the Romantic mode cannot be reconciled with the "militant," questioning activist of the sixties and seventies, the result being that an irreparable dichotomy exists between the earlier and later poetry. In a word, her detractors insisted, Levertov had either betrayed her own aesthetics or lacked the "poetic power and authority" to maintain a unity between her social concerns and her aesthetics.

*　*　*

Conversely, in an analysis of "American Underground Poetry Since 1945," Samuel Charters discussed the climate of American art at the time that Charles Olson, the new American giant, came to the attention of the American public and literary critics. Olson, a major American poet and scholar, became the mentor for a whole generation of poets that included Denise Levertov. "American poetry," Charters wrote, "comes out of a society that is uncertain and uneasy and the poetry has always had some of this uneasiness. . . . It always seems to be beginning, and every poet seems to be the beginning of a new American poetry. Olson, with his sense of having found a place [had] the range and strength of force—in his own way—to be this kind of beginning, this kind of new American poet." He then continued, "The first place a poet has to find is the ground he stands on—then he has to go out and find the distances to the places where other poets have decided to stand—to the place where they stand in the culture, and the place they stand in the society."[40]

In another study of Olson, Robert Creeley added, "The local is not a place but a place in a given man—what part of it he has been compelled or else brought by love to give witness to in his own mind. And that is *the* form, that, the whole thing as it can get. Thus Olson adopted the voice of Ishmael, the witness."[41]

I have cited these comments on Olson, who epitomized the dilemma of the post-modernist poets, in that they were "fiercely involved in the uniqueness of the American experience," as Ann Charters notes.[42] On the one hand, they celebrated America in a

Whitmanesque mode, while on the other they abhorred human greed and the exploitation of natural resources. They were ripe for the kind of disillusion engendered by the acceleration of an already unpopular war: Vietnam.

The critics who understood their ambivalence and the aesthetic dilemma of not only "witnessing" but recording in poetry—poets like Levertov, Kinnell, Bly and others—became their most active defenders. This was the argument put forth by a distinguished poet, Louis Simpson.

> The 1960's were different from previous years in that poets began talking from the platform about political matters. There were poetry readings against the war in Vietnam, and readings of black poetry. Poems were read at meetings to help the children of Biafra, and poems were read during sit-ins. Some of the poets who read against the war travelled from place to place and exposed themselves to a great deal of discomfort and to some abuse. The names of Galway Kinnell, Robert Bly, Denise Levertov are respected today not only because they are fine poets, but because they have shown qualities of self-sacrifice and courage. It may be said that these qualities, however admirable, have little to do with the quality of poems. I don't agree. In the hands of a poor writer, a cause is likely to produce bad art; he would have produced bad art anyway. But if the writer has intelligence, his political activity is an extension of his awareness, and, if it does not produce masterpieces at once, in the long run it is bound to add to his writing—as will everything he does.[43]

Simpson quoted Senator Eugene McCarthy who referred Americans to Camus' dictum: "If we intervene as men, that experience will have an effect upon our language. And if we are not artists in our language first of all, what sort of artists are we?" McCarthy concluded, "In 1968, the artists served their land and language well."

Writing again of the sixties, Ralph Mills devoted a chapter to Denise Levertov, in which he characterized such poets as Gary Snyder, David Ignatow, Robert Creeley, Galway Kinnell, and Denise Levertov, among others:

> as aiming at an expression of the personal kind of experience, an authentic statement about themselves, what they see and know, suffer and love, their responses to the things, relationships, and heightened instants of their lives. . . . Denise Levertov stands out as one whose art, fresh and compelling, convinces her of her genuine rapport with the reality she presents at its core. . . . Thus she engages very naturally in a persistent investigation of the events of her own life—inner and outer—in the language of her own time and place, and completes that investigation in the forms emerging from what she discovers as it is translated into words.

Miss Levertov shares the spirit of Martin Buber, for she always says 'thou' to the persons, occasions, and objects she encounters; that is her imagination's essential humanizing gesture toward every aspect of existence.[44]

While Mills' study preceded the publication of Levertov's war poetry, his understanding of her commitment to that inner/outer world would have encompassed her later stand. He concluded in this essay, "Poetry, if it will earn its name, must never begin with experience at second hand, but with a steady eye on what surrounds us everywhere."

Todd Gitlin makes an even more positive assertion: "The return or renaissance of political poetry is a happy by-product of the 1960's." Gitlin defended Levertov's *Relearning the Alphabet* as "beautiful, for it presents political sensibility purely, the place where the inner person meets the outer reality." He noted the union of form and content, image and motion.[45]

Walter Sutton, in discussing the modern revolution in poetry, has defined the artist's dilemma.

> In recent years, the sense of social involvement and responsibility has deepened. In a nuclear age, the pressing consciousness of the interrelationship of societies throughout the world and the shared responsibility for destructive power and questions of a public morality will not allow the luxury of alienation. The opposing demands of personal perception and public conscience may often impose a strain upon the poet, as they have in the career of Denise Levertov. But in the long run, the interfusion of social and personal concerns should enrich rather than limit his work if he resists the surrender of his authentic voice to the cliches of the forum.[46]

Julian Gitzen believed that Levertov had successfully reconciled the opposing demands Sutton alluded to above. Gitzen reviewed Levertov's past accomplishments, comparing her to Wallace Stevens and his belief that "imagination seldom fruitfully transcends reality, but performs a vital service in illuminating or modifying the real. . . ." As Gitzen wrote, "The imagination, then, as Levertov conceives it, is the power of mentally recreating reality." He then made this conclusion.

> Her efforts at political and social reform are entirely consistent with her personality and outlook, for her practice of counting the misfortunes and wrongs of others as her own intensifies her social consciousness, while her belief that vitality is synonymous with change encourages her to assume that social and political change is likely to be beneficial.[47]

In reviewing *The Poet in the World*, Susan Hoerchner also felt that
Levertov had satisfactorily explained the harmony between the artist
and her political commitment. Hoerchner expressed her sense of
Poet's importance this way:

> Denise Levertov's new prose work, *The Poet in the World*, is a valuable,
> almost necessary, book for the writer and reader of poetry, and indeed
> for anyone sensitive to the motivating and celebratory quality of
> words. . . . In *Poet*, Levertov responds to the most insistent issues for the
> contemporary poet: the function and technique of poetry, the artist's role
> in the classroom and political arena. . . . As a poet Levertov feels she
> must act in the world. As a maker and instrument of poems she also
> struggles to bring forth her unique celebration of life. . . . *The Poet in the
> World* fills the gap that too many writers leave open, the chinks between
> their poetic, personal, and political ideas. . . . Levertov presents a holistic
> vision of the poet in her surroundings. At the very least Levertov answers
> the persistent question about how she can reconcile her poetry with her
> political activism. At the most the book awakens us sleepers and commu-
> nicates some of the energy which enables us, too, to live creatively in the
> world.[48]

In another study of Levertov's poetry, Joan F. Hallisey viewed her
as within the Emersonian tradition, as a poet "who refuses to be
silent in times of political and social crises." Hallisey believed that
Levertov's long family tradition of social consciousness "committed
[her] to justice and reconciliation" as it had her forebearers in their
"life-long search for community." Like Emerson, Levertov reveals
the belief that "Man is a center for Nature, running out threads of
relation through everything." In addition, writes Hallisey, the poet
is a missionary, . . . the "visionary pulse" of the tradition of Biblical
prophets present in some of this poetry of dissent, violence, and
pacifism."[49]

As one would expect, some critics, among them Sandra Gilbert,
Suzanne Juhasz, and Marjorie Perloff, have chosen to discuss Levertov's war poetry within the context of "women's literature." But it
is crucial to realize that ultimately Levertov and other women poets
are to be judged as poets in the light of universally accepted criteria.

In a similar context, Kenneth Rexroth, discussing Levertov in his
major work, *American Poetry in the 20th Century*, wrote the following:

> The contrast between Denise Levertov and the women poets of the
> early part of the century is startling. In comparison with her poetry, theirs
> makes being a woman in itself at the best a form of neurasthenia. Denise
> Levertov writes at ease as a woman about love, marriage, motherhood,

deaths in the family. The universal round of domestic life is transformed by the sensibility and moved into the transcendent setting of 'wholeness, harmony, and radiance,' yet this is only a portion of her work, a group of subjects lying naturally to hand and left easily for other subjects as diverse as can be—poems of social protest, of nature, of meditation and contemplation, of vision.[50]

As evidence of the continuing interest in this debate, Jerome Mazzaro has recently published an essay on Denise Levertov's political poetry in Linda Wagner Martin's *Critical Essays on Denise Levertov*.

Mazzaro's fine analysis of Levertov's poetic technique in the war poetry from *The Sorrow Dance* to *To Stay Alive* is meticulous and insightful. In discussing the early lyric war poems he recalls Levertov's own statement that they are "without personae: nakedly, candidly . . . in the poet's unmediated character" (*Cave*, 119–29). This permits "a submergence of self to larger linguistic and social issues" since "no fictive persona emerges." In his detailed reading of *To Stay Alive*, Mazzaro notes the poem's "aesthetic shifts" (narrative, quasi-narrative, lyric, imagistic flashes of actual events) as providing variety and renewed interest by changes in rhythm, form, and theme. Four kinds of "shifting" effectively produce important *distancing:* temporal, personal, generic, and emotional—offering a complexity revealed in dramatic juxtapositions. "The poet constructs a world shaped by a twofold dialectic of flowering and destruction." He then observes Levertov's use of montage, myth, the function of language, and touches upon Levertov's belief in spiritual energy. Through art, dream, and past experience, Mazzaro believes, Levertov reveals all the facets of her experience—both inner and outer. "The sanity, intelligence, and generosity that emerge in the process engage readers' sympathies in the conditions that unfold, and however nightmarish and disordered things become, the speaker knows to keep herself trustworthy by keeping her accounts accurate, believable, and realistic."[51] Mazzaro's essay is informed, sensitive, and extremely astute.

Throughout this maze of criticism, it is often easy to fall prey to a scholarly blindness that bedevils critical endeavor—that is, to lose sight of the poet's own "vision" of her aesthetic role. So it seems fitting to recall here Denise Levertov's early articulation of her own artistic goals. She wrote, early in 1961:

> I am interested in writing poems in which the dynamic interplay of objective and subjective experience is manifested. . . . Whatever affects us or that we affect may give rise to a poem; but no live poem can be made where there is no real affect. [*sic*] . . . The more intense the affective relationship and the more acute our perception of it the more chance for

intense life the poem has—given that the poet has enough craftsmanship to know he is dealing with live forces, and to handle them accordingly. Craftsmanship is a midwife, not a begetter or a mortician.[52]

Although *all* of the critics of Denise Levertov's poetry could not possibly be included in this study, it seems clear that there is great disagreement about the central argument: To what degree can the poets in the modern world permit their political and social consciences to be the centerpiece of their art? Some of Levertov's severest critics would claim that poetry is not the arena for "protest" (although Levertov disdains that term), while equally respected critics believe artists must speak their consciences. Still other critics believe that aesthetics are too often held hostage by a poet's moral convictions. Most twentieth century artists have declared *all* experience to be the fit subject for their creative endeavors, but equally clear is the need for poets, painters, novelists, or musicians to be true to their *artistic* principles.

3

Early Poems of "Awareness": "Westward through danger to the shores of peace"

The early poetry of Denise Levertov—the poetry written until 1965—has been called Romantic, in the tradition of English Romantic poetry of the nineteenth century. To use C. M. Bowra's definition,[1] this would suggest a poetry that strongly emphasizes the "Imagination" as the well-spring of the poet's art. Such an imagination draws its strength from religious and metaphysical sources. It is touched with the mystery of immanence—a "divine" gift, a numinous presence in the chosen poet. So strong was the "Imagination" of the poet that he often spoke in the voice of a prophet, a seer, a creature endowed with transcendent knowledge. But Romantic also meant truth to the emotions, or sentiment, a strong belief in the individual self, and the conviction that "poetry deals in some sense with truth." To Coleridge and Wordsworth, poetry was the "union of deep feeling and profound thought; the fine balance of truth in observing, with the imaginative faculty in modifying the objects observed . . ."[2] Bowra noted, "Every poet has to work with the world of the senses, but for the Romantics it was the instrument which set their visionary powers in action."[3]

In essence, the Romantics were basically revolutionary: revolutionary in their perception of man and the artist-as-seer, revolutionary in their "lover's quarrel with the world,"[4] revolutionary in their adoption of a new language for poetry, revolutionary in their new forms and tone. And their subject matter was not only the inner reality: for Blake it was "the outcast and the oppressed" for whom he felt infinite compassion; for Wordsworth it was the humblest creatures of the countryside. We know Shelley's own commitment to revolution. His Prometheus suffers in chains and is deeply "troubled by the images of cruelty and evil which have attacked him."[5] Both *Queen Mab* (1813) and *The Revolt of Islam* testify to Shelley's preoccupation with "revolution."

Thus, the Romantic poets must also be remembered as poets who were committed to the world they lived in—however fragmented and evil it might have appeared—and they never lost faith that the poet had a role in explaining the world of visible things.

It is interesting that Levertov in defining the *lyric* wrote, "We are to ask, then, of the political poem (which in our time means relatively brief, and therefore ostensibly lyric, poems that deal nevertheless with social observations and even opinions, such as the lyric *used not typically to deal with*) [emphasis mine] that it affect our senses and engage our aesthetic response just as much as one with whose content—spring, love, death, a rainbow—we can have no argument."[6]

There is little disagreement with the observation that the early poems of Denise Levertov followed a tradition long enduring in English poetry. Yet, as we have seen, the criticism levelled against Levertov is that she surrendered her Romantic tradition for an anti-war polemic in the sixties—a stance that stripped her poetry of its grace, its form, its beauty, its themes of nature and the simple life, of celebration and harmony. To make such a charge is to interpret too narrowly the English Romantics who frequently went beyond Browning's celebration in "Pippa Passes": ". . . God's in his heaven / All's right with the world."[7]

Denise Levertov is well within the Romantic tradition, but grew beyond it when she came to America and assumed a new voice, an American voice, and a "critical" perspective that led to her writing "engaged poetry." She has said that the changes from her earlier poetry have been largely the outcome of her American experiences and the growth and stimulation of her intellect as it responded to the challenge of the tumultuous decades of mid-century America and the new poetic initiation.[8]

But, as we shall see, the process was one of accretion. Levertov never lost the threads that are traceable from her Romantic beginnings: the capacity for wonder, the delight in the numinous quality of the inner world, the need to celebrate life's cycles and seasonal change in the external world, and a reverence for the qualities that make man both interesting and ennobling. And always, the social consciousness that was inherent in Romanticism itself, in her own family tradition, and in her intrinsic nature would deepen and grow and gain in complexity as both she and the events "came to maturity" in America.

In the early poems, the structures were often "traditional"; the familiar stanzaic patterns, regular metrics, frequent end-stopped lines, and rhymed patterns were part of her inheritance; young poets usually imitate their mentors and hers were the Romantics dear to every budding English poet in the early twentieth century. These early poems are generally brief, impressionistic, and lyrical. Yet an examination of many of the early volumes are interesting for the variety of meter and pattern with which, no doubt, she was experimenting. Nature is frequently the setting for her musings on her inner experiences, especially when she measures the impermanence of man against the permanence of nature. The early poems are replete with the music we associate with Romantic poetry—the rhythms provided by alliteration, repetition, internal rhymes, and the tropes that give a lyric richness to many of her utterances: similes, metaphors, pesonification; and the reverberation of audial as well as visual images. She *listened*, and her ear was sure. The speaker in her early poems was alternately romantic and dreamy, friendly and open, celebrative and poignant, thoughtful and nostalgic. At times, the world seemed distant and remote to the young girl in her solitude; at times she was warmly encircled and protected by those around her. She wrote about dreams, work, love, the beauty of life, being a woman, marriage, poetry, her family, and death as a romantic, rather distant, place. Her penchant for biblical and mythic materials both augurs her lifelong preoccupation with myth and fantasy and the mystical and provides her with a wealth of images to draw upon.

The landscape often reflects the inner experience of the speaker and is often dark, disordered by man, disturbed by ominous occurrences but always there—everlasting, perennially a reminder of nature's *ultimate* supremacy over man. The landscape is not always limited to nature in a primitive form—at times, the landscape may be the city. It is a sensitivity to **locale** that is often a hallmark of Levertov's poetry—we are acutely conscious of **where** we are. Many of the early poems make us aware of the speaker, often the "I" who observes, records, and reacts to the world around her. She is most often alone—an accepted state of "solitude" which Levertov admits has been her most frequent condition in life: not "loneliness" but "aloneness."[9] At times she yearns for friends who have left or experiences nostalgically recaptured. Alone, she is often dreamy, romantic, eye and ear alert to the experience within and the state of the world without. Thus the act of listening is central to the act of writing poetry, and silences are as significant as sound—much like the Rav, her illustrious ancestor, who "listened well." An examination of just a few poems from this early period reveals Levertov's response to Romantic tradition and touches themes with which she will be associated in the future from these "beginnings." "Durgan" is such a poem.

Written in 1945, it is considered by Levertov to be one of her poems of adolescence.[10] The theme is the melancholy one of lost childhood, for the bond between the young is irrevocably shattered and the speaker, adrift on the sands of Durgan's shore, moves from loss and longing to nostalgia and reflection; finally there is no desolation but acceptance.

Both in theme and in form, the poem is traditionally Romantic. It is lyrical in its metrical regularity (varying iambic tetrameter and pentameter), in its several feminine endings and enjambed lines, and in its use of figurative language: personification, metaphor, and simile. The music depends, as well, upon the use of anapests, alliteration, and repetition. The poem abounds in dramatic opposites: darkness and light, youth and maturity, land and sea, friendship and loss, sound and silence. It is replete with color. The tone is enigmatic; at first one would think the tone as one of longing, but the overall tone approaches more closely one of reflection as well as nostalgia, and ultimately acceptance of nature's immanence in the sounding sea. For Levertov, "dark" is not desolate; nor "each alone" as an occasion for despair—though this is a first impression. By the poem's end, the key words are eloquence and serenity and the gleam of the sand as the tide recedes. "Durgan" encapsules the experience of nature with the experience of the girl on the shore in the familiar and accepted place. As an early poem, it prefigures Levertov's sensitivity to nature in all its seasons; the lyrical power of her later utterance; and the penchant for juxtaposing opposites that often approach oxymoron. By 1945, Levertov had already proven herself to be a poet of some promise.

Written in the same period, "The Flight," "Sarnen," and "Interim" reflect Levertov's tendencies in these formative years. "The Flight" is Blakian in that Levertov has explained that the poem originated in a dream in which she heard Blake speaking the words: "The will is given us that / we may know the / delights of surrender."[11] The poem centers on an incident at once casual and significant. A bird, trapped in the poet's room at night, flies in a crazed state to escape—finally collapsing "huddled half-dead on the shelf . . ." But with morning, finding the opened window, the bird is reborn; it "gathered itself and flew / straight out / quick and calm (over the radiant chimneys—" The poem, written in 1945, is another example of Levertov's fine eye for detail—the image of the battered bird, the fight for freedom, the act of surrender, and the final "quick and calm" flight. The presence of Blake helps to retain the poem's dream-like quality. Yet the **action** is desperation and violence—ending in radiance. The form of the poem follows the erratic flight of the trapped bird; the swooping, battered victim is mirrored in the broken lines.

"Interim" is another poem that began in dream and is replete with both dark and glittering images. The poem is Denise Levertov's revelation of how the poet may conceive the poem, but the poem also touches on the familiar themes of solitude, transformation, the magical quality of words, and the act of listening. Critical is the expression that the creative life of the poet begins in that necessary "solitude." The poem contains an irregular meter, enjambed lines, and a flowing form that, like the "black page of night," flutters like a leaf through the poem—from hollowness to emanations and echoes to the glitter and gleam of the words that will be the poem. The flowing quality of waking, sleeping, listening, longing, falling, hesitating, dreaming, affording—all evoke the filling of the hollow mind "as an iron cup . . . would . . . fill with rain."

Denise Levertov's perennial interest in nature, the effects of nature on man, and the emotional states which she anatomized in these poems written before 1960 also included poems of love, marriage, friendship, and the act of writing: the wide trajectory of her experiences would eventually be revealed in all her poetry. But we cannot forget that, like many of us in the twentieth century, Denise Levertov was aware of war and knew war—if not at the front lines—as an ever-present reality from 1940 to the present; it became a pervasive theme of her art—war with its accompanying violence, loss, tragedy, cruelty, unreason, and the desecration of the delicate but necessary relationship of man to man.

The Early War Poems

Denise Levertov's first published poem, "Listening to Distant Guns," was written in 1940 when she was seventeen years of age. The place is Buckinghamshire, where, Levertov tells us in the "Author's Note," she had been evacuated, but the guns of Dunkirk were pulsing on the French coast, an ominous portent of the havoc that awaited England. Yet there is a distancing in the poem, a sense of impending violence but lacking the immediacy that violence will assume in her war poems of the sixties and seventies. Although the poem is restrained and highly condensed, the act of listening to the distant guns impinging on the quiet shores of England evokes its own kind of terror.

> The roses tremble; oh, the sunflower's eye
> Is opened wide in sad expectancy.

Westward and back the circling swallows fly,
The rooks' battalions dwindle near the hill.

That low pulsation in the east is war:
No bell now breaks the evening's silent dream.
The bloodless clarity of evening's sky
Betrays no whisper of the battle-scream.

One is immediately aware of the reductive affect of war—though distant—on nature: disturbed, awaiting future disorder. The poem juxtaposes the traditionally tranquil season of blooming roses, wakening sunflowers, circling swallows, perching rooks with the portentous sounds of war. An ambiguity remains in the overtones of the final words. While evening's dream and evening's sky remain aloof from the horrors of war, that horror is hinted in the language of the poem in the "battle-scream" of dying men on the field of battle.

Historically, Dunkirk was a successful military maneuver, in the sense that the majority of the landing force in France was rescued, but to the young woman uninitiated to the terrors of war, the spectre of that retreat must have been haunting.

The form of the poem suggests techniques Levertov would use during this early period: regular stanzas, alliteration, the personification of nature and a mind for verbs: tremble, dwindle, breaks. The images are often drawn from war itself: battalions, the pulsation of guns, betrayal, and battle-scream. In this and other early poems, the "I" speaker has not yet fully emerged, but like the speaker in countless other poems, she is engaged in listening—listening within and without as the experience becomes transformed into the poem.

Critics have noted the romantic exploitation of nature, for example, in the trembling roses and the open-eyed, sadness of the sunflower. But though such images are sentimental and do not enhance the poem as do the final lines—"The bloodless clarity of evening's sky / Betrays no whisper of the battle-scream"—this *first* published poem is successful in its visual and aural images, in its condensation, and in the hint of the chaos to come. Moreover, we are sensitive to the listener for whom war would ever be disruptive, ominous, tragic. No matter that few would disagree that World War II had to be fought; war is always a universal tragedy though the reasons be just.

Other poems that do not treat war *overtly* nevertheless reveal Levertov's unconscious sense of the war in the imagery, the disordered "real world," the despair in reflecting a lost Eden. Such a poem is "'They Looking Back All Th' Eastern Side Beheld,'" written in 1943, a year of suffering and hardship in war-torn England.

Like other poems during the war and its aftermath, "Fable" more than hints at the dark world but does not make overt reference to it, unless one is sensitive to the images of war and peace present in many of the poems of this period. At this time, when Denise Levertov was twenty-one and still living in the very private world of the self—the world of emotions, loves, losses, joys, the interim before meeting the world of the emerging adult—it is important to realize that war and violence were still outside the immediate periphery of her consciousness. That the war was there is a fact, and the images of war were part of her *unconscious,* and this does not deny their presence. Yet, for the young Denise Levertov, whose spirit would rise against inhumanity and terror, the actual horrors of war were still too remote from her immediate experience.

"Fable" was written in 1945; like another poem of this period, "To The Inviolable Shade," it is a love poem set against a hostile world. Yet "Fable" is persistently hopeful against all the realities of the external world—the darkness, the biting night air, the ravishment, the danger and the terror—undefined but present. The striking analogy of the children saved by a swan in the fable is central to the poem if—like the children—the lovers are to save themselves: "There still are forests we must penetrate."

"Fable," written barely at war's end, is a metaphor for a world yet in darkness. The images are of darkness, violation, death, pain, cries for release, pain, division, and indirection. The war was over, but there was still desolation and lifelessness: "impenetrable forests." The lovers are destined to separate, unless rescued like the innocent children in the fable. Thus, although the subject of "Fable" is not war, the aftermath of war is here. Although not yet as mature as the "voice" would suggest, the poet assumes the role of observer, lover, one who wishes to move forward bravely as revealed in the determined voice in the opening line: "There still are forests we must penetrate." The vision of the children at the poem's conclusion illuminates the way for the lovers who also "must not fear."

The form of the poem is a compressed, one-stanza statement of the need for direction, of urgency. The frequently enjambed lines, the repetitions, the intensity of the alliteration—still, silent, stricken, slow, strong, sea, south, storm—flow toward the climax where the soft, murmuring w's contain an intimation of whispered hope and peace: wallow, westward, wings of wisdom. Violation and peace here become the correlatives for the inner experience of love, loss, and "recovery" against the backdrop of the natural world—both hostile and benevolent. There is still, however, a romantic note here; in later poems about war and violation and the desecration of the land it is not love alone that will save us. A more supreme effort will be called forth. "Fable" is a lovely early poem, echoing other myths and fables: the Zeus-swan who captured Leda; the swallow, transformed Procne whom the gods saved from the hands of Tereus; and, of course, the many mythological children stolen (by creatures) who then miraculously find their way back to love and wisdom.

"Christmas, 1944" and "The Conquerors" represent Levertov's looking back on a time that demanded the courage and strength that England did, indeed, reveal as the war proceeded inexorably and death permeated even the safest places of refuge. These poems, written between 1944 and 1946, center on themes and images that will be more explicitly developed in later poems: chaos and death, courage and fear; the world in its natural state and the world in wartime. In "Christmas, 1944",

> Bright cards above the fire bring no friends near,
> fire cannot keep the cold from seeping in.
> Spindrift sparkle and candles on the tree
> make brave pretence of light; but look out of doors:
> Evening already surrounds the curtained house,
> draws near, watches;
> gardens are blue with frost, and every carol
> bears a burden of exile, a song of slaves.
> Come in, then, poverty, and come in, death:
> this year too many lie cold, or die in cold
> for any small room's warmth to keep you out.
> You sit in empty chairs, gleam in unseeing eyes;
> having no home now, you cast your shadow
> over the atlas, and rest in the restlessness
> of our long nights as we lie, dreaming of Europe.

As we will come to expect in Levertov's poetry, the gleaming "candle in the dark" (stanza 11) is all that lies between death and violation and a sense of order. The poem turns on the central irony of Christmas, the traditional season of celebration and new life and the darkness of war hovering over those huddled against the venomous wind.

The poem is replete with images of death and sorrow and violation: there is only a "pretence of light"; the carols "bear a burden of exile, a song of slaves"; the speaker invites poverty and death to come in: "this year too many lie cold, or die in cold." The last line is a balance of the two opposed realities Levertov recognizes in the human condition. Which one will win out? It would be difficult to say that hope and despair are perfectly balanced throughout the poem, for the images of darkness, death, venom, and plague outweigh the celebration of the Christian Coming; and while the festival season is not enough to dispel the fear and anxiety of what lies ahead, nonetheless the "voice of love" *is* the final phrase and we cling to its promise against the facts that threaten. It is interesting to note that in all the poems that directly or indirectly bear upon the second World War, there is rarely the emotion of anger or protest. The tone is sometimes fatalistic as England, nature, lovers, the speaker—all are the victims of conditions they cannot control. Sometimes, the mood is melancholy, reflective, poignant, or fearful. One would have to have lived in England during its throes of suffering in 1944 to understand the suffering that permeated every level of experience. Yet there was also, as we know historically, the toughness of England's stand and the everyday courage and uncelebrated acts of bravery that carried her people through the worst days.

"The Conquerors" also invokes the imagery of war. The real world is not much different than in earlier poems—all is in chaos: "Love lies bleeding / alone, / alone" and the tone of despair is reinforced by images of darkness and death. Such words as sombre, sunken streams, ever-darkening wine in throbbing veins of stone, the reddening evening pools—all suggest not only the final rays of the sun but blood as love itself lies bleeding. Again, nature is an objective correlative for the state of the speaker. As the poem proceeds, the microcosm is inhabited by "conquerors" who fear each other, by sinister intent, by empty streets. "The invaders lie awake / tormented by the treason in their hearts"; but here the speaker moves to a final attitude of hope and confidence:

> but love alone and deaf to their despair
> lies like a rock
> an island in the sorrow of the air

The final line is the hallmark of many Levertov poems as she seeks an island in "the sorrow of the air." Never disowning the facts of the world, the poem moves frequently to a bulwark against the chaos: love as an island, the lighting of a candle, the return to writing a poem, the stubborn but necessary search for possibilities. Like several of the poems we have looked at, the images are of war, violation, and death. It is as though the chief metaphors in these early poems are love is peace ("an island in the sorrow of the air") while dislocation, chaos, violence, and the division of human beings are always war.

World War Two ended, and in 1946 Denise Levertov—the fury and the violence and the fear of that traumatic event still echoing in her memory—found peace, as she always did, in the season in Corn-wall. "A Dream of Cornwall" reflects that quietude.

Like all of England, Denise Levertov turned her back on the war that had been her daily condition since the age of sixteen, but unconsciously that experience would never leave her. By the time she went to America in 1948, other social issues would trouble her and climax during the Vietnam crisis.

Perhaps some attempt to summarize these poems that consciously or unconsciously reflect war is needed in order to challenge the "leap forward" perceived by the critics of Levertov's later Vietnam poems. On the whole, the poems *are* romantic, nostalgic, reflective, and, in form and metrical patterns, reminiscent of some of her predecessors. Yet it cannot be denied that Levertov *lived through a war* in a country almost brought to its knees in suffering despite its unbelievable cour-age and readiness to act. The bombing of England—more widespread than is commonly known though less dramatic than the famous Blitz of London—touched every life. While it is true that many of the poems seem to be distanced from the physical "horrors" of war (Lev-ertov had been removed for a time from London as many youths were in the forties), there is nevertheless the omni present sense of war's devastation and disorder. The colors in these poems are blacks and grays and "tarnished gold"; nature is rarely sunlight and gleaming water—more often "every rock cries out to be released." Relation-ships are overshadowed by events; hope is ephemeral and "celebra-tion" of even traditional rites is attenuated and unsatisfying. A pervasive darkness more often sets the tone than joy or ebullience. If Denise Levertov did not see the broken bodies, she did see skele-tons of bombed-out houses; she knew well the effect upon the indi-vidual. After a period in the countryside, she had returned to her family in London. She lived through the bombings, but today she feels that the effects upon her were largely unconscious.[12]

On the whole, the poems are successful because of Levertov's sharp images of color, of tones, and of the pervasive darkness, as well as her ability to sustain the tone of the *entire* group of poems—pre-cisely because of the harmony she achieves between external events and her inner experiences.

Between the Wars

Between 1946 and 1960 Denise Levertov published four volumes of poetry: *The Double Image, Here and Now, Overland to the Islands*, and *With Eyes at the Back of Our Heads*. Some of the early poems, like

"Durgan" and "Christmas, 1944," were collected in *The Double Image* (1946) and "The Flight" in *Here and Now* (1957). In this poetry, spanning a period of fourteen years, Denise Levertov grew into a mature, highly accomplished poet. Her adolescence was over; her nostalgic enthusiasm for the Romantic poets was more subtly revealed in her poetry. But most important, her wide trajectory of experiences in the "new world," first expressed in *Here and Now*, had an important impact upon her poetry. Her diction changed as did her relation to reality. For the first time, the poet dealt substantively with immediate reality—less the imaginative dream world of the adolescent girl and more the confrontation with the exciting, stimulating, and sometimes vexing world outside herself. Hence, one detects a shift in subject matter and an ever-widening interest in her external life with the resulting expansion in her art.

More frequently, Levertov experimented greatly with form: meter, line pattern, enjambment, as well as subject, image, and tone. In *Here and Now* are gathered her poems about the city: "People at Night," "Xmas Trees on the Bank's Facade," "Central Park, Winter, after Sunset," and "Poem from Manhattan" whose unusual stanzaic form and choral endings are enhanced by the sharpness of the images and her gift for capturing the city's essence in sight and sound.

In another vein, "Everything that Acts is Actual" is Levertov's tribute to the imagination: "We are faithful / only to the imagination. *What the / imagination / seizes / as beauty must be truth*." The volume also contains two of her "marriage" poems and the beautiful and unusual poem, "Laying the Dust," a ritual of work lovingly and painstakingly done. Its central image of the water like a cat "arching its glittering back" is sharp and memorable.

By the advent of *Overland to the Islands* (1958), Levertov's poetry spanned not only subject but space itself. The volume included several poems she had published on Mexico ("Overland to the Islands," "A Supermarket in Guadalajara, Mexico," the often reprinted "Scenes from the Life of the Peppertrees")—a country whose beauty haunted her as one can see in the several Mexican poems in *With Eyes at the Back of Our Heads* (1960).

But *Overland to the Islands* also reflected Levertov's experimentation with verse forms, metrics, free verse, and theme. The banality of everyday life is offered tongue in cheek in "The Dogwood," and her personal vision broadens in "Merritt Parkway" as she muses on the mechanization of modern highways. Numbed, she writes about the death of children. She dances her losses in "In Obedience" and eulogizes the old and dying in "Pure Products,"—the title evoking, no doubt, William Carlos Williams's poem "To Elsie." Probably the most widely known poem of the collection is "Illustrious Ancestors" which was discussed earlier. The poem—condensed, witty, wise, and memorable—not only suggests Levertov's own "two worlds" but has much to suggest about the writing of poetry.

On the whole, one is struck by the range of emotion in the poems in *Overland to the Islands:* joy, humor, wonder, pain, and a sense of bereavement; but also thoughtfulness, worldliness, and wit. Images of dancing abound—whether reflecting joy or sorrow, or "—a radiance / consorting with the dance," in "Overland to the Islands," or in "I dance / now that work's over and the house quiet:" and "Let my dance / be mourning then, / now that I love you too late," in "In Obedience." Technically, Levertov was on a voyage of discovery, and the poems are a merging of the experience with the form the poem takes as the whole is transformed into art.

With Eyes at the Back of Our Heads (1960) is the last volume I should like to touch upon before I consider the significant step Denise Levertov took toward what she has called "poems of engagement" in *The Jacob's Ladder.* Levertov's frequent use of myth, characteristic of many of her poems, appears in these early works. Using fairy tale or parable, the volume introduces many poems illuminating Levertov's awareness of the needs of women, their prerogatives and their conflicts, as in "A Letter, " "The Wife," and "To the Snake." This last poem is rich in myth and fantasy. The sensuality of the poem is new in the poetry of women in the twentieth century, and the joy—which leaves "a long wake of pleasure" as the speaker awakens—fades with the dream into grass and shadows.

Later, in *O Taste and See* (1964), Levertov will further develop her self-awareness as a woman in such poems as "Song of Ishtar" in which "creativity and love are inextricable from the body," and "About Marriage," "The Ache of Marriage," "Hypocrite Women," and "Love Song." While it is sometimes tempting to think of Levertov as a feminist poet, this would be a mistake, for the breadth and depth of her experiences—while including those of being a woman—trace a wider trajectory than these poems suggest.

The Ladder

The Jacob's Ladder, published in 1961, represents a *turning point* in Denise Levertov's poetry: a focusing on larger social concerns; a commitment to "stand on common ground" while searching for those "shining pebbles" uncommon men have left; and a boundless belief that nature is restorative and nostalgic for one "who now in a far country / remembers the first river, the first / field, bricks, lumber dumped in it ready for building, / that new smell, and remembers / the walls of the garden, the first light." *The Jacob's Ladder* is a book of renewal, of hope, yet qualified by one who has already become a poet in the world. It is informative to look again at the volume's epigraph.

> Rabbi Moshe (of Kobryn) taught: It is written: "And he dreamed, and behold a ladder set up on the earth." That "he" is every man. Every man must know: I am clay, I am one of countless shards of clay, but "the top of it reached to heaven"—my soul reaches to heaven; "and behold the angels of God ascending and descending on it"—even the ascent and the descent of the angels depend on my deeds.[13]

The poem, "The Jacob's Ladder," takes its text from Buber, and is the key to the shift in Levertov's perspective:

> The stairway is not
> a thing of gleaming strands
> a radiant evanescence
> for angels' feet that only glance in their tread, and need not
> touch the stone.
>
> It is of stone.
> A rosy stone that takes
> a glowing tone of softness
> only because behind it the sky is a doubtful, a doubting
> night gray.
>
> A stairway of sharp
> angles, solidly built.
> One sees that the angels must spring
> down from one step to the next, giving a little
> lift of the wings:
>
> and a man climbing
> must scrape his knees, and bring
> the grip of hands into play. The cut stone
> consoles his groping feet. Wings brush past him.
> The poem ascends.

Levertov cites "The Jacob's Ladder" as her favorite poem among the many she has written. First the extended metaphor carries a dual meaning. Climbing Jacob's Ladder is universal aspiration: the difficulty of achievement, an easy feat only for angels. More personally for the poet, it is the painful, yet rewarding, task of writing poetry. If successful, the poem—like the angels—will ascend to one's aspiration, but—as all poets have confessed—the harsh reality is arduous.

What strikes us in this poem is the language—a continuum of the change already noted in the poetry since *Here and Now*. Levertov uses the extended metaphor of climbing a ladder. "*toward* Heaven" as Robert Frost noted in "After Apple-Picking," to describe the overwhelming challenge of creating a poem. Levertov reiterates a theme that has preoccupied her since *Here and Now*. Also notable is the change in Levertov's forms. The tone is more conversational, the images sharp—almost tactile, the lyrical quality more controlled—present but husbanded for the final lines: "Wings brush past him. / The poem ascends." But such achievement is possible only after climbing the sharp stairway, scraping one's knees, and bringing the grip of one's hands into play—all physical images of persistence and power.

The titles of other poems in *The Jacob's Ladder* suggest Levertov's expanding interests: "The World Outside," "The Rainwalkers," "From the Roof," and "During the Eichmann Trial"—(three poems that look back on the Nazi horrors). The forms are freer, the verse more experimental, the language a melange of allusion—mythic and classical—and the American idiom. Yet there is also present here the preoccupation with nature and men as they interact, Levertov's gift for collages of images, and her penchant for cameo poems like "The Tulips," "Resting Figures," and the Mexico poems.

In her continuing interest in social action and the persistent and haunting remembrance of things past, "Three Meditations" is an important poem for our consideration here. In many ways it a transitional sequence—the sense of social responsibility evident in the epigraph to the three poems—and the poems both looking forward to purpose and power and looking backward—suggested not by the content but by the images—to the "battlefield, stirring / with unheard litanies, sounds of piercing / green half-smothered by / strewn bones."

"Three Meditations" is a poem about the complexity of being, and the verbs dramatically emphasize the invitation posed by the poet: "Breathe deep of the / freshly gray morning air"; the planting will bear leaves and the leaves will "light up the death-mirrors with / shining petals." The reader is urged to "Stand fast in thy place," and to "Live / in thy fingertips . . ." Though shadows are everywhere, "Barbarians / throng the straight roads," and "There is darkness in me," the speaker ends this second poem with a statement of "multiplicity." Levertov, in explaining this poem, reveals her faith that we all incorporate a multitude. Whitmanesque in spirit, each of us is beautiful. The speaker in these final lines are both the "I" and the "We".[14]

> I, I, I, I.
> I multitude, I tyrant,
> I angel, I you, you
> world, battlefield, stirring
> with unheard litanies, sounds of piercing
> green half-smothered by
> strewn bones.

The final poem is a beautifully balanced "response to the creative wonder" as the epigraph to this third section declares, quoting D. H. Lawrence. The poet is brought back to song—to sing of death *and* life; "energy / being in him a singing." To be what he is, "filling his whole space," is the destiny of the poet. The Whitmanesque quality here of the poet-singer both celebrating and elegizing *all* experience adds a new dimension to a poet who has opened up a new world in these meditations.

The Eichmann Trial in Israel brought back all the horrors of the Nazi Holocaust the world wished to forget in the fifteen years that had elapsed since World War II. The three poems that comprise "During the Eichmann Trial" are important in that they signal dramatically Denise Levertov's newly sharpened and intense concern with social issues. Of course, the poem revives the war itself, and surely—for our purposes here—emphasizes the poet's larger canvas. We are haunted in these poems "When we look up / each from his being" (Robert Duncan), by such phrases as "we are members / one of another," and "the veils / are rent in twain" (The Passion of St. Mark, 15:38). "Are these the veils that have screened us from the horror of events?" Levertov seems to be asking. In any case, in the final glare of "Crystal Night," the poet recreates the desecration in the violent events when white hailstones become "each a mirror / for man's eyes." There is more in these poems than Eichmann's guilt—Levertov believes there is the shared guilt of all *civilized* mankind.

The first poem, "When We Look Up," touches upon the enigma of universal guilt. It is a complex vision Levertov perceives here, as she pictures the man in the booth in Israel, facing trial for the murder of millions of Jews.

> He had not looked,
> pitiful man whom none

pity, whom all
must pity if they look

into their own face (given
only by glass, steel, water

barely known) all
who look up

to see—how many
faces? . . . .

The question is posed: "Here is a mystery, / a person, an / other, an I?" seems to suggest more than the "man" but all of us. Levertov talked about this poem with me, repeating the questions: "How many / faces? How many / seen in a lifetime? . . . Shall we pity them?" she asked, and answered, "Only if we look into our own faces."[15] The mystery, as the poem looks into the heart of the Eichmann trial, poses: How many faces am I really seeing? For all of us—like the man in the booth—are, the poet believes, isolated, removed. The poem gives us the man and his defense, which, ironically, is indefensible. He merely *obeyed*. The poem is terse—stripped of any emotion save that which is produced by what we all remember and must not forget. The power here lies in the stark portrait of the man in the bulletproof glass booth. The images play upon reflections—in a glass, water, a mirror. The criminal does not understand as he recites his mechanical speech, "And what would disobedience / have brought me? . . ."

The images in the poem are not so much shocking as evocative—the yellow Star of David, the blood gushing from the earth, the metaphors of birth and death. The tone of the poem is one of pity: not so much pity for the apparition in the booth but for those who not even know "we are members / one of another," reverberations of Donne's tolling bell.

The poem's succinctness is accented by the brief, two-line stanzas, while its coldness and objectivity are reinforced by images of glass, steel, water, mirrors. The tragedy of both recollected horrors and the trial itself are equally enigmatic. Some of those who watched the drama of the trial unfold in Israel, as Levertov has revealed in the poem through the unanswered questions, also sensed the atmosphere of universal guilt, but, even more disturbing, the mystery of man's inhumanity to man.

"The Peachtree," the second Eichmann poem, is the account of a crime: the Jewish child who steals the yellow peach, the killing of the child by Eichmann. The covetous "mister death" who would have relished the peach with sour cream and brandy stands in sharp contrast with the final lines. The poem is a series of images; the action is brief, dramatic, swift, the comment sparse.

> Son of David
> 's blood, vivid red
> and trampled juice
> yellow and sweet
> flow together beneath the tree
>
> there is more blood than
> sweet juice
> always more blood—mister
> death goes indoors
> exhausted

Levertov tells us in her notes to the poem[16] that the account was envisioned by her as it might have happened, not a report of what did happen; indeed, the images of the poem, the emphasis on color, taste, sight, and the sound of "trampled" juice create a surreal flood of merging yellow and reds—colors evoking both life and death. In this moving account, the image "more blood than / sweet juice" lingers in the memory and conjures up for us the trauma of the Holocaust—more immediate for most of us in the killing of one small boy than in the abstract figures of millions—difficult for the human mind to conceive.

Perhaps the most aesthetically memorable poem in this sequence is "Crystal Night." Many of us who lived during this horrendous event know that Crystal Night was the name given to the infamous destruction of all of the Jewish businesses in Germany by the Nazis. The "crystal" evokes the tons of shattered glass that accompanied the desecration of storefronts and was a grim foreboding of the fate of six million Jews in the coming years. Now, as Eichmann stood to defend himself—the "apparition" who admitted, "They were cast out / as if they were / some animals, some beasts," the memory of Crystal Night hovered over the trial in Israel.

Denise Levertov's poem is an imagistic recreation of the infamous Crystal Night in tones of darkness and light, the emanations that come from "crystal"—piercingly bright—"splitting and splintering the silence," and the merging of violation and death in the "blood-light." The poem opens in darkness, emptiness—"dark within dark"—as the curfew leaves the streets desolate and still. The silence is broken by screams as the attack begins and the images that follow reflect the horrors created there. The language electrifies the poem as chaos and tumult seem to carry us to world's end: the screams, the broken temples, the "floodlights of their trucks," the smashing of windows, the "knives of glass," the "whiteness scattering / in hailstones." "Crystal Night" is a design of terror—the lines are uneven in length; few are end-stopped as the flow of action parallels the random nature of the attack itself, suddenly rearing up in the darkness. The light in the poem is unnatural light as "the veils / are rent in twain." Even "terror has a white sound / every scream / of fear is a white needle freezing the eyes." The poem is a collage of images that lose their traditional connotations and succeed in recreating the indescribable, the unutterable. The final lines merge the three poems by reiterating the recurrent motif: "each a mirror / for man's eyes." The poems bring us back to universal responsibility, communal guilt, the tragedy that man is capable of catastrophe such as this.

In contrast to Levertov's former poems on war and violence, the language is stronger, the sense of social conscience more immediate, the urgent need to see oneself in that mirror effectively "smashing the windows of sleep and dream / smashing the windows of history." The sleepers will awake; this is Levertov's faith, one that will remain with her into the present.

O Taste and See

By 1964, Denise Levertov was more than a "presence" in American poetry. The leading poets of the era, Charles Olson, Kenneth Rexroth, Robert Bly, Robert Creeley, Allen Ginsberg, Muriel Rukeyser, David Ignatow, and many other respected her as a fellow artist for her poetic accomplishments and her stature as an articulate voice of poetic theory. She had already published many essays on organic form and the technical aspects of poetry which would appear later in her two important prose works: *Light Up the Cave* and *The Poet in the World*. William Carlos Williams, some years before, had already recognized her gifts and had proclaimed to anyone who would listen that Denise Levertov would be America's poet of the future. Her reputation grew in stature with the regular publication of her work, both in magazines and collections. By the time *O Taste and See* appeared—her sixth volume of poetry—critics expected not only a lyric quality at its maturest, but wide-ranging and ever-deepening thematic variations. They found them in this new volume of poems that were experimental in form, diverse in tone, and both personal and universal in their choice of subject. Here there is dream and fantasy in the "Song of Ishtar," (written in 1959) and realism in "The Ache of Marriage" and "Hypocrite Women." Feminists seized upon those poems that grew from the female perspective and, to this day, Levertov's poems about her experiences as woman are frequently anthologized. Yet, as I have already suggested, Levertov's interests were broader than these particular poems might suggest. The social consciousness that had been a part of her experience since childhood now made its way subtly into her poetry. She did not as yet write about war and violence with the explicitness that would come in *To Stay Alive,* but the sense of being a "poet in the world" is clearly present in *O Taste and See.* It is present in "To The Muse" and in "The Old Adam" and in "A March." The clarion call in the volume is the poem that gives the book its title: "O Taste and See."

The poem begins with an ironic reversal of Wordsworth's lines: "The world is too much with us late and soon." The problem as Levertov sees it is that "The world is / not with us enough. / O taste and see." The poem calls sleepers to awaken to life.

The images are richly sensuous and the invitation to breathe, bite, savor, chew, swallow is to "transform / into our flesh our / deaths." To taste and "savor" the world is to know the pleasure and the pain, and the copious fruits are fitting images for the intensity of experience we are summoned to engage.

Although Denise Levertov has never, to the present, relinquished her passion for dream and the inner life, for stillness and solitude, "O Taste and See" is a warm invitation to engage life at every level. The final prose poem of the volume, which the poet says was given to her in a dream, emphasizes the growing conviction that one must know one's world if one is to know oneself.

Denise Levertov was already poised to reach the next important step of her journey—the creation of what she herself has called "engaged poetry." The seeds are already here in *O Taste and See* and will grow in *The Sorrow Dance,* where her most widely known Vietnam poem appears: "Life at War."

4

Vietnam and the Sixties: "la selva oscura"

> . . . what gives a poet the right and the ability to write a political poem is that the political event is personal to him or her. . . . one is personally implicated in it in some way, not necessarily by being there. . . . It's only out of that degree of *intimacy* with the political or topical—that internalization—it's only out of that good political poetry can be created.
>
> —Interview with Author, 10/9/82

The Sorrow Dance, Levertov's first volume which reflected her strong protest against the horrors of the Vietnam War, appeared in 1967— three years after America's active engagement in the war had begun and six years before its ending. As she tells it, her "personal involvement" in the war did not necessitate her being there, and, indeed, Levertov did not go to Vietnam until 1973. But, as she asserts, she was "intimate" with the "political" events in Vietnam through her own efforts on this side of the Pacific, so that it had become "internalized."

In his highly enlightening study of presidential constitutional authority, *Undeclared War: Twilight Zone of Constitutional Power,* Edward Keynes devotes a chapter to the Vietnam War, "Vietnam: Entering the Twilight Zone of Concurrent Power." He begins the chapter as follows.

Unlike the U.S. Civil War, the Vietnam War did not erupt or spring ". . . forth suddenly from the parent brain, a Minerva in the full panoply of war." Almost two decades before the Gulf of Tonkin incident on August 2, 1964, the Vietnam conflict began as a guerilla war between the Vietnamese and the French who attempted to reestablish their authority in Indochina after the Second World War. For more than twenty-five years five U.S. Presidents from Harry S. Truman to Richard M. Nixon committed the nation's resources to armed struggle in Indochina. . . . America's involvement in the Vietnamese conflict resulted from joint congressional-presidential action that began long before the first army combat troops arrived in Vietnam in 1965. American decisions to engage militarily in Vietnam resulted from a foreign policy consensus that committed the U.S. to security agreements with forty-two other nations.

Keynes notes that by the "final phase of American participation in the Indochinese War. . . . public fatigue and frustration with the war intensified" and Congressional support "ebbed." America's participation in the Vietnam conflict ended in 1973.[1]

By 1965, Levertov expressed her opposition in public to the tragedy and horror of Vietnam, while thousands of Americans had yet to raise their voices against the war. The enlightened Americans who kept close watch on events, the artists and poets who had served in Vietnam, either in combat or as conscientious objectors: poets like William Eastlake,[2] Walter McDonald,[3] William Ehrhart,[4] and John Balaban among countless others, were chronicling, protesting, charting the events of the war in Vietnam at the same time that a large majority of Americans committed themselves to America's role in the conflict.

No one could have said *when* the involvement became serious. As Keynes notes, five American presidents from Truman to Nixon supported some form of commitment to the war in Indochina. Only when the war entered American living rooms with the evening television news broadcasts and American youth demonstrated their defiance and refusal to be drafted did the country "experience" Vietnam. Too many Americans were poorly informed. Believing that America could never lose a war and unable to understand, while accepting, the theory of a "domino effect," many Americans lagged behind events and were baffled by the rising protest of the young on college campuses, the burning of draft cards, the exodus to Canada. It is *still* not clear to many Americans what Vietnam was all about—hence our increasing preoccupation with the Vietnam War and its aftermath that occurred more than thirty years ago. In his speech upon receiving an Oscar for directing the film *Born on the Fourth of July* in 1989, Oliver Stone noted ". . . the Vietnam War is not over, though some people say it is."[5]

As gradual as our involvement in the war, so gradual as well was the protest that erupted finally in the late sixties. The impatience with Americans, on the part of Levertov and others, must be tempered by an understanding of the optimistic, good-news perspective of Americans who listened to "kill ratios" in the media without a full awareness of the significance of those figures. It would be years before they heard of napalm, agent orange, the total obliteration of the landscape in Vietnam, and the tragic dilemma of the Vietnam vet who returned not a hero but an alien in his own country. "Waking sleepers" was a goal for those who found their voices in the sixties—in the merging public outcry of the young, and in the reports from those who *were* there!

In June 1966, Levertov's "Life at War" appeared in *Poetry Magazine*. Living in the tension of protest marches, demonstrations, military intervention on college campuses, and the dramatization by the press of the Vietnam conflict, Denise Levertov—whose knowledge of war and strong social consciousness were already part of her inner experience—would have found it impossible to remain a "banked fire."[6] Thus the question of her choice of theme is not at issue here. The issue, as I noted earlier, is whether she sacrificed her aesthetics for polemics, whether in her involvement with her theme her "form" failed her, as some of her critics assert.

The word "polemics" of course raises another critical issue: the term comes from "war"; and the assumption is that a polemicist is at war with, in controversy with, an antagonist. Whatever Levertov's *private* actions during the Vietnam conflict, much of her poetry cannot be called polemical. In most of these early Vietnam poems, she reports; she sympathizes with victims; she mourns the desecration of the land; she documents man's inhumanity to man; she reaches out to her courageous compatriots; she looks toward peace, toward returning—as she later says in "Candles in Babylon"—"from this place of terror / home to a calm dawn and / the work we had just begun." At times, unfortunately, she is "didactic"—a perspective that is anathema to many readers. But polemical is an unfortunate sweeping adjective chosen by her critics. As we examine the poems that appeared in *The Sorrow Dance* and later volumes, we can judge whether they are successful artistically. We are not here to question her themes but to determine whether her artistic judgment was held hostage by her politics.

Olga Poems

The Sorrow Dance was dedicated to the memory of Olga Levertoff, the poet's sister, who died in 1964, and the "Olga Poems" are important not only because of their intrinsic value as fine elegiac poetry, but because of the way in which they explain and mirror Levertov's ever-increasing social conscience. In an interview in 1971, the poet spoke about the importance of structure: ". . . in other works of art which I value I often see echoes and correspondences. . . . It's the impulse to create pattern or to reveal pattern. I say 'reveal,' because I have a thing about finding form rather than imposing it. I want to find correspondences and relationships which are there but hidden, and I think one of the things the artist does is reveal."[7] It is those echoes and correspondences that hold special interest for us. It would therefore be simplistic to view the Olga poems, as one critic has, as Levertov's absorption with the theme of death.[8] While the poems are nostalgic and often lyrical—for unredeemable time, for the "older sister" clearly a "presence" in the life of the younger child—they are more than this. The poems are also a "portrait," an observation that "everything flows," a painful recapitulation of Olga's death (at which the poet was *not* present), and a search for "a clearing in the selva oscura"—a reference not only to Olga's favorite poem "Selva Oscura" by Louis MacNeice but an oblique reference as well to Dante's "dark wood." For our purposes, the poem is a crucial road sign in the development of Levertov's social consciousness, for Olga was a political activist; and, indeed, in later poems about anti-war activity, Olga appears like a benevolent ghost on the fringes of the crowd. The poems are part of a larger section, "The Sorrow Dance," and the first mention of Olga comes in "A Lamentation" preceding the "Olga Poems." In the poem, it is Olga who dances "Sorrow" and the younger sister who dances "Summer":

> That robe or tunic, black gauze
> over black and silver my sister wore
> to dance *Sorrow*, hung so long
> in my closet. I never tried it on.
> And my dance
> was *Summer*—they rouged my cheeks
> and twisted roses with wire stems into my hair.

"A Lamentation" is grief, recollected joy of youth, and grief dismissed. It is something of a prelude to the six poems that follow. As often in Levertov's most troubled poems, there is a hint of the leavening moment—of joy, of nostalgia, of humor: "(and the little sister / beady-eyed in the bed— / or drowsy, was I? My head / a camera—)"—to balance the "bones and tatters of flesh in earth." The "Olga Poems" offer a portrait of a headstrong, idealistic, intelligent, fated woman who set herself against the world to "shout the world to its senses."[9] Olga's social conscience evoked here swept in the great inequalities around her that she could not deny and militated against. The poet traces Olga's journey in search of "a clearing / in the selva oscura": ". . . What rage for order / disordered her pilgrim-age—so that for years at a time / she would hide among strangers." Olga's tortured story is interspersed with memories of childhood that persist. "Your life winds in me," the poet writes, remembering child-hood pleasures. The poem is replete with visual and tactile images of Olga's striking beauty framed by her intellect and sensitivity: "Your eyes were the brown gold of pebbles under water. . . . And by other streams in other countries anywhere where the light / reaches down through shallows to gold gravel. Olga's / brown eyes."

The moving final lines of the poem are not only a glowing collage of the golds and browns and olivewood of the entire sequence, but a poignant reminder for the mature Levertov, her own sense of protest aroused by the "human shame" *she* now experienced, poised on the threshold of decision, yet still looking toward Olga for guidance:

> I cross
> so many brooks in the world, there is so much light
> dancing on so many stones, so many questions my eyes
> smart to ask of your eyes, gold brown eyes,
> the lashes short but the lids
> arched as if carved out of olivewood, eyes with some vision
> of festive goodness in back of their hard, or veiled, or
> > shining,
> unknowable gaze . . .

The metaphors in the poem—Olga herself, the figures of "danc-ing" and Sorrow's black and silver tunic—deepen the otherwise per-sonal utterance. Olga is inspiration, keeping "compassion's candle alight," and this is the Olga whom Levertov will recall. In this crucial poem, Levertov has revealed the source of her own pilgrimage—social consciousness but one leavened by compassion and hope and vision. This was her own interpretation of Olga's legacy.

Thus the "Olga Poems" are both personal and universal—as fine elegies are meant to be. The theme is both private and public, for it addresses the poet's own problem of finding a "clearing / in the selva oscura," and the dilemma posed by the need for the artist to speak out of the experience within, responding to the disorder of the world without. The language of the poems is controlled and evoca-tive, sensuous at times, coldly realistic at times, the figurative lan-guage both immediate and symbolic in its overtones.

> On your hospital bed you lay
> in love, the hatreds
> that had followed you, a

> comet's tail, burned out
> as your disasters bred of love
> burned out,
> while pain and drugs
> quarreled like sisters in you—

The emotion is strong, but it is reigned in by the necessity of looking past the poet's grief for her dead sister and toward the immediacy of her own concerns as both artist and "poet of the world." The "Olga Poems" testify to the belief that Levertov was able to combine her aesthetic gift with what would become now a lifelong concern: the need to give expression to her social consciousness, careful not to betray her artistic calling.

Olga is a haunting echo in Levertov's poetry—a motif that appears and reappears as Levertov groups her poetry—not according to chronology, she points out, but according to theme. Thus, in as late a volume as *Breathing the Water*, a poem "To Olga" appears. It is a poignant backward glance at childhood, before they spoke "less and less." Most moving is the penultimate stanza that reveals Levertov's remarkable ability for portraying the sisters "benighted but not lost":

> I felt the veil
> of sadness descend
>
> but I was never afraid for us,
> we were benighted but not lost, and I trusted
> utterly that at last,
> however late, we'd get home.
> No owl, no lights, the dun ridges
> of ploughland fading. No matter.
> I trusted you.

Whatever Levertov's personal feelings about her "brave . . . lost" sister, Olga shines in her petry like an exiled spark.

The War Poems

In a lecture given in 1970, "Great Possessions" (later reprinted in *The Poet in the World*), Denise Levertov commented about "revolutionary poetry":

> I believe our survival demands revolution, both cultural and political. . . . for a poet the attention to things and people, to the passing

moments filled to the brim with past, present, and future, to the Great Possessions that are our real life, is inseparable from attention to language and form. And he must recognize not only that poetry is intrinsically revolutionary but that it is so not by virtue of talking *about* any one subject rather than another (though if he has political concerns they may not be excluded, and *not* to have political concerns—in the broad and deep sense of the term—is surely impossible to the aware adult in the last quarter of the twentieth century).[10]

I cite this statement because it goes a long way toward our understanding of Levertov's first explicit poem about Vietnam, "Life at War." The poem gives its title to a grouping of nine poems that center upon the Vietnam War and, more specifically, the expansion outward of Levertov's explicit reaction to events that had long disturbed her. In a word, these are poems of "engagement" as the facts are revealed with graphic vividness and coupled with the poet's inner response. Crucial to Levertov's view is her oft-stated insistence on the indivisibility of her subject (things and people and those passing moments filled to the brim with past, present and future) and language and form. This is her model for successful poetry—the inseparable quality of the "subject"—that which is "important to the aware adult"—and form and language.

The poem that introduces the series, "The Pulse," moves from Levertov's "inner world" of dream and mystical lights and shadows to the "outer world" that appears to be "resplendent" and glittering.

The Pulse

Sealed inside the anemone
in the dark, I knock my head
on steel petals
curving inward around me.

Somewhere the edict is given:
petals, relax.
Delicately they arch over backward.
All is opened to me—

the air they call *water,*
saline, dawngreen over its sands,
resplendent with fishes.
All day it is morning,

all night the glitter
of all that shines out of itself

crisps the vast swathes of the current.
But my feet are weighted:

only my seafern arms
my human hands
my fingers tipped with fire
sway out into the world.

Fair is the world.
I sing. The ache
up from heel to knee
of the weights

gives to the song its
ground bass.
And before the song
attains even a first refrain

the petals creak and
begin to rise.
They rise and recurl
to a bud's form

and clamp shut.
I wait in the dark.

One of the most lyrical of Levertov's poems, "The Pulse" is, on one hand, the celebration of the delicate radiance of the natural world, and, on the other, the condition of the poet, aspiring toward that world but weighed down by her own humanity. The cycle from darkness to light, from joy and celebration of the glittering world, from the ache of weight to the song, and—finally—from light to darkness once more constitutes the "experience" of the speaker. The unusual metaphors of the poem serve to emphasize the tension between the sense of imprisonment in blackness and the brilliance of the natural world: the "steel petals" of the anemone that seals one up; the glitter of night that "crisps the vast swathes of the current"; the "seafern arms" reaching for the world all dramatize the conflict. At the end, left waiting in obscurity, the poet is closed out of that luminous world.

"The Pulse" is a prelude to the poems that follow and prefigures the tragedy to come when the beauties of nature are obliterated by the blackness. In its form, the pulsing that is the opening and closing anemone symbolizes the pattern of imprisonment on one hand, and the freedom to sing on the other. The dreamlike quality of the poem that never mentions Vietnam or its horrors hints at the tragedy that will envelop the land and leave all in the obscurity of death.

The poem, "Life at War," immediately followng "The Pulse" is, perhaps, Levertov's best-known Vietnam poem and addresses itself to the ominousness hinted in "The Pulse":

> The disasters numb within us
> caught in the chest, rolling
> in the brain like pebbles. The feeling
> resembles lumps of raw dough
>
> weighing down a child's stomach on baking day.
> Or Rilke said it, 'My heart . . .
> Could I say of it, it overflows
> with bitterness . . . but no, as though
>
> its contents were simply balled into
> formless lumps, thus
> so I carry it about.'
> The same war
>
> continues.
> We have breathed the grits of it in, all our lives,
> our lungs are pocked with it,
> the mucous membrane of our dreams
> coated with it, the imagination
> filmed over with the gray filth of it:
>
> the knowledge that humankind,
>
> delicate Man, whose flesh
> responds to a caress, whose eyes
> are flowers that perceive the stars,
>
> whose music excels the music of birds,
> whose laughter matches the laughter of dogs,
> whose understanding manifests designs
> fairer than the spider's most intricate web,
>
> still turns without surprise, with mere regret
> to the scheduled breaking open of breasts whose milk
> runs out over the entrails of still-alive babies,
> transformation of witnessing eyes to pulp-fragments,
> implosion of skinned penises into carcass-gulleys.
>
> We are the humans, men who can make;

whose language imagines *mercy,*
lovingkindness; we have believed one another
mirrored forms of a God we felt as good—

who do these acts, who convince ourselves
it is necessary; these acts are done
to our own flesh; burned human flesh
is smelling in Viet Nam as I write.

Yes, this is the knowledge that jostles for space
in our bodies along with all we
go on knowing of joy, of love;
our nerve filaments twitch in its presence
day and night,
nothing we say has not the husky phlegm of it in the saying,
nothing we do has the quickness, the sureness,
the deep intelligence living at peace would have.

The poem turns on Rilke's metaphor of the "overflowing heart." The theme: the anger, the anguish, the experience of "life at war" speaks for itself in this poem in which the visual images shock and finally numb our senses. We need make no further comment on Denise Levertov's strong emotional commitment for peace and against war. I should like to point out, instead, those formal qualities that enhance the poem's theme. The basic tension in the poem rests upon the *duality* of mankind: all he can "make" and all the inhuman acts he can perpetrate. The images are balanced precisely on this duality. Against the images of violence, destruction, and unimaginable cruelty, there are images of the heights of human potential. It is the imagery that orders the poem's structure, dictates the tone that vibrates between despair and hope, and is responsible for the great emotional impact of the poem. The title itself is an oxymoron, and prefigures the "impossible" juxtapositions perceived by the speaker.

Levertov has chosen a form that reflects the objects before her eyes: fragments, broken lines, enjambed lines, arrhythmic patterns to reinforce the chaos of war and its casualties; and, in contrast, structured, often end-stopped lines, patterned meters to mirror the order and significance of human life in time of peace and sanity. The poem plays on irony, reinforced by frequent repetition. Images evoking strong emotion are juxtaposed to "statement": "We are the humans, men who can make"; and the control in the poem depends upon the double vision of the speaker and the alternation of tone from horror to speculation to—in the end—the quietness of a desired peace.

No less important is the *effect* upon us as readers: the effect of seeing and *knowing* all that is engendered by war, the effect of *knowing* ourselves as we seek to attain our potential, the effect of trying to reconcile a dual image of man that defies reconciliation, reminding us of Shakespeare's great portrait: "What a piece of work is a man . . ." But at the moment that Hamlet declares man's potential, he despairs: "yet to me, what is this quintessence of dust? Man delights me not . . ."[11]

Levertov's poem ends with the need, in the face of the desecration of war, to remember the joy and the love intrinsic to the human condition. This is the faint hope for a dark moment in human history, but the final lines look *toward* living in peace. Levertov's statement on the rhythm of the "inner voice" that controls the rhythm of the poem is particularly relevant in "Life at War."

> . . . a poet, a verbal kind of person, is constantly talking to himself, inside of himself, constantly approximating and evaluating and trying to grasp his experience in words. And the 'sound' inside his head, of that voice, is not necessarily identical with his literal speaking voice, nor is his inner vocabulary identical with that which he uses in conversation. At their very best, sound and words are song, not speech. The written poem is then a record of that inner song.[12]

The response to "Life at War" has been varied. Clearly, it is one of Levertov's most anthologized poems, and while a minority of critics have felt the language too strong or the subject taboo, the majority have cited the poem's immediate effect of war on our psychology, philosophy, and language. James F. Mersmann has made the point, "It is the loss and contradiction of vision that makes the war horrible to Levertov, and this may be said without any denigration of her compassion or humanity."[13] Mersmann bases this evaluation on the lines in the poem that the "imagination / filmed over with the gray filth of it," represent the poet's loss of vision; indeed, Levertov herself has admitted in the poem that the "awareness" of war's horrors—*threatening* the imagination—precludes the poet's *certainty* that all that lies within man's power for goodness will reappear. Nor is the poem's dual vision an unfortunate (if understandable) impairment of her aesthetic power. The Vietnam War staggered the imagination of all but the totally insensitive, but ultimately it was Levertov's very strong belief in the unity that lies beneath the world of visible things that supported her "vision" and her form, demonstrated earlier. Levertov's poetry *was* a "poetics of order" as Mersmann asserts, but the form should not be confused with the chaos she has chosen to depict. As to Mersmann's reference to Levertov's own "admission" that she had lost her vision and poetic form, we need to hear the poet's response: "those who turn away from concern for the commonweal to cultivate their own gardens are found to have lost touch with a nourishing energy. Better a bitter spring than no irrigation at all. Ivory towers look over deserted landscapes."[14] Levertov had never looked over "deserted landscapes" but here, for the first time, her eyes turned toward matters that demanded response, and her poetic powers were in no way impaired by her apprehension of the grim realities of Vietnam.

Another critic, Marjorie Perloff, does not see a split between subject and metaphoric mode in Levertov's war poetry, though she does observe it in a large majority of American verse.[15] As Susan Hoerchner has said, succinctly, "As a poet Levertov feels that she must act in the world. As a maker and instrument of poems she also struggles to bring forth her unique celebration of life."[16] These twin impulses remain the hallmark of Levertov's poetry to the present. She believed the poet had an obligation to society, and in 1960 she wrote that "they [the poets] are . . . *makers,* craftsmen: It is given to the seer to see, but it is then his responsibility to communicate what he sees, that they who cannot see may see, since we are 'members one of another,'"[17] Later, in this same essay, she wrote, "I long for poems of an inner harmony in utter contrast to the chaos in which they exist. Insofar as poetry has a social function it is to awaken sleepers by other means than shock." Thus it is well to distinguish between the disorder of modern life and the "supposed" disorder in the aesthetics of Denise Levertov.

"Didactic Poem," also written in the sixties, appears in *The Sorrow Dance* immediately after "Life at War." Later, in 1975, Levertov wrote, "The poetry of political anguish is at its best both didactic and lyrical."[18] We need to remember that the word "didactic" means "morally instructive," and, although today it has an unfavorable connotation, we should also recall that poets have always been didactic. Nonetheless, the word has an unpleasant evocation, and the poem reveals *indirectly* what Levertov might have omitted in her title. The successful artist need not preach if the subsumed message of the poem is communicated through the structure and language—"the dynamic of sensuous forms." We have only to hear the poet-prophet Ezekiel in Eliot's *The Waste-Land* to remind us of the role of moral instructor frequently played by modern poets: "What are the roots that clutch, what branches grow / Out of this stony rubbish? Son of man, / You cannot say or guess, for you know only / A heap of broken images," and it is the richness of Eliot's imagery here—borrowed from Scriptures—that saves these lines from didacticism.

Thus Levertov's poem is better than that which is promised in the title. The poem rests upon the duality of death and life. Death must be conquered, refused. The many images of giving, inventing, dancing, and creating are life images, juxtaposed to what we must refuse: feeding our dead spirits, our infamous deeds, heeding the deathknell of past atrocities. The alliteration of the opening lines—the resounding effect of "dead, drink, deeds, and dead spirits—suggesting a tolling deathknell is contrasted with the language of creativity in the poem: [positive] deeds, imagination, speech, invent, and dance. The speaker enjoins us all to heed our own "will to live," to give expression to our "imagination of speech," to create our lives. The alternative is too horrifying to contemplate should we fail: "we shall thirst in Hades, / in the blood of our children." "Didactic Poem" is strong, positive, alive with our potential to *refuse* the dead and elevating as we are invited to "dance / a tune with our own feet." The poem testifies to Levertov's commitment—despite past experience—to respond to life's challenge, a theme that will remain with her through her most despairing moments.

The litany with which the poem opens is in sharp contrast to the lines which follow, "Refuse them!" The opening lines are a kind of dirge; the lines in the second part of the poem a kind of dance as the poet urges us to "create our lives, / invent our deeds, do them, dance / a tune with our own feet." The verbs emphasize a "way to be," for in the midst of despair, Levertov keeps faith with possibility—no matter how impossible the dream.

The rest of the poems that comprise section VI of *The Sorrow Dance:* "Life at War," are various perspectives on the war in Vietnam, but reflect as well Levertov's *inner* response to the events *outside*. The last poems in this series were written during the late sixties. As we might expect there are recurrent motifs and the repetition of the horrors that are engendered by war, but otherwise they differ greatly one from the other—in tone, image, metaphor, form, and perspective. It is almost as though we see the war through different eyes, but one central theme prevails: the ironic contrast, already dramatically presented in the poem "Life at War," between the chaos, destruction, and death and the "possibilities" that are the gifts of peace. Levertov never lets us forget the waste—not only of human life—but the wasting of nature in the destruction of a once-beautiful land.

In "What Were They Like?" the poem rests upon a dialogue between an innocent—the questioner—and the speaker who "knows" all:

1. Did the people of Viet Nam
   use lanterns of stone?
2. Did they hold ceremonies
   to reverence the opening of buds?
3. Were they inclined to quiet laughter?
4. Did they use bone and ivory,
   jade and silver, for ornament?
5. Did they distinguish between speaking and singing?

There are few metaphoric overtones in this first part; Levertov is dealing with the "facts" of Vietnamese life. The responses comprise the remainder of the poem. The "answers" ironically pick up the language of the questions, and the perversions of wartime are revealed in the "distortions" of a once-revered way of life. What emerges from the answers is the summation of war's inevitable outcome expressed as metaphors: "hearts turned to stone," children killed, bones charred, bombs smashing mirrors so that "there was time only to scream,"—the destruction of the human spirit. The final stanza—the final answer—strikes a poignant note as an echo of the past haunts the present:

> There is an echo yet
> of their speech which was like a song.
> It was reported their singing resembled
> the flight of moths in moonlight.
> Who can say? It is silent now.

One might question the format of the poem—a pseudo-journalistic and deliberately cold approach to the catastrophe of Vietnam (so effectively emphasized by the repetition of "It is not remembered"), but the device is reminiscent of the reportage of the Vietnam War in interviews on television. Equally absent from this poem is the presence of metaphor and symbol in the earlier part of the poem—something we have come to associate with Levertov's later poetry. True, there is a value in the poem's "understatement" and lack of intensity that is present in "Life at War," but the horror and the tragic waste of a civilization are present here. The final stanza offers an added dimension of recollected beauty in the image of the flight of moths. One is struck by the reportorial voice of the first six questions contrasted with the graphic images and the poignancy of the final lines. After her visit to Hanoi, as we shall see, there is a subtle shift in tone that reinforces this note of empathy. The silence that closes the poem is juxtaposed to the "echo," which *echoes* in our minds. This is a poem not of anger but of anguish.

"Enquiry," one of "Two Variations," presents us with another perspective—that of a Vietnamese woman who watches the atrocities of war in silence. The omniscient speaker, whom I assume to be a mother, addresses the "killers," those who carry on the "scheduled" destructive business of war and yet sleep at night. The first poem closes with the ominousness of the lidless eyes watching and the reminder that "She will outlast you." The form of the poem—the short lines, sharp images, juxtapositions of burning flesh, writhing, dying children and lidless eyes with the eating, sleeping, buying, selling killers—creates the tone of bitterness. There is no hope here, save that the woman will outlive the killers. And there is little solace from that observation. Here, Levertov allows herself the temptation to preach to the killers—a tone that flaws the first part of the poem. But in "The Seeing," the power of the suffering victims is reminder enough of the inhumanity of killing children indiscriminately. In this poem Levertov reaches the nadir of despair. The tone—not the theme—will change in later poems, but the sheer horror of *seeing* what war wreaks upon the innocent—women and children—cannot be assuaged.

The mother "sees" even with "hands over my eyes" the living and the dead; ironically, the dead are "as if alive" and the living as if dead. Death comes from the skies releasing "wet fire, the rain that gave / my eyes their vigilance." There is no overt emotionalism in the poem, but the fragmented images, the terse lines, the act of "seeing" give emotional weight to the poem. Mere survival itself seems a pyrrhic victory.

Levertov has been censured as "hysterical," over emotional, lacking control and order which she so highly prizes. There is anger but not "hysteria" in the poems in *Life at War.* Yet, the immediacy of the Vietnam War in these poems cannot be dismissed, and the sharp visual images capture the violence and the human indifference to the ravishment of the human body and soul. The images of burned human flesh, lidless eyes, babies nursing at dry breasts, and charred bones are the realities of Vietnam, and the tone of the "Life at War" poems, while at times bitter, incredulous, poignant, or despairing, is always controlled. The order that Levertov assumes is the antithesis of the horrors she describes—in vivid image collages, in rhetorical structures (such as "What Were They Like?") in measured rhythms and repetitions. That order, for Levertov, is to be the underpinning of her poetry, to be sought and found, as she reaffirms again and again.

"The Altars in the Street" begins with the poet's notation that on June 17, 1966, the children of Vietnam built altars in the street as part of a Buddhist campaign of nonviolent resistance. The altars become a symbol of transformation as their presence change the war-ridden city into a temple: "fragile, insolent, absolute."

The form of the poem is highly structured in three-line stanzas, contains more end-stopped lines than in the previous poems, and follows a more patterned metrical design. The poem, like the altars, is an "edifice" to the effort of the children to create a structure of *positive* resistance to the "oncoming roar / of tragic life that fills alleys and avenues." The images of the children's efforts are a cause for hope: the green dawn, the altars, the prayers, the "hale and the maimed" working together, the dreams, and, finally, a temple. The final line encompasses Levertov's faith in the order that ultimately overrules the corruption and the bloodshed: absolute though fragile, an artifact of man's resilience and Buddha's silent power.

For the first time in these Vietnam poems, the poet reveals her hope in the conjoined effort of God and man—here the innocent committed children. "The Altars in the Street" will be the touchstone of Levertov's response to the apprehension of war and violence. Although at times, her own faith may hesitate and falter, the overwhelming evidence is on the side of the "people" rising to the challenge "at green dawn nimbly to build."

One senses that Denise Levertov's sister, Olga, an activist through most of her brief life, is ever present in Levertov's consciousness—and particularly when her themes are driven by conscience. "A Note to Olga, 1966" is the poet's account of a peaceful rally to "Stop the War." The hue and cry had already spread throughout the country. Olga is the ghostly presence supporting the demonstration as the haunting words of "We shall Overcome" linger in the air:

> Though I forget you
> a red coal from your fire
> burns in that box.

The lost sister seems to be one with the "limp and ardent" protesters dragged off in the police paddy-wagon. As I have already noted, the poet conjures up the vision of Olga in her own moments of "engagement," who would have proudly marched with those who shuffle along in the dark snow. From this point, Levertov recounts her role as an activist in an already popular cause. The poem is yet another perspective on the war—group action—which Levertov chronicles in future poems. While this is history, it is also poetry, because "A Note to Olga" with its poignant memories and comparisons of past and present activism is also reinforced by the form of the poem: its stanzaic pattern, its regular meter, and its sharp and unusual images—especially the opening image—visual and tactile—which sets the tone of the poem:

> Of lead and emerald
> the reliquary
> that knocks my breastbone,
>
> slung round my neck
> on a rough invisible rope
> that rubs the knob of my spine.

The final poem in the group, "Living," corresponds to the first, "The Pulse," in that the scene once again is nature. Levertov's discussion of this poem in an interview is especially illuminating. When she was asked, "What does religious mean to you?" she responded in this way:

> The impulse to kneel in wonder. . . . The impulse to kiss the ground. . . . The sense of awe. The felt presence of some mysterious force, whether it be what one calls beauty, or perhaps just the sense of the unknown—I don't mean "unknown" in the sense of we don't know what the future will bring. I mean the sense of the numinous, whether it's in a small stone or a large mountain. I think at this particular point, that sense of joy which you've mentioned in my poems, and which I think is very real to me, and has been, at a very low ebb.
>
> I think of my poem called "Living". . . . There's a certain apocalyptic sense in that, but there's also a kind of joy in the marvelousness of that green fire in the grass and leaves, and in the beauty of the little salamander. My feeling this winter . . . is doom-filled, the sense of time running out is pretty much squashing my sense of the beauty of the ephemeral being ephemeral.[20]

Yet the theme of the ephemeral quality of life in nature gives a special poignancy to the scene that celebrates the final moments of beauty: "The fire in leaf and grass / so green it seems / each summer the last summer." The poem juxtaposes images of life with images of impending death: "the leaves / shivering in the sun, / each day the last day." The salamander, so close to death, moves as in dream. "Each minute the last minute," and although this poem could easily be the poet's celebration of nature's *desired* yearly cycle, it appears in *Life at War*—presaging the end of life as it was known in "What Were They Like?": "Did they hold ceremonies / to reverence the opening of buds?"

Closing the series on a note of "anguish and despair"[21] brings to a pause Levertov's "imagined" first stage of the journey of life and death in Vietnam. In *Relearning the Alphabet*, Levertov is still, at times, in the "selva oscura": yet she is also still awed by the beauty in nature and affirms her faith in that hidden order where marigolds—the resurrection flower—continue to bloom in Vietnam—though one is still weighted down by the "Disasters / of history," the "anguish of mortality."

Relearning the Alphabet (1970) is a continuation of Levertov's longing for the "here and now": a living-in-the-present. Vietnam is still with us, inexorably, in the present, and, indeed, many of the poems in the volume were written during the late sixties as were those in *The Sorrow Dance*. But the title of the collection suggests other themes: getting back to "basics"—relearning the tools of one's craft; "tentatively exploring new directions," as Charles Altieri noted, but as importantly, continuing one's pilgrimage to "awaken" insensitive sleepers to the events taking place a continent away.[22]

In yet another sense, "relearning the alphabet" is a ritual: it is the activity of going back to beginnings to reaffirm the terms upon which we create our values, our priorities, our future direction. For Denise Levertov, a very large part of this activity is a return to language—the words which give flesh to her inner experiences.

Thus the opening poem "The Broken Sandal"—similar to Dante's sense of being lost in the "selva oscura"—is a "statement" of the condition that will call for a relearning process and provides a clue for the direction the volume will take—a pilgrimage.

The Broken Sandal

> Dreamed the thong of my sandal broke.
> Nothing to hold it to my foot.
> How shall I walk?
> 	Barefoot?
> The sharp stones, the dirt. I would
> hobble.
> And—
> Where was I going?
> Where was I going I can't
> go to now, unless hurting?
> Where am I standing, if I'm
> to stand still now?

That the experience occurs in a dream prefigures the "inner voyage" ahead. As in many dreams that reflect unconscious emotional, psychological, and spiritual states, the dreamer admits to being "lost"—at some mysterious crossroad where movement forward is difficult if not impossible and memory of the quest is obscure. The images attest to the questing nature of the dreamer who, in this moment in time, stands still, seeking her direction, hampered by the "broken sandal." The terrain is difficult; the voyager full of questions and frustration.

Altieri had written that "The Broken Sandal" reveals that "Every step is no longer an arrival as [Levertov] replaces confident assertion with a series of questions. . . . This poet of place and attention now can neither stand peacefully nor follow a purposive path. . . . she perceives in the present at least as many inescapable reminders of suffering and pain as causes for awe and religious acceptance."[23] The broken sandal is a metaphor for the dreamer's spiritual and psychological condition before embarking upon a voyage of difficult terrain: a condition of "stasis."

"Indirection" and "immobility" are universal conditions, described by numerous poets, that impede a voyage of discovery. That Levertov, quoting Rilke, wrote "Every step in an arrival," emanated from the belief that one *always* knows the direction; but this is often not the case. Two poets whose "journeys" are marked by "stations" of doubt, of loss, of impaired vision, who might well have asked: "Where am I standing, if I'm / to stand still now?" are T. S. Eliot and Frost. In *Four Quartets*, the traveller muses.

> In order to arrive at what you do not know
> You must go by a way which is the way of ignorance.
> In order to possess what you do not possess
> You must go by the way of dispossession.
> In order to arrive at what you are not
> You must go through the way in which you are not.
> And what you do not know is the only thing you know
> And what you own is what you do not own
> And where you are is where you are not.[24]

This is part of the speaker's spiritual journey of a pilgrim whose has already gained the knowledge that every step is *not* always an arrival. In Robert Frost's poem, "Directive," written at a late stage in his life, he can still assert the need to lose oneself to find oneself.

> Back out of all this now too much for us,
> Back in a time made simple by the loss
>
> Of detail, burned, dissolved, and broken off
> Like graveyard marble sculpture in the weather,

There is a house that is no more a house
Upon a farm that is no more a farm
And in a town that is no more a town.
The road there, if you'll let a guide direct you
Who only has at heart your getting lost.

. . . .

And if you're lost enough to find yourself
By now pull in your ladder road behind you
And put a sign up CLOSED to all but me.

. . . .

Here are your waters and your watering place.
Drink and be whole again beyond confusion.[25] (emphasis mine)

Frost's process of loss and recovery is close to Levertov's, although the reasons may be quite different. Levertov will again find her direction, but her sense of loss here and in "Advent 1966" are the direct outcome of her crisis of faith in man initiated by the Vietnam War for Levertov as well as other artists.

Perhaps more significant is that aesthetically "The Broken Sandal" is controlled and ordered. The questions form the rhetorical structure of the poem, the image of the sandal an affective metaphor, both for the speaker's moment of crisis and for the evocation of a journey to be made. If the sandal is a vehicle for travel, the speaker will have to find another "form" to convey her on her pilgrimage. Levertov will use the metaphor of the sandal again in her latest volume, *A Door in the Hive,* in the poem, "A Traveler": "If it's a chariot or sandals, / I'll take sandals / . . . "I'll chance / the pilgrim sandals."

In "The Broken Sandal," the order is not yet perceivable, but not because the order is not there; the poet-dreamer must find a new means for discovering it. Levertov confronted this problem at the beginning of the poem, "Relearning the Alphabet," appending the words of Heinrich Zimmer, "The treasure . . . lies buried. . . . And yet . . . only after . . . a journey to a distant region, in a new land, that . . . the inner voice . . . can make itself understood by us."[26]

Thus, with the writing of *Relearning the Alphabet,* not only a *new* direction of her pilgrimage, but a renewed "inner voice" is summoned. The tone of "The Broken Sandal" is pragmatic: the moment is one of temporary "loss," one of searching for the form and the direction which necessitates pain and sometimes the frustration of standing still.

It is not clear to me why Levertov's severest critics could consider a poet's apprehension of anguish and tragedy that was Vietnam—inescapable and relentlessly present—as a serious "failure" of both her vision and her aesthetics. Given Levertov's social consciousness, her attitude toward war, and her innate sensitivity to human waste and suffering, her momentary "lapse" of direction is understandable. Moments of hesitation and doubt have always been the pilgrim's experience.

The key question here is whether Levertov's state of "involvement" seriously hampered her poetry by sacrificing her aesthetic vision. Poem after poem testifies to Levertov's sustaining vision, though admittedly there were moments of serious introspection and the need for renewed faith in man. If her belief in man "faltered," it did not follow that the poet had lost control of her poetic sense. I believe I have indicated above that the form of the poem, the symbols of pilgrimage and sandal, the repetitions, the alliteration, and the rhetorical device of the "questions," attest to the poet's command of her poetics. As to the aesthetic "pleasure" of the poem, it rests upon the use of the homely image of the broken sandal and the reminder that all has been a dream.

After the anger, the despair, and the visions of babies burning in Vietnam, the poet rediscovers an order, a coherence, a place of peace and wisdom to which she can return. The discovery also reveals the form that has always been there, though "The treasure . . . lies buried."

But the poem that goes a long way toward explaining the crisis of "The Broken Sandal" by revealing the experience and the "blurred" vision of the poet is "Advent 1966."

> Because in Vietnam the vision of a Burning Babe
> is multiplied, multiplied,
> > the flesh on fire
> not Christ's, as Southwell saw it, prefiguring
> the Passion upon the Eve of Christmas,
>
> but wholly human and repeated, repeated,
> infant after infant, their names forgotten,
> their sex unknown in the ashes,
> set alight, flaming but not vanishing,
> not vanishing as his vision but lingering,
>
> cinders upon the earth or living on
> moaning and stinking in hospitals three abed;
>
> because of this my strong sight
> my clear caressive sight, my poet's sight, I was given
> that it might stir me to song,
> is blurred.

> There is a cataract filming over
> my inner eyes. Or else a monstrous insect
> has entered my head, and looks out
> from my sockets with multiple vision,
>
> seeing not the unique Holy Infant
> burning sublimely, an imagination of redemption,
> furnace in which souls are wrought into new life,
> but, as off a beltline, more, more senseless figures aflame.
>
> And this insect (who is not there—
> it is my own eyes do my seeing, the insect
> is not there, what I see is there)
> will not permit me to look elsewhere,
>
> or if I look, to see except dulled and unfocused
> the delicate, firm, whole flesh of the still unburned.

What the poet *sees* in "Advent 1966" refutes the poet's own admission of "blurred vision." She sees only too painfully the truth in the death and mutilation of babies and the horror engendered by what she "see[s] is there." The poem is itself a laceration, but it also is a powerful poetic expression of the poet's experience. The evocation of the symbolic sacrifice of the Holy Infant, a ritual of redemption, is ironically juxtaposed to the real *human* sacrifice of babies in Vietnam. The recurrent litany of "multiplied," "repeated," "infant," "ashes," "cinders," and "vanishing" reinforces the wrenching truth of war that does not spare the innocent. The dual vision seems the creation of a "monstrous insect," but is, instead, *reality*—seeing what is there. The hypnotic power of such horror would seem to curb the poet's vision, but in the last lines, even though "dull and unfocused," the eyes see "the delicate, firm, whole flesh of the still unburned." What finally remains in this poem of shock and disbelief is the abiding vision of the Passion of Christmas Eve. Not to be dismissed too hastily is the poet's "clear, caressive sight, my poet's sight I was given / that it might stir me to song." The events in "Advent 1966" preclude "song" but the strong sight, the caressive sight—however unfocused—prevails in the end in the image of the whole, inviolate, delicate "Babe."

The technical excellence of this poem cannot be stressed sufficiently. The litany—a song itself—is a deathsong, not the one the poet was prepared to sing. The distancing in the poem by juxtaposing the sacred ritual with the infamy of Vietnam relieves the poem of sentimentality and "personal" emotion, though we never lose sight

of the "observer-recorder" who is capable of "vision." The images
carry the weight of sensuous appeal. Like the poet we are compelled
to *see*, and what we see is carved in the mind. The other oppositions
in the poem are dramatic: the furnace in which souls are wrought
into new life contrasted with the beltline on which "more, more
senseless figures" are set aflame. The "advent" of Christ's birth at
Christmas is ironically paralleled by the cauldron of flame that is
Vietnam in 1966. The poem is, indeed, an elegy for the innocent.

The poems that remain in *Relearning the Alphabet*, as one would
expect, cover a wide spectrum of experiences as the poet responds
to events in the outside world. The themes that run through them
are "elegiac": for the suffering in Biafra; for the moment that "the
heart / breaks for nothing" as the disasters weigh upon it; for "Life
yet unlived"; for love recollected and lost; for the mourning of a
stranger—added pain—while visiting the grave of a friend's child;
and always for the suffering in Vietnam. These are "deathsongs," yet
at the close the poet renews her love for life, her joy in the cold
spring.

"Biafra" recalls Vietnam. Again, Levertov dwells upon the sacrifice
of innocence, massacre, and violence, but we have become inured
after Vietnam. The poem leaves the world with no hope, sluggish,
dull, 'getting used to' the horrors of those distant tragedies. In many
ways, "Biafra" is a frightening poem as it testifies to our own loss of
compassion, our inability to take action, and our indifference. Yet I
do not feel this is one of Levertov's more successful poems. Although
the reality is played out in the poem, "we are / *the deads*" because
we "do nothing," there is an unconvincing joining of the dying babies
in Biafra and the dying children on Vietnam. The massacre of the
Ibos seems distant from the expending of life in the Vietnam War,
but perhaps even more signficant, there is a tendency for the poet
here to *state*, to *chastise* (because we do nothing), and the emotional
impact is lessened. The poem, for all the compassion of the speaker,
does not move us as countless others do when the images, the
rhythms, and the irony of opposed visions (as in "Advent 1966")
create a successful poem.

I also would question Levertov's departure—"no room / for love
in us . . ."—from the vast number of her poems in which she always
returns to what man is capable of and, into the present, maintains
her faith in humanity. Although she does "waiver" in some instances,
more often, as in "The Wings of a God," she writes the following:

> I am felled,
> rise up

> with changed vision,
> a singing in my ears.

In "A Cloak" she tells us, "I walked naked / from the beginning / breathing in / my life, / breathing out / poems." The metaphor of "breathing" is important in Levertov's lexicon. "Breathing is life": breathing in experience and breathing out poems. One of her latest volumes is titled *Breathing the Water.*

The journey in relearning the alphabet will be an arduous one, but Denise Levertov knows the path and has the means. Her poetic as well as her personal journey continues in this volume.

In "A Marigold from North Vietnam," we find poignant images of life and death. The form of the poem is unusual—a single stanza with long breath pauses within the line. The marigold is a resurrection flower, and the movement of the poem is from death to life, through love. Nature's seasonal cycle is reflected in the life, death, and resurrection of the earth. Notably life is *resilient*—even there in Vietnam—a promise perhaps for the future. For the poet, the marigold she nourishes is a symbol for nourishing new life in that tragic land. For the first time, a poem on Vietnam closes with a thread of hope: "to the root-threads cling still / some crumbs of Vietnam." The poem is delicate, lyrical, imaging the beauty that one day must return to that stricken country. The repetitions accrue in meaning, and the entire tone of the poem suggests the tentative but promising peace that lies ahead. In a 1966 essay, "Writers Take Sides on Vietnam," she wrote the following:

> It is hard to be an artist in this time because it is hard to be human: in the dull ever-accumulating horror of the war news, it is more difficult each day to keep remembering the creative and joyful potential of human beings, and to fulfill that potential in one's own life, as testimony.[27]

* * *

Heart breaks but mends like good bone.
— "Staying Alive"

The long poem, "Relearning the Alphabet," is preceded by Levertov's poem on "revolution or death" and its crucial message: *"Life that / wants to live. / (Unlived life / of which one can die.)"*—this last the words of Rilke. She "chooses" revolution in "From A Notebook: October '68–May '69" but importantly, she writes, "I want the world to go on / unfolding." In this way, the poet heralds the journey of recovery, the recapture of "seeing," the voyage that will ultimately lead to the house that "yawns like a bear. / Guards its profound dream for us, / that it return to us when we return."

"Relearning the Alphabet" is a very beautiful poem of the journey from "anguish" to "ardor," the search for renewal by means of a return to beginnings. The central image that binds up the movements from part to part is fire, and, as we might expect, fire becomes the symbol for life, cleansing, illumination, the cycle of life *and* death, love, the imagination, "transformation and continuance," and the mysterious voice of God.

The tone is at times tentative, delicate, lyrical, guardedly hopeful, and often joyous. The form ingeniously hides a numinous word in each stanza of the "Alphabet." We know that learning the alphabet is a child's earliest experience with words, and the ritual—for it is a ritual—is a kind of incantation, as the poet moves painstakingly from letter to letter as though each were a signpost on her journey and her own return to language.

Most original in this long poem are Levertov's tonal effects as each "letter" encompasses a poem made up of alliteration, assonance, and consonance. Thus, "A" contains not only "anguish" and "ardor" but "ah!", "as," and "ashes." This continues throughout the poem, and a few examples are notable here. "C" echoes with "clear," "cool," "comes," and "core." "E" contains repetitions of "endless," "ember," "returning," and "revolution," "dream," and "delight." "I, J" is replete as well with evocative sounds: "I" is repeated throughout, as well as "imagination's," "jester," "joy," "Jerusalem," and "jealous." "M" again echoes and re-echoes not only "moon," but "man," "moving," "moonwater," "half-moon," "luminous," "come," "humbled," "warm," "myself," "mouth," and "home." The entire "alphabet" becomes a lesson in language.

The poem is reminiscent of William Carlos Williams's respect for the magic of language. To "make a start" in Williams's poetry is of necessity to name. "The only means the artist has to give value to life is to recognize it with the imagination and name it."[28] So it is that "Relearning the Alphabet" is a poet's need to return to the imagination, the words. The opening lines of the poem set forth the purpose and set the tone in the final lovely image.

> Joy—a beginning. Anguish, ardor.
> To relearn the ah! of knowing in unthinking
> joy: the beloved stranger lives.
> Sweep up anguish as with a wing-tip,
> brushing the ashes back to the fire's core.

The poem moves from its "beginning" to the "magical" stages of the

journey of illumination: "To be," to delight and dream, to the fire of
the mind. Again I hear an echo from Eliot's *Four Quartets:* "Not
fare well, / But fare forward, voyagers,"[29] as Levertov intones, "Not
farewell, but faring / forth into the grace of transformed / continuance." The voyage continues with its images of harvesting, "Imagination's holy forest," and though the speaker stumbles she makes her
way toward her origins, joy, Jerusalem. She recalls the "time of isola-
tion" and wakens to the luminousness of nature: "I am / come back, /
humbled, to warm myself, / . . . . I'm home." There she is loved,
enfolded, trusted, and transformed. Toward the end of the poem,
the voice strengthens in its resolve as the way becomes clear:

> Relearn the alphabet,
> relearn the world, the world
> understood anew only in doing, under-
> stood only as
> looked-up-into out of earth,
> the heart an eye looking,
> the heart a root
> planted in earth.

The poem is replete with original and memorable images and
metaphors: to "sweep up anguish as with a wing-tip"; the cycle of
"revolution of dream to ember, ember to anguish, / anguish to flame,
flame to delight, / delight to dark and dream, dream to ember /
that the mind's fire may not fail"; the "vowels of affliction"; the
"somnolence grotto"; the "clicking of squirrel-teeth in the attic." It
is words—language—that give the poem its new life, a reinforcement
of Levertov's own conviction that to relearn the alphabet is to relearn
the world.

The end of the journey will be rediscovered vision, praise, and the
waiting dream. As for the rest of the world, "Vision will not be used. /
Yearning will not be used. / Wisdom will not be used. / Only the vain
will / strive to use and be used, / comes not to fire's core / but cinder."
Yet the poet, calling upon the household gods, Lares, entreats them
to "guard its profound dreams for us, / that it return to us when we
return." Clearly the voyage had not ended, but there is a destination
in sight and in *To Stay Alive* Denise Levertov will "step by hesitant
step" move toward "continuance into / that life beyond the dead-
end" where she was lost, so that once again she can affirm: "Every
step [is] an arrival" *(Overland to the Islands).*

* * *

To Stay Alive

While the war drags on, . . .

—"Staying Alive"

To Stay Alive, Denise Levertov explained in the "Author's Preface,"[30] is "one person's inner / outer experience in America during the '60's and the beginning of the '70's, an experience which is shared by so many and transcends the peculiar details of each life, though it can only be expressed in and through such details." Many of the poems were written while Mitchell Goodman, Dr. Benjamin Spock, and three other war resisters were on trial in the spring of 1968. But the volume also contains several poems, under the section titled *Preludes,* that had been included in *The Sorrow Dance* and *Relearning the Alphabet:* "Olga Poems," "A Note to Olga (1966)" (Olga had died in 1964), "Life at War," "What Were They Like?" "Advent 1966," "Tenebrae," and "Enquiry." The justification for their inclusion, Levertov explains "is esthetic—it assembles separated parts of a whole. . . . that whole being seen as having some value not as mere 'confessional' autobiography, but as a document of some historical value. . . ."

It appears to me that another advantage in including these earlier poems is to give coherence to Levertov's progress in her poetic journey: from "awareness" and empathy for the suffering of those in Vietnam, to her "speaking out" against the war, and then to the beginnings of activism and the experience of interacting with the "revolutionary young" who were making a "statement" about Vietnam in their personal sacrifices. No longer removed, as many troubled adults had been from the activism of the young, the poet traces her growing sense of being a part of contemporary history in "Staying Alive."

Among other things, "Staying Alive" is a ritual of *naming.* These were the young who took upon themselves a moral posture toward the war in a concrete way and they are called by name: de Courcy Squire (18 years), Dennis Riordan, Chuck Matthei, Bob Gilliam, David Worstell, and Jenny Orvino. And there were the others: Dan Berrigan; Mitchell Goodman, the poet's husband; and poets Robert Duncan and David Bromige, as well as the nationally known Dr. Benjamin Spock; and those who became two of many victims of police brutality: James Rector, killed on 5 May 1969; and Alan Blanchard, an artist who was blinded while protesting the violence at People's Park. There also were those referred to only by their given names: Judy, Richard, Boat, Neil, and others.

The poet comes to understand the choice—"revolution or death"—and speaks out as artist *and* human witness to the pathos, the courage, the excitement, the sacrifice, and the hope of those who were fighting that the nation might stay alive, in peace.

There is more here in "Staying Alive"—not the least of which is the poet's sense of the richness of constructive "engagement" and "the sense of community, of fellowship, experienced in the People's Park in Berkeley in 1969." Levertov and other artists and scientists in America had come from the safety of their universities, studios, writing desks, laboratories, and their inherent privacy to join the efforts in the public arena and—in the case of the creative poets—to transmute that experience in their work.

The experience itself was alternately exhilarating, painful, violent, encouraging, and equally unsatisfying and satisfying, as events marched in their inexorable way until the war overseas and the violence at home finally came to a halt. This was a part of the story that needed to be "recorded," but as importantly, "Staying Alive" was a stage in Levertov's poetic career that—in the interest of her aesthetics—needed to be chronicled.

In another way, "Staying Alive" is different from Levertov's previous poems in the sixties. The *scene* has shifted from Vietnam to the "war" taking place in America: the young protesters and the adults who supported them against the powers that prevailed to continue the conflict in Southeast Asia. With a "You are there!" immediacy, "Staying Alive" brings us all into the streets, recalling for many readers with vividness the "revolution" from which America would never quite recover. The period of civil disobedience is not a page in American history books but a proud *and* painful part of our national consciousness.

No small part of the success of "Staying Alive" results from the poet's *first-hand* experience. Previous poems on the war in Vietnam were based on news reports, the messages brought home by Vietnam vets and conscientious objectors in Vietnam, and the portrayal of suffering on television screens. Levertov did not visit Vietnam until 1973 to see first-hand what the ravages of war had left. This is *not* to suggest that the Vietnam poems that appeared in *The Sorrow Dance* and *Relearning the Alphabet* were not sincere responses to the *reality* communicated by both reporters and the media—they constituted Levertov's only available "experience" to this point, and became the raw material for her poetry. And given her own knowledge and feelings about war, in addition to her strong sense of the poetic, she was able to bring to her subject all the conviction and sensibility necessary to achieve successful poems.

Yet the sense of immediacy I have noted in "To Stay Alive" adds a special quality of intensity and identity to the events in the poems, and endows the whole with a high level of aesthetic value. There is a vitality in "To Stay Alive" that is intrinsic to Levertov's most successful poems. She is in the act of "doing," and then of transmuting that energy into a dramatic work of art. As important as the subject matter is the complex form of "Staying Alive." The poem is a verse drama in four acts: the Prologue and Four Parts divided by "Entr'actes" or intermissions. This form heightens the reality of the experience comprised of action, character, and the remembrance of things past.

I have already mentioned the admixture of poetry and prose, "testimony" and lyricism. In many respects, this long, multidimensional poem is one of Levertov's most ambitious modern works; she combines a variety of dramatic situations (in which we hear the cries of the protesters) juxtaposed to scenes of stillness and serenity (to which she often retreats for reflection and speculation). The effect is a collage—snapshots of action alternating with meditation, dream, and recollected tranquillity. The verse is at times carefully measured in couplets, stanzas, and entire sections unbroken in patterned forms; elsewhere the verse is free, and still elsewhere, she reflects, whether consciously or unconsciously, William Carlos Williams's three-stepped line.

Always, there is an awareness of sound and silence, of activity and experiences recalled. Levertov is particularly adept in her use of slant rhyme and her own version of enjambment (in which, as she has explained many times, the voice pauses as if for a half-comma before continuing). In the passages where *seeming* choices must be made, the rhetoric of the verse echoes the variation of the themes: revolution *or* death, revolution *or* poetry, revolution *or* love. But the final choice has been made:

> O holy innocents! I have
> no virtue but to praise
> you who believe
> life is possible . . .

Although an examination will reveal both the structure, the thematic continuity of "Staying Alive," and the beauty of the individual "poems," I should like to note that the whole sequence is a tribute to Levertov's aesthetics, although it would be impossible to reproduce the entire work here. The metaphors are sharply pictorial and mind-numbing at times: "the soul dwindles sometimes to an ant / rapid upon a cracked surface; / lightly, grimly, incessantly / it skims the unfathomed clefts where despair / seethes hot and black." At other times, the beauty of Levertov's images—a "coral island"—of peace, of silence, of the sea, of the mind's "dream eye," of nature's restorative powers enrich the poem with the poet's sense of the ineluctable mystery of life and the need and desire to live—the *"Love of living. That wants to live."*

The delicate, lyrical passages are more stirring when set against the heroism and suffering of the activists and the shocking knowledge of the invasion of Laos. It is indeed the juxtaposition of opposing images, emotions, and worlds of war and peace that creates the complexity of tone of "Staying Alive" and that increases its dramatic intensity. Action is directly contrasted with moments of quiescence when the poet escapes the exciting but draining atmosphere of political activity. Thus, poems like "Casa Felice" create an oasis of peace, stillness, and beauty, filling the poet with thankfulness and calm.

Levertov traces the wide trajectory of thought and feeling that attended the historical experience in "Staying Alive" to reveal, finally, the experience within. Apart from the importance of its subject, "Staying Alive" is one of Levertov's finest and most artistic compositions. Because the poems in *Preludes* have been discussed earlier in this chapter, I will examine "Staying Alive" as an integrated stage of Levertov's "pilgrimage."

As I have noted, the larger poem is composed of several sections. "Prologue: An Interim," is made up of seven parts of varied length, rhythm, and pattern, including a "prose" passage. "Part I" is comprised of six parts—again, extremely varied in rhythm and length, with an admixture of prose and verse. "Entr'acte" is composed of four largely lyrical passages. "Part II" is a single long, diverse poem with pauses between its several passages, followed by a kind of broadside, "WHAT PEOPLE CAN DO," and closes with a lyrical passage. A second "Entr'acte" is composed of several poems: "At the Justice Department, November 15, 1969," "Gandhi's Gun (and Brecht's Vow,)" "The Year One," "Looking for the Devil Poems," "Today," "Casa Felice (I and II)," "Revolutionary," and "I Thirst."

A marked shift occurs in "Part III" as the poet takes us into the summer of 1970; this section, made up of nine untitled parts, takes place far from the demonstrations in America and, in some respects, is a "hymn" to life. This is followed by a brief Entr'Acte centering upon "revolution" and "poetry"—recollected in tranquillity. Finally, "Staying Alive" closes with "Part IV," a poem of four sections, replete with recent history, the voices of the young revolutionaries—and Olga—echoing in the mind. The poem is a return to beginnings—a going home with a renewed affirmation for life, love, and resolution. "Staying Alive" concludes with the end of a journey, although for Levertov there still is a far distance to traverse.

The forms, the tone, the language, the shift from lyricism to fact to colloquialism to memory and desire—all coalesce in "Staying Alive" around the moods of hope and despair engendered by events, and provide an intricate and unusual design of inner and outer experience.

"Prologue: An Interim" occurs in historical time, as Levertov explains in her notes when Mitchell Goodman, Dr. Benjamin Spock, and three other defendants, identified as Richard, Boat, and Neal, awaited trial. Thus the poem opens on a note of irony as the "events" reflect the moods of impatience and frustration with the almost insensate banality of everyday life:

i
While the war drags on, always worse,
the soul dwindles sometimes to an ant
lightly, grimly, incessantly
it skims the unfathomed clefts where despair
seethes hot and black.

ii
Children in the laundromat
waiting while their mothers fold sheets,
a five-year-old boy addresses
a four-year-old girl, When I say,
'Do you want some gum? say yes.'
'Yes . . .' 'Wait!—Now:
Do you want some gum?'
'Yes!' 'Well yes means no,
so you can't have any.'
He chews. He pops a big, delicate bubble at her.

O language, virtue
of man, touchstone
worn down by what
gross friction . . .

Encapsulated here in the innocuous conversation of small children is the reductive quality of everything—language, feeling, communication (yes means no; it is necessary to destroy a town to save it)—induced by war. As the war takes its toll, man himself is reduced. All is eroded as "the war drags on . . .":

iii
Language, coral island
accrued from human comprehensions,
human dreams,

you are eroded as war erodes us.

The history of the activists follows, interspersed with evanescent glimpses of a calmer, quieter, better time—peacetime. Levertov had written in the "Author's Preface": "In 'Prologue: An Interim,' some of my heroes—that is, those who stand for integrity, honesty, love of life—are draft resisters who go to jail in testimony of their refusal to take part in carnage. In the same poem I invoked the self-immola-tors—Vietnamese and American—not as models but as flares to keep us moving in the dark. I spoke with love—a love I still feel—of those who 'disdain to kill.'" The intermittent return in dream to other scenes: childhood, the sea, the quiet, the peace, the "black butter-flies at the lemon blossom," the pleasure in another's warmth are interspersed with the violent activities of the present.

Yet there are "other" dreams—the speaker dreams that she herself is on trial: "they led us through the streets, / dressed in our prisoners' robes— / smocks of brown holland— / and the people watched us pass / and waved to us, and gave us / serious smiles of hope." Thus throughout the despair and the desperation, there is the hope that the *people*—distinguished from the cruel and indifferent establishment—understand and will rally to the aid of the protesters.

The poem alternates between prose, that offers factual events and personal reactions, and the poetry that communicates the spirit of the protesters, the emotions of the speaker, the pathos of those that make sacrifices. These moments are relieved, as I have suggested, by the "remembrance of things past" and constitute some of the most lyrical passages of not only the prologue but the remainder of the poem. The theme is frequently rebirth: "To repossess our souls we fly / to the sea . . ." There is beauty here and comfort and calmness and regeneration. It is a mystical and mysterious presence in nature that offers man its recuperative powers. So it is that this first part of "Staying Alive," "Prologue: An Interim," relives the rite of revival, and against the sacrifices of the young for the conviction of their beliefs, there is also the hope "to expand again" but not to forget. The tone of the poem varies so that at the end it is more reflective and sober—not anger but remembrance.

"Part I" turns on the theme of "Revolution or death." "Death" is Mayor Daley and the chaos at the Democratic Convention in 1968; it is the mindless, indifferent public yelling at the marchers. Death, to Denise Levertov, as to Rilke, is the unlived life. (Rilke's words are among Levertov's favorites. As she explains in the "Notes," the phrase, "Unlived life / of which one can die," is taken from *Notebook of Malte Laurids Brigge*.)[31]

Ever present in this part of the poem is the theme of the challenge of life: in Lori's attempted suicide, who "has died and risen," leading

the poet to affirm, "If she can live I can live"; in recollection of her
counterpart, the teacher Bill Rose who led her to the question: "How
to live and the will to live," and who continued—a lone figure—to
teach until his death.

Thus, much of "Part I" is an affirmation. Revolution is action; it
is Albert Schweitzer's "Life" that wants to live. (Levertov quotes
Schweitzer: "I am Life that wants to live, among other forms of life
that want to live.") It is "engagement" with public issue. It is danger
and death and the human scream. It is the Spring and Fall of Gerard
Manley Hopkins's Goldengrove. It is the poet's reach back into her
childhood of Grimm and Anderson, Dickens and Keats, whose
"drowsy numbness" is an invitation to death against the plea for life.
Finally, revolution *is* life, because the alternatives are unacceptable.
More significantly, though she is "beginning to learn," the poet is
haunted by what was always there:

> *Love of living.*   *That wants to live.*   *Unlived life.*
> whisper
> of goldengrove . . .

"Entr'acte" is the interim between the violent acts of war and
revolution and the silence and peace of life in nature. In the hushed
beauty of October, the poem's tone is reverential—spiritual both in
its rituals and in its quiet affirmation to poetry that becomes transformed through its images into prayer.

> Last of October, light thinning
> toward the cold. Deep shadow.

The entire scene is one of oncoming darkness, the shadows of winter,
the death of nature. Against the images of "moving darkness," the
advent of November's first snowstorm, "we find candles. / We light
up the woodstove which was all we / used to have anyway, till a few
weeks back." Candles, for Levertov, are always important images of
light and enlightenment and recur throughout her poetry until they
become a major symbol in "Candles in Babylon." Here, too, light
and darkness reverberate in nature. Against death and dying in nature, there is also the sound of the brook "under and out from / thin
ice." In the stasis of winter, "All things muted; deprived / of color,"
yet in the terror of eclipse there is also promise of resurrection as
forgetting is resisted and remembering is re-living:

> What pain! What sharp stabs of recall! What revelations!

The black taste of life, the music
angel tongues buzz when my paws nuzzle it
out into light!

For the poet, the moments will all be captured in a poem, not
only verse but *song*. The first "Entr'acte" closes with a transcendent
moment of joy. "Entr'acte" is a ritual of life against the backdrop of
death, characteristic of Levertov in her finest poetry. Although her
step falters—even in "Part I" when she thinks, "I choose / revolution
but my words / often already don't reach forward / into it—/ (perhaps)" the poet, in this interim between revolution and artistic creation, closes with the prayer "To make / of song a chalice," and the
religious imagery reinforces the supernal quality of that creation. For
Denise Levertov, the dedication to what she firmly believed as moral
choice is indivisibly united with her equally profound commitment
to poetry—so beautifully harmonized in this final poem.

"Part II" is again a temporary setback. "Revolution" is in need of
definition, so the poet is forced to "dig down, / to re-examine," and
that speculation takes her to the sounds of revolution permeating the
air, to the examination of language and its origins: "*Revolution* / implies the circular: an exchange / of position, the high / brought low,
the low / ascending, a revolving, / an endless rolling of the wheel.
The wrong word." A familiar theme of poets is the inadequacy of
words, because there is *no other* word but "revolution." Resorting
to actions where words fail us, the poet traces the activities of the
"revolutionaries," among them Chuck Matthei—carrying with him a
poem by Levertov about Mitchell Goodman. The poem casts an
interesting gloss on the activists, marching to *their* own song:

> 'A Man'
> Living a life—
> the beauty of deep lines
> dug in your cheeks
>
>   And ends,
> you pick out
> your own song from the uproar,
>
> line by line,
> and at last throw back
> your head and sing it.

A cacophony of voices declaiming the slogans of the "revolution":
the need for new beginnings, the need for social change, the need

to lay down arms, the need for cooperation and mutual aid, alternates
with the hesitancy and the questioning voice of the poet who appears
to find *events* more comprehensible than rhetoric. It felt good to work
beside students in People's Park: "everyone doing, / each leaf of
grass near us / a new testament." Working side by side, their love
grows stronger than mere slogans can effect. The poem ends with
action—the demonstration, the violence, the terror of bullets, clubs,
and gas: "The War / comes home to us . . ." The "us" is not ambiguous. As the young marched and were driven back, America knew the
war had come home. The final verse is stark, frightening in its simplicity and concreteness: "clubs, gas, bayonets, bullets"—the poem
echoes the war that had *seemed* so very far away. This was 15 May
1969, the crucial year in the protest against the war in Vietnam.

What follows is a set of guidelines: "What People Can Do," then
followed by long, impressionistic, often fragmented echoes of the
"revolution": words, music, gestures, but also a definition in images
from nature itself: "Revolution: a crown of tree / raises itself out of
the heavy flood." And in this landscape, the human forms:

> A hand, arm,
> lifts in the crawl—
> hands, arms, intricate
> > upflashing—
> > > a sea full of swimmers!
> > their faces' quick steady
> > lift for air—
> Maybe what seems
> evanescent is solid.
>
> Islands
> step out of the waves on rock feet.

Thus the poet has—with the power of vivid metaphors and sharp
visual, audial, and tactile images—defined the revolution: a branch
pushing against walls of air, but, as she concludes, *solid*. As always,
when Levertov departs from slogans and uses her power with language to trace an experience, the result is poetry: pure in its visual
impact, rich in its emotional complexity, true in its integrity.

The second "Entr'acte" is another "station" on the poet's journey
of political activism. All of the fruits of action are here, both bitter
and sweet. It is a collage of both events and voices from the past, of
the young activists and old sages: Gandhi, Brecht, and Jose Yglesias.
It begins in the chaotic atmosphere of the Justice Department on 15
November 1969—the entire picture an almost surreal nightmare of

stumbling, retching, blinded protesters, despairing yet *together* in the experience of the bitterness and joy of their convictions. The scene is followed by the echoes from the past: Gandhi's injunction: "Never / run away from the stormcenter," Brecht's rallying cry: "Keiner / oder Alle, Alles / oder Nichts!" (No one or everyone, all or nothing.) As the poet is "born" to revolution, she finds the experience "ecstatic anguish." In a passage that is both amusing and serious—"Looking for the Devil Poems"—the poet, now strong, searches the familiar streets for the Devil, seeking to define him but to no avail. The images the Devil evokes are repellent, unhealthy, malevolent, but they are images of the "modern" city: garbage, flies, fetid water, and not the Devil. Was the Devil apathy or "the inexorable / smog of tedium," or ". . . was he / the toneless ignorance all that I saw / had of itself?"

Then, as one expects in Levertov's journey, the mood changes to one of sheer joy—the sensation felt in the bone and the heart, of being "human." The almosts tactile sense of cloud and sky and "taciturn winter buds"—as she is free for the day—complements her own sense of life.

> Human, a kind of element, a fire,
> an air, today.
> Floating up to you I enter, or you
> enter me. Or imagine
> a house without doors,
> open to sun and snowdrifts.

As always in Levertov's poetry, the sheer exhilaration of *being alive* surpasses all chaos and despair.

The poems "Casa Felice (I) and (II)" (Happy House, the home of a friend on Cape Cod), afford moments of respite from the stirring but exhausting periods of demonstration. As often in Levertov's poetry, peace is offered by the sea—the dreaming tides, the silent gulls. From desperation to peace—this is the theme of "Casa Felice (II)." Imagining a conversation with one of the activists, she asks this question:

> Would you feel new
> coldness towards me
> because this April morning, gentle light
> on the unglittering sea and pale sands,
> I am not angry and not tense?

Nature is restorative; it drains the emotions and there is a mystical sense of the presence of God in the "blessed blue." As the poet gratefully notes in the poem: "I drop / plumb into peace for a day—" In the next poem, "Revolutionary," one can discern a clear conflict between the speaker's inner state and the outside world, but as the "curtain of sorrow" parts, she renews the "struggle to move" but not alone! In the final poem of "Entr'acte" (II) "I Thirst," an echo of Christ's thirst, the religious overtones continue. The poem is replete with Christian symbols: the wooden cross, the re-enactment of the crucifixion, the silence of "witnessing." Against the singer's injunction, "We must *not* be angry, we must / L_O_O_O_V_E!" the poet understands that "there comes a time when only anger / is love."

"Part III" takes place in 1970. The place is Trieste, Italy. The poet is "on holiday from causes": "Silver summer light of Trieste early evening." The entire scene is suffused with silver-gold-grey light; there is peacefulness here, quiet, beauty . . . a necessary respite from the activity, the violence, the surging emotions of the previous experiences in People's Park or at the Justice Department or in the demonstrations in "the 90-degree shadeless Washington midafternoon." The five poems set in Trieste are filled with images of Italian changelessness: cups of espresso, the soft intonation of Italians speaking, the cafes and the sea, and the Triestino dusk "(and Amerika / far away / tosses in fever)." Bits of recollected conversation echo in the silent twilight: the voice of a friend, David, in England asking, "What's a cop-out? Is it / the same as / opting out?" and the response, "Yes, but / opting out sounds like / cool choice / and copping out / means fear and weakness." But for these chance ruminations, Trieste takes over and the scene becomes alive with daily life: couples and their babies, the nightly *passegiata* when the men "still prowl as they used to," and then the memory—now in 1970—of Spring 1948 when the poet was a young bride waiting for her husband in Florence. The scent of the Italian voyage lingers. Back home in Boston, "at my unhappiest," the impact of a violent America returns and the poet longs for oblivion . . . but not for long. Her thoughts circle about the "*approaching* sound of terror" and even Olga returns to the consciousness, Olga—rushing back and forth beneath the "dreamy lamps / of stonyhearted Oxford Street—" working "in her way for Revolution." The poet recalls the gentleness that seems synonymous with England, the kindness, the expectation of love that was part of her native land, and compares it to a sick America.

The passage closes with a strong affirmation of life and for the "love for / what happens." Taking her cue from William Carlos Williams's delightful "Danse Russe," Levertov declares: "I bless / every stone

I see, the / 'happy genius' not of my household perhaps / but of my solitude . . ."

The final part of the poem reviews the poet-as-voyager: to Rijecka (Fiume), to Jugoslavia, to an Adriatic island, all the time reflecting, reading, sifting for truth in Jose Yglesias, in her meetings with young revolutionaries and dreamers until she turns home to England, to Dorset. There a friend tells her,

> Make a place for yourself
> in the darkness
> and wait there. *Be* there.

And yet another friend says,

> Get down into your well,
> it's your well
> go deep into it
> into your own depth as into a poem.

Thus ends this stage of her journey with the wisdom of those who knew that only in transformation and the "fiery stillness" within would Denise Levertov *realize* the peace that seemed to come only in dreams. She would find within herself, as Emily Dickinson had found, "that undiscovered continent / No settler had the mind."

The final "Entr'acte" is titled "Let us Sing Unto the Lord a New Song," and, indeed, the poem is a song. The verbs of pulsing, rippling, breaking, singing are reinforced by the rhythms of the poem. The theme unites revolution and poetry and gives to each a new life and significance. Revolution is Richard and Poetry is the persona. Life shall cease without both revolution *and* poetry. The pulse that beats through both must not be allowed to falter or weaken. Levertov declares with affirmation:

> But when their rhythms
> mesh
> then though the pain of living
> never lets up
>
> the singing begins.

The final act of "Staying Alive," titled "Report," emphasizes the poet's renewed dedication to poetry. She will dive deeper into the self for hope. No longer angry—not Kali ("There comes a time when only anger is love"), she has come to think in terms of love for husband and child. This final section is the "return." Although news from America is not a "fiery fusion" but "an atomistic bleakness," the poet is in England—home to the "objects of dailiness." Haunted always by Olga, "she in the flare caught, a moment, her face / painted, clownishly, whorishly. Suffering." The words echo in her mind: "It's your own well. / Go down / into its depth."

The passage that follows is characteristic of Levertov's resiliency and urge to *live*. "Happiness" is just that —the entire poem is suffused with the joy of being: dancing, swaying, the declaration, "The reason for happiness is, / happiness exists," as the poet discovers within herself, "even in the very midst of / winter, an invincible summer." Happiness is, in the words of the hymn, "amazing grace." In the midst of this ecstacy there is the memory of Judy who committed suicide as she recalls Judy's words, "If you would write me a poem / I could live forever." And so, both the joy and the tragedy of the entire revolution comes back forcefully. "Revolution or death," and the young student "raged bursting with life into death." The poet concludes, "Yes, I want / revolution, not death . . ." Anger transformed becomes the theme of this final section, and, characteristically, Levertov turns to her mentors. Mayakovsky had written,

> "Life
> > must be
> > > > started quite anew,
> > when you've changed it,
> > > > then
> > > > > > the singing can start up"—

"Staying Alive" ends with the conviction that approaches a supernal belief: "When the pulse rhythms / of revolution and poetry / mesh, / then the singing begins." For a moment the figures of Berrigan and Etheridge Knight appear and fade, for the poet ends only as a poet can, as Williams believed, to *praise*.

> O holy innocents! I have
> no virtue but to praise
> you who believe
> life is possible . . .

Now, at the end of a journey, the poet will serve in the only way she knows well: to praise, to make the impermanent permanent through art, in poetry. At the close of "Staying Alive," Denise Levertov has accepted the role she always knew to be both valid and true: to inscribe her experiences, her hopes, her indecision, her fears, her anger, her feelings of love for the courage and bravery and sacrifices of the young in the best way she knew as an artist, as well as a moral being, in poetry that would unite both her inner and outer journeys.

As one might have expected, *To Stay Alive* received mixed reviews. Those who opposed what they viewed as "poetry and polemics" felt the volume to be "problematic." Cary Nelson in his review of *To Stay Alive* felt that mysticism was in conflict with Levertov's real world. "She avoided," he wrote, "encountering the larger myths of our history and kept her poetic territory elsewhere and self-enclosed."[32] But other reviewers praised Levertov for both her artistic accomplishment and her ability to chart the dramatic events of her times. Hayden Carruth analyzes the volume as the poet's life as a political activist, as the exploration of the sense and temper of the years, and as the attempt to locate and express the poet's own complex feelings, particularly with regard to "artistic responsibility." He sees *Alive* as "a creation of poetic analogues to the inner form, *the inscape*, of that momentous 'historical present.'"[33]

Denise Levertov believed that for political poetry, as for any other kind, the *sine qua non* is that it elicits 'the poetic emotion.'"[34] One part of Denise Levertov's journey had come to a close with "Staying Alive," but her commitment to the "poetry of engagement" continued into her later work. It is interesting to note that in her next published volume, *Footprints*, she included poems that had been written during the same period as *To Stay Alive*. She wrote: "About two-thirds of the poems in this volume were written concurrently with the 'notebook' poem that gave its name to my last book, *To Stay Alive*. The rest were written—some in England during the summer of 1971—since then, except for a few which got 'lost' during the compilation of earlier volumes."[35]

She would write again about Vietnam, activism, El Salvador, Chile—wherever human rights were violated. And later she joined other voices round the globe against nuclear testing and the build-up of nuclear arms. There was much to do to arouse the sleeping conscience of the world, and America in particular. She would light candles and as always in her poetry would keep alive the celebration and the wonder. In *Footprints*, *The Freeing of the Dust*, and *Life in the Forest*, the continuity of Levertov's life-long quest for a world in which poets could return "home to a calm dawn and / the work we had just begun," would be realized.

5

Poems of the Seventies: Echoes and Footprints

. . . it is the poet who has the language in his care; the poet
who more than others recognizes language as a *form of life* and a
common resource to be cherished and served as we serve and
cherish earth and its waters, animal and vegetable life, and each
other.

—*Poet*

As late as 1968, Denise Levertov—under censure from some critics
for writing "political poetry"—felt it incumbent upon her to define
the poet's function as the caretaker of the language. As her poetic
journey continued, Levertov's sense of language as "a form of life"
became increasingly more apparent, and the volumes that follow *To
Stay Alive* are particularly notable for the poet's reverence for life
and reverence for language as a form of communion. She had said,
"Communion is at the base of living humanly,"[1] and living humanly
is the message of both *To Stay Alive* and the volumes that followed.

It is a compelling thought that while Levertov was writing *Footprints*, her private notebooks were forming into a body of poems she
would later publish as *To Stay Alive*—the account largely of her public
involvement in the protest movement against the Vietnam War.
Thus, though *Footprints* takes us further into the Seventies (and indeed was published in 1972—a year after *Alive*), many of the poems
in these two volumes were written simultaneously. The series of
poems in *Footprints:* "A New Year's Garland for my Students/
MIT:1969–1970" is close in spirit to *Alive* with Levertov's characteristic warmth for the young: their beauty, mystery, courage, humor,
trustfulness, and Puckish charm. Yet there is no activism revealed
here, no "Revolution or Death!" These are the young students to
whom she writes: "I hunger for a world / you can / live in forever."

There are other similarities, of course. The suffering of the Vietnam people is in keeping with previous war poems that had appeared in *Alphabet* and *To Stay Alive*. As in earlier volumes, she writes about nature, defeat, rebuff, love that fails and love that fulfills, hurt and healing, and—always present in Levertov's poetry—individuals recalled with fondness and admiration. Most familiar in Denise Levertov's poetry, those recurrent experiences touched by ineffable mystery and dream—the poet's inner life—reappear here. In form, there is always the sense of the journey—of a new and unknowable threshold that we found in *Alphabet*—"Someone / entered the dark wood."

Yet, *Footprints*, despite its echoes, *is* different. Notably, the tone is more meditative—at times questioning, at times pensive, more controlled, less angry, and more descriptive. In "Staying Alive," there is a wonderful sense of felt life—reminiscent of the music of the sixties which reverberates in the rhythms of Levertov's poems— and the sheer joy in living *in spite of* the suffering, the disillusion, the tragic circumstances of war, the young dying for and against it.

The Vietnam poems continue to present the bitter and unforgettable images of that tragedy. At the time *Footprints* was published in the fall of 1972, Denise Levertov went to Vietnam with the poet Muriel Rukeyser and Jane Hart, the wife of the late Senator Hart of Michigan. Doubtless, her report contributed to the many voices calling for a close to that chapter in American history. The war ended a year later.

Thus the Vietnam poems in *Footprints* (many of which were written in the late sixties) testify to Levertov's preoccupation with that experience, and, in a way, perpetuate a theme woven into *The Sorrow Dance*, *Relearning the Alphabet*, and *To Stay Alive*. The War also would become part of the fabric of subsequent volumes such as *The Freeing of the Dust* and *Life in the Forest*.

I had suggested that one part of Levertov's poetic journey had come to a close: her "group activism" continued in her private life but does not figure significantly in *Footprints*. This is not to suggest that Levertov's public commitments had ended; they still figured largely in her consciousness and she reiterates, to this day, that humankind must ultimately save itself. Thus her social conscience never diminished, but the tone of the subsequent volumes had undergone a sea change.

Apart from the themes of war and the pain concomitant with it on both sides of the Pacific, there is an expansion outward, as well as a deepening of Levertov's themes. Nature is always important, but we return to an almost Wordsworthian simplicity, the mysterious yet restorative powers of a nature that is still unknowable. There is an intimation of a supernal power—ambiguous, inscrutable, but present. Joy is thematic; suffering and rejection are thematic; and love shrouded in its own enigma both affirms and denies, gives pain as well as pleasure and the nostalgia of ephemeral delights.

If echoes take us backward in time to the public poet in the world at large, *Footprints* also reveals Levertov's continuing journey forward. "The Roamer" is metaphoric as the world in the guise of the wandering dog is "impatient to assume the world."[2] Equally significant is the theme of the "Soul's dark Cottage," in "The Old King" and dreams assume their ever-present importance. As always in Denise Levertov's consciousness, the role of the poet is never forgotten. The poet—personal or public—sings her didn't and dances her did.

In form, *Footprints* is innovative as Levertov varies the line, spacing, stanza, and length. There are fewer traditional forms and more freedom. Many poems capture the magical brevity of *haiku;* some poems are colloquial while others are measured by longer syllables, alliteration, and a reflective quality as in "The Malice of Innocence." Clearly, in its content and in its form, *Footprints* is a credit to the poet who wrote, "for a poet, the attention to things and people, to the passing moments filled to the brim with past, present, and future, to the Great Possessions that are our real life, is inseparable from attention to language and form. . . . *song that suffices our need* . . ."[3] So in *Footprints* and *The Freeing of the Dust,* as in *Relearning the Alphabet,* language becomes the poet's source of creativity—resulting in those fleeting moments of beauty Levertov could capture so well as in "February Evening in Boston, 1971."

> It was the custom of my tribe
> to speak and sing;
> not only to share the present, breath and sight,
> but to the unborn.
> Still, even now, we reach out
> toward survivors. It is a covenant
> of desire.

*   *   *

The individual poems in *Footprints* reveal a contrast of light and darkness as the poet embarks on the next stage of her journey. The themes move from night to day, defeat and rebuff to love and fulfillment, indirection to purpose. As always in Denise Levertov's poetry, at the moment of despair and loss, ("Wondering / where the hell to go."), the road turns her toward a sense of "being alive," to a need to affirm—a need, as she writes "to refocus." Thus the first poem, which gives the volume its title, is extremely enigmatic.

> *Someone crossed this field last night;*
> *day reveals*
> *a perspective of lavender caves*
> *across the snow.   Someone*
> *entered the dark woods.*

"Someone," deliberately ambiguous, does not *seem* to be the poet, but can only be the poet, or the soul of the poet, voyaging out into the dark woods. (Interestingly, the volume's cover reveals the legs of a walker standing on a promontory in the snow.) The Dantean echo suggests the "pilgrim's" spiritual condition in the opening lines of *Inferno;* but here we are aware of the speaker's sense of *both* indirection and the revelation at daybreak. The poem is a design in color: lavender, black and white. There is a suggestion of a mystical transformation revealed by day, coupled with the reminder of Dante's dark wood. In a later poem in this volume, we are told that "Life is Not a Walk across a Field" (quoted by Boris Pasternak from a Russian proverb),[4] but the poem concludes with the same sense of miracle we discover in "The Footprints."

"The Footprints," as an epigraph to the volume, conveys the predominant motifs of this stage in the poet's experience: a journey through the "dark woods" and the wondrous illumination revealed by daylight. Yet despite the ambiguity, a sense of threshold prevails— the image of "footprints" evokes pilgrimage. Later, the poet will be urged forward in "Life is Not a Walk" to "To be at the hollow center of a field / at dawn; the radius / radiant. Silver / to gold, shadows / violet dancers." The lavender of "The Footprints" and the violet of "Life is Not a Walk" are, interestingly, Dante's sacral colors at dawn and sunset when the presence of a divine spirit is most deeply felt. As an epigraph, Levertov leaves us her footprints in the snow, on the threshold of discovery.

"Threshold" is an invitation: "Enter, who / so desires." By night, one can see "through smokehole, / the star." Clearly, "Threshold" and the poem "Hut" are what Hemingway has called "the good place." These two poems that open the world of *Footprints* can be better appreciated after reading the entire volume. There is a great desire to escape the world, a great need to "refocus" and to renew one's direction so that, as she suggests in the final poem in the volume, she will know the way—like the dove who "takes flight / boldly, / and flies fast."

The Vietnam Poems

All that once hurt
(healed) goes on hurting
in new ways.

—"Joie de Vivre"

"Intrusion," written in August 1969 at the very height of anti-war fever—as the evening telecasts left on the mind indelible images of death and dismemberment—reflects the growing mood of the country:

After I had cut off my hands
and grown new ones

something my former hands had longed for
came and asked to be rocked.

After my plucked out eyes
had withered, and new ones grown

something my former eyes had wept for
came asking to be pitied.

The poem is terse and ironic. The words are prosaic, but they only serve to reinforce the shock of hands cut off and eyes plucked out. The voice is that of a victim, called upon by other victims. There is violation here and pathos, but the poet makes no comment. The stark words evoke the terrible images: the only emotional echoes are in "longed for," "wept," and "pitied." Since the Vietnam War was brought home for Americans in pictures rather than words, so here too Levertov's effect comes from the seen and the heard, and comment is gratuitous. There is neither anger, nor blatant protest, nor commentary—only the message conveyed by the images and the two central verbs: "*asked* to be rocked" and "*asked* to be pitied."

"Overheard over S.E. Asia" contains an immediacy that comes from first-hand report. The poem is a question and an answer. The subject is the devastation wrought on innocent populations by the dropping of napalm in Vietnam. The question is almost ingenuous: "White phosphorous, white phosphorous, / mechanical snow, / where are you falling?" The answer that is given is heavy with irony: the "snow" seems to fall "impartially," "recalls rich seas," elicits "luminous response." Its name evokes "a whisper of sequins. Ha! / Each of them is a disk of fire," but here is only destruction and mutilation,

not beauty or light—death, not life. The final lines suggest the amorality of the napalm, sent by *men*:

> I fall
> wherever men send me to fall—
> but I prefer flesh, so smooth, so dense:
> I decorate it in black, and seek
> the bone.

The tension between seeming beauty and the fact of death, "I am
the snow that burns," is further accented by the design of black and
white in the final lines, and the effect is enhanced by the repetitions:
white, snow, fall, and fire (in luminous, "disk of fire, and burn").
"My name recalls rich seas on rainy nights," has an almost hypnotic
effect, until one realizes with a shock that this snow is death, "falling
impartially on roads and roofs, / on bamboo thickets, on people."
(There is a Joycean echo in the deadly snow, falling, falling "impartially." At the end of "The Dead," Gabriel hears "the snow falling
faintly through the universe and faintly falling, like the descent of
their last end, upon all the living and the dead."[5])

The two poems are interesting for subtle changes in Levertov's
poetic technique: they present sharp visual images without "commentary." The tone is dominated by irony that is *removed* from the
speakers but evoked by the images. There is condensation here and
immediacy because both poems are related by an "I" persona. The
verse forms are characterized by enjambed lines—emphasizing the
unembellished rhythm of colloquial language, and, indeed, "Overheard" is a form of dialogue. But this is a deceptive "simplicity," for
careful examination reveals Levertov's consistent use of assonance,
alliteration, and repetition.

"Scenario," another study in irony, juxtaposes the unnatural "con-
joining" of death and life—here in a marriage. The poem is a conceit
as the title suggests a stage setting. The opening lines remind us of
"The theater of war. . . ." As the symbolic drama begins we hear,
"Offstage / a cast of thousands weeping." The wedding—a cruel and
tragic parody of a new life—is played out. The dead and the dying
form the wedding party as the Bride enters. She is Vietnam—not
pure and virginal or beautiful, but mutilated, tarnished, hobbling.
The emotion generated by the young soldier when he first sees her
rises in intensity in the final lines: "he begins to shudder, to shudder, / to ripple with shudders. Curtain." The conceit—succinct, imagistic, unembellished by comment—is set against the shudders of
the uninitiated soldier. The future is only violation, death, and dying
for the young and hopeful in Vietnam.

Levertov's technique in this poem has been criticized as forced, lacking realism. But Levertov believed that the real world of Vietnam she was recreating in the poem *was* dismemberment and despair. If for aesthetic purposes, the form she chose here is surreal, this does not invalidate the truth that the scenario exposes. As a tour de force, "Scenario" is successful because of its use of the conceit—distancing the emotions of the poet: the images of violation are given almost as "statistics," and tension is created between the "factual" report and the bridegroom's horror. The conciseness—a "play" in eighteen lines—adds a special power to "Scenario."

"Time to Breathe" is exactly that:

> Evenings enduring, blending
> one with the next. Oceans calmly
> rocking reflected docks and those
> indecipherable roads that
> inscribe themselves in sky
> way above trajectories of the swifts.
>
> That freshness, over
> and over: summer
> in folds of your dress, mysterious fabric.
> And in the disturbing
> gentle grace of your neck.
> The same summer shadow
> looking out of your eyes.
>
> Night seems to stop short
> at the horizon. Perhaps it never
> will quite arrive. Perhaps,
> renewed in the breath of these
> first summer days,
> we shall leave off dying.

The epigraph tells us the poem is an adaptation of a prose poem by Jean-Pierre Burgart, so we can only speculate about the speaker's female companion. What is significant is the placing of this poem— one of respite—after the painful evocations of the Vietnam War. There is the sheer delight of giving oneself over to the joys of nature, after the surfeit of repulsion and despair that follows the previous war poems. The persistent desire to "be alive"—for renewal, for peace, and, *implied*, for a return to the work awaiting the speaker—is characteristic of many of Levertov's poems that end with a wisp of hope: "We shall leave off dying." As she writes later in this volume, in "Sun, Moon, and Stones":

> And we were born to that sole end:
> to thirst and grow
> to shudder
> to dream in lingering dew, lingering warmth
> to stumble searching.
>
> But O the fountains,
> where shall we find them.

The poignancy of these last lines reinforces the emotions evoked by the reminder of our complex human condition: to thirst, to grow, to shudder, and to dream. The tension in this poem rests on stumbling and searching for fountains. Thus we are prepared for a change in tone after the shock of "Scenario," and it comes in "Hope It's True." The poem presents two ways of living: the "charmed life" of the 'Hunza' who, Levertov tells us, are "residents of a small mountain kingdom in northwest Kashmir, noted for their health and longevity,"[6] and, in contrast, the life she knows in a corrupted world. The evocation of this paradisal Shangri-La in the Himalayas is a bitter reminder of the suffering, pain, and complexity around *her*, so that all she can hope is that the Hunza idyll is true. The poem is a design of antitheses: "limbs anointed with oil of apricot, almond milk, and sesame" have overtones of Biblical paradise, opposed to Nevada whores, starving babies in Mississippi, and the war where "'small clashes' rip human guts per / daily usual, closer to Hunza-land than here . . ." The tone of the poem is speculative at first, almost colloquial with its lack of the grammatical "I": "Hope It's True" and "Wonder if this very day the Hunza / are leading their charmed lives," but the tension increases as the language intensifies: blast, shatter, grunt, die, clashes, 'rip human guts.' The poem ends with the speaker's seemingly guileless question: Is the apricot taster who checks on bitterness, making sure that "no Hunza, / the length of the land, shall eat sorrow?" The cynicism emerges in the unspoken question the reader asks: Does America's royal "apricot taster" make sure no individual, *the length of the land,* shall eat sorrow?

In Levertov's poem, the sense that no one is in charge, that no one will prevent us from eating sorrow, that there is no suggestion of either direction or succor, is in bitter contrast with the "royal apricot-eater." Denise Levertov never loses her own consciousness of ceaseless and gratuitous suffering whether it be in Vietnam, Mississippi,

or Las Vegas where the bomb and the unreal gambling-whoring life
co-exist.

"The Day the Audience Walked Out on Me, and Why" is a whimsical title that belies the seriousness of this poem. Written in 1970
on the occasion of Levertov's poetry reading at Goucher College
in Maryland, the poem begins a narrative with the colloquial tone
suggested in the title.

> Like this it happened:
> after the antiphonal reading from the psalms
> and the dance of lamentation before the altar,
> and the two poems, 'Life at War' and
> > 'What Were They Like?'
> I began my rap,

Much of the wit in this opening rests on Levertov's creation of the
churchly atmosphere of the setting, the university chapel. This was
a poetry reading, not a sermon, but a sermon is precisely what the
poet delivers: "Yes, it is well that we have gathered / in this chapel."
This is a speech to raise the social conscience of the audience, but
it was one that clearly the audience objected to and one that did
not please critics who dislike sermonizing in poetry. In groups, the
"audience walked out"—the poet noting the symbolic turning of their
backs to the altar. Impervious, the poet continues until almost the
last person departs, accusing the speaker of desecrating a holy place.
As an ironic afterthought the poem ends:

> And a few days later
> when some more students (black) were shot
> at Jackson, Mississippi,
> no one desecrated the white folks' chapel,
> because no memorial service was held.

In a way, the sermon at Goucher *was* a memorial service—a reminder of those who had died in their efforts to stop the war. Most
striking in this poem is the ambiguity of "desecration": who had
desecrated a holy place and who continued to desecrate human life?
The whimsy of the opening lines of the poem gives way to the seriousness and controlled outrage revealed in the remainder. Levertov
exposes an American public immune to chastisement, immune to the
assumption of responsibility, immune to the killing taking place when
moral outrage rose among the young. In another poem ("Memories
of John Keats"), Levertov refers to Keats' words: "the Genius / of
Poetry must work out / its own salvation in a man." Like Keats, she

"leapt . . . / headlong into a sea . . ." and the courage to do so rested upon her sense that a poet *should* recreate the experience into a poem, "we make our actions their memorial, / actions of militant resistance,"—even as the audience walked out!

But, although one cannot contest the poet's right to choose the theme of her poem, one can judge the artistic success of that endeavor. For all the humor of the opening lines—"Like this it happened"—and the whimsy of seeing oneself in this situation, the poem is not a poem but a "rap" as the speaker reminds the audience of the painful events of Kent State and other police violations of human rights. What is present here is anger and protest; what is not here is the emotion-charged language that resonates through most of Levertov's poems of conscience. "The Day the Audience Walked Out on Me" *states* much and *moves* too little. There is little "mystery" here, as suggested in "Conversation in Moscow" by the Russian poet.

As I have suggested, *Footprints* is a point-counterpoint of hope and despair: on the one hand, the persistent images of mutilated bodies in Vietnam where the war dragged on, the sacrifice of young Americans protesting on college campuses, and the indifference of too large a share of the American public; on the other hand, the need to renew oneself, the need to love and celebrate, to find the regenerative fountains. One poem that poses this dichotomy within the poet's consciousness is "The Old King."

The poem opens with the words of the poet Edmund Waller:

> *The Soul's dark Cottage, batter'd and decay'd,*
> *Lets in new Light through chinks that Time hath made.*

As an epigraph, the lines suggest the experience of moving from darkness to light, from the abyss to the hearthblaze.

> And at night—
> the whole night a cavern, the world
> an abyss—
>
> lit from within:
>
> a red glow
> throbbing at the chinks.
>
> Far-off a wanderer
> unhoused, unhouseled,
> wonders to see
> hearthblaze:
> fears, and takes heart.

Here, in a series of sharply opposed visual images that define the destiny of the wandering Soul, Denise Levertov has opposed the abyss of the palpable world to the inner world lit with the "red glow / throbbing at the chinks." Light—enlightenment—can penetrate the darkness, and the wanderer, ever searching for the sacral light, can perceive it, though "unhoused" and "unhouseled"—this last an echo of Hamlet's ghost who dies without benefit of sacrament. Fearing, the Soul still "takes heart." The poem is mystical, religious, yet corresponds to Denise Levertov's dual perceptions: the decay and chaos of the world and the wholeness, warmth, and order that the hearthblaze suggests.

I include this poem, because it comes at an important stage of Levertov's pilgrimage. "Staying alive," "taking heart," warming oneself at the hearthblaze are enduring and positive values of a poet who often despaired of the world while *refusing* to be conquered by it. It recalls her own favorite lines from Rilke who spoke of "unlived, disdained, lost life, of which one can die." Rather, the lines of Olga Levertoff's poem that closes *The Sorrow Dance* will guide the way.

> The dance of peace it will never cease till life
> has conquered death.[7]

One of the more delightful and original poems in the volume is "The Roamer" which touches on a central theme in all of Levertov's work: the wanderer, the pilgrim, the quester, and, here, the roamer-come-home. It is the *world* that comes back to the poet—here in the form of a dog with wanderlust. The tone of the poem is witty and whimsical. The metaphor of the world like a weary, affectionate dog "concocted / of phantasmagoric atoms" gives a wonderful sense of felt life to the poem. The dog has a irresistible personality of its own: eager and hungry, making its way home without the help of kindly strangers, scratching at the door, nudging the dreaming poet with wet nose—"flumps down, deeply sighing." The dog brings the aroma, the earthiness of life: muddy streams and "thrown-away treasures." The roamer conveys Levertov's abiding love of the earth and of life. With humor and wisdom, she knows the world communicates through odors, not words. And finally, she asks herself,

> Where have I been
> without the world? Why am I glad
> he wolfs his food and gathers
> strength for the next journey?

So the world, like the poet, journeys but always returns home—to rest, to eat, to "flump down, deeply sighing." Always the next journey, but finally, as she will tell us in "Candles in Babylon," "home to a calm dawn and / the work we had just begun."

"The Roamer" is one of Levertov's most delightful poems of celebration, of the joy of "being alive." Most memorable are the lines: "I let in blue / daybreak, / in rushes the world," and we are struck with this recurrent motif, for Denise Levertov is never so deep in dream that the world cannot rush in. The images of the poem are palpably real—anyone who owns such a roamer knows the smell of muddy streams and the feel of a wet nose. When she asks later, "But O the fountains, / where shall we find them," we do not know *where* but we are sure the poet *will* seek and find.

The final poem of the volume, "Knowing the Way," testifies to that renewed sense of purpose revealed in nature.

> The wood-dove utters
> slowly
>   those words he has
> to utter,
> and softly.
>   But takes flight
> boldly,
> and flies fast.

So, too, the poet will utter the words *softly*, but like the wood dove will "take flight, boldly," and fly fast. Always alert to nature's symbolic guidance, the poet too will "know the way."

The Freeing of the Dust

> I am tired of 'the fine art of unhappiness.'
> —"The Wealth of the Destitute"

The Freeing of the Dust (1975) will probably stand as one of Denise Levertov's finest poetic achievements. At the very height of her maturity as a poet, Levertov reveals, in the sixty poems in *Dust*, her uncontestable power at the cutting edge of American poetry: the crystalline quality of her language; the precision of her poetic craftsmanship; the new and familiar themes; the penetrating depth and breadth of thought; and the irrepressible joy in "celebration" and a reverence for life despite experiences that sadden and leave one again and again "in the dark wood."

The poems are varied in line, rhythm, tone, and perspective. The lyrical is juxtaposed to the reflective; designed stanzaic poems are followed by irregular, freer forms; the mood of the speaker covers a wide trajectory of emotions. It is this volume that won the distinguished Lenore Marshall Poetry Prize in 1975.

What is interesting, though not unexpected, is the response of the critics who, again embracing Denise Levertov with the publication of *The Freeing of the Dust*, assiduously passed over her war poems, her poetry of engagement, and praised her gifts admired more than a quarter century earlier. They noted, as one would expect, her "lyric intensity and delicacy," and an undefined "growth as a poet."[8] *Dust* was viewed as her "consummate achievement" because of her "clear, spare diction and her sense of rhythm and tone."[9]

A poet himself, David Ignatow observed that Levertov had launched into new, vital areas, recognizing that "The bitterness, like the dust, must be swept away. . . . For Levertov," he wrote, "the circle of human frailty has been completed and forgiven and even blessed, because of life. . . . her power to move us has not diminished." *The Freeing of the Dust* was the culmination of the growth of a poet over a period of almost thirty years. William Carlos Williams's prophecy that Levertov would be America's poet of the future appeared to have reached fulfillment.[11]

By 1975, the war had been over for two years, but the scars were still fresh; there were the veterans in the aftermath of violence, returning to an America that chose to put Vietnam behind it as a bad dream. There were new problems to be confronted: the impingement of technology on nature with all the ominousness those inroads augured; there was the embarrassing presence of destitution, "the wretched of the earth"—rootless, homeless people in "Bountiful America." On a more intimate level, there was the erosion of a marriage and divorce to be faced and the new experience of "living alone" with "only knowledge of silence." But Levertov's strength, her tenacity of spirit and taste for life—for "staying alive"—urged her through bleaker moments. There was the need "to live / beyond survival." As we shall see, her outer world had extended to a wider circumference, while her inner world of the spirit had plumbed a depth of profound faith.

Thus, *The Freeing of the Dust* encompasses the varied experiences of a poet who engaged the "world" at many levels; she writes of Vietnam and the haunting tragedy that will not disappear; she writes of love in its complexity; she writes about what it means "being born a woman"[12]; and she writes about nature in all its awesome beauty and mystery. Whether writing of dreaming or living alone or of places and friends, she gives us a sense of "voyaging." But *Dust* is also a voyage of the soul, as Levertov makes her way—more clearly than she has formerly expressed—toward the life of the spirit, toward what Ignatow noted as "the acceptance of the self."[13] I do not agree with Ignatow that Levertov changed. All the threads of her most cherished ideas are woven into *Dust*.

What is different is the shift in tone that will be revealed as we look more closely at individual poems, as well as the willingness to experiment with poetic forms. What is different is the acceptance of imponderable limits; yet Levertov is a poet in control of her emotions and her materials, and a poet ever aware of the simultaneity of darkness and light, death and life, pain and ecstacy, as part of the experience of living.

And there is the renewed purpose that is imagined in the theme of "rebirth." So it is that ultimately *The Freeing of the Dust* is a work of *celebration* and quiet rapture. And, as if to testify to that "vita nuova," she writes about the "matter" of poetry and the poet more reflectively than in the past (with the exception of her prose works *The Poet in the World* and *Light Up the Cave*). This is a rich and revealing work, and the technical accomplishments are equal to the thematic breadth in their great variations in language, tone and poetic form. *Dust* is rebirth after death, as she affirms the "fragrance"—the good smell / of life." And herein lies the central theme suggested in the title. For this reason, I should like to consider the title poem first.

"The Freeing of the Dust" begins with the ritual of freeing death from life. The poem goes back, in a way, to beginnings—to Egypt and the ancient rite of preserving the body of the dead in a winding sheet. This opening image takes on symbolic significance for the poem and the entire volume:

> Unwrap the dust from its mummycloths.
>
> . . . .
> Let the dust
> float, the wrappings too
> are dust.

"Dust unto dust" echoes in the mind, as the poem suggests both death and resurrection. Levertov juxtaposes earth and spirit in the forms of Caliban and Ariel (Shakespeare's dual spirits in *The Tempest*). At first, dust and death—"ashes of what had lived"—coexist with the seeds that symbolize the beginning of life. It is interesting that the entire poem is a series of *gentle* imperatives: "Let Ariel learn / a blessing for Caliban / and Caliban drink dew from the lotus / open upon the waters." Thus, the "weightless Spirit"—Ariel—will bring

new life to Caliban through blessing, and Caliban's rite of renewal
will be enacted by his drinking dew from the lotus. There are clear
contrasts here: the dark river and the fresh dew, the dust of the
mummycloths and the "pure dust" that is "all in all"—a reference
perhaps to both the "good earth" and our own humanity. The poem
concludes with the dual imperative: to Ariel to give his blessing, to
Caliban to drink from the lotus. The images are striking and moving,
as the speaker urges rebirth. The command to Caliban, "Drink,"
echoes Tennyson's Ulysses who vows, "I will drink / life to the
lees . . ." for, like Ulysses, the poet will voyage again as the first
poems of this volume suggest. The poem's images emphasize the
need for rebirth in the ritual of drinking; the alliteration, consonance,
and repetitions create the rhythm flow of liquid—especially in the l's
in almost every line: let, learn, Caliban, lotus, slow, lips, light, float,
lived, all, and calyx. The repetition of *all* reinforces the "dust unto
dust" echoes in the "ashes of what had lived" and in the "pure dust
that is all / in all." Added to this are the enjambed lines and uneven
accents which re-enact in form the *freeing* process and the float of
both air and river. In this poem, earth, air, and water contribute to
make "new life."

   "The Freeing of the Dust" is a rite, and thus has mystical implications, but early in her poetic career, Levertov had revealed a penchant for rituals. In 1969, Richard Howard noted: "Gently . . . Miss
Levertov undertakes the approach to life as a continuum and to poetry as a rite by which its rhythms may be recorded. . . . The longing
for rituals, the need to 'transform into our flesh our deaths' is the
subject, then, of all her later poems . . ."[14] In this same essay, he
speaks of her "longing for miracles" and "otherness that was
blessed."[15] Howard had indeed touched a chord in Levertov that
would go far toward understanding her later volumes of poetry.

   The three poems that open *The Freeing of the Dust* set the tone
for many of the poems that follow: "From a Plane," "Bus," and
"Journeyings." These are both real and internal voyages, the first her
historic airtrip to North Vietnam. The first journey is presented as
though it were a painting in tones of green, brown, and silver. From
the plane, Vietnam seems serene, untouched, though it only *appears*
that the great body is "not torn apart, though raked and raked / by
our claws." The second is a bus ride on the turnpike that has cut
across nature, leaving no history, no memory, a haven only for drivers.
The third is internal and touches a theme that will recur throughout
this volume as we travel "through the overcast":

Majestic insects buzz through the sky

bearing us pompously from love to love,
grief to grief,

expensively,
motes in the gaze of that unblinking eye.

Our threads of life are sewn into dark cloth,
a sleeve that hangs down over
a sinister wrist. All of us.
It must be Time whose pale fingers
dangle beneath the hem . . .

Solemn filaments, our journeyings
wind through the overcast.

All of us, Levertov emphasizes, journey from love to love, from grief
to grief, our quests always a winding "through the overcast." "Ways
of Conquest" is a poem about love, but the language pointedly rests
upon an analogy between love and war. The speaker accuses her
loved one: "You invaded my country by accident, / not knowing you
had crossed the border," and then confesses, "I invaded your country
with all my / passionate intensity." As we follow the experience of
love to the speaker who lives in the "suburbs of the capital / incog-
nito," who listens to the dreams of adolescents in the dusty park,
who *is* the "stranger who will listen," we are reminded of the poet's
experience with the protest movement, with the "voice" of the invaded country. Finally, the truth of both the experience of love and
that of the tragedy of Vietnam comes in the last lines. "What I invaded has / invaded me."

War metaphors have appeared in Levertov's poetry as early as "The
Conquerors," but here the references invite us to think of "conquest"
as the title suggests. Invasion, crossing borders, running inland "toward the hills," pontoons and parachutes—all evoke Vietnam. Finally, speaking as "America," with the words, "What I invaded has /
invaded me," the poet reminds us of a bitter truth. There are many
"ways of conquest" whether between individual lovers who invade
each other's spiritual being—that "undiscovered continent" Emily
Dickinson writes of—or between countries who confess that, ultimately, invaders are themselves invaded with memory, love for the
"enemy," or an overpowering sense of becoming a stranger. Whether
Levertov *intended* "Ways of Conquest" to touch these chords we cannot know, but the language suggests that Vietnam in these years in
never far from her consciousness.

Part 4 of *Dust* begins with America's own tragedies: racial tension, the plight of the poor and deformed and a city's sounds of fear. In "Photo Torn from *The Times*," we discover the tragic story of a boy trapped in the crossfire of racial conflict. As always, Levertov is caught up with the human condition "after" the facts: the poignancy of a mother who says: "Nothing else / can happen to me / now that my son / is dead." But what the poet creates with her own incandescent language is the power of the unforgettable face:

> But the power is there to see, the face
> of an extreme beauty, contours
> of dark skin luminous
> as if candles shone unflickering
> on beveled oiled wood.
>
> Her name, Alluvita,
> compound of earth, river, life.
>
> She is gazing
> way beyond questioners.
>
> Her tears
> shine and don't fall.

After Hanoi

The poems that grew from Denise Levertov's experiences in her participation in demonstrations at home and her journey to North Vietnam have that special stamp of truth that comes from first-hand knowledge: the unexpected beauty of the land and the desecration almost invisible from the air; the violence of demonstration "to block traffic from the air-force base"; the woman weeping for her lost right arm; the POWs who, as pilots dropping bombs, did not quite comprehend what they had committed; the horror of the tiger cages. These are accounts in which "You are there," and the immediacy of the *seen* is balanced only by the poet's control—over her emotions, over her language, over her poetic forms.

As Harry Marten has noted in his recent and revealing study, *Understanding Denise Levertov,* her "eye witness testimony of the human cost of war" was more devastating that even she could have imagined.[16] She heard, she saw, she feared. Marten writes: "Sights at Bach Mai Hospital in particular prompted the searing verses, terrifyingly and tenderly wrought . . ."[17] An examination of the Vietnam poems, in some detail, reveals a poet still haunted by the horrors of

Vietnam that could only be exorcised—as Marten declared—in "searing verses" that fifteen years later have the power to move us.

In "The Distance" we are in two places *simultaneously:* in the United States, where group protesters are carried off "to jail to be processed," and in Vietnam, where all the chaos, violence, suffering, confusion, and fear that actual war creates is produced in harsh visual images: "Over there the torn-off legs and arms of the living / hang in burnt trees and on broken walls."

The poem first appeared in *Poetry* in September 1972 during the same season when Levertov made her trip to Vietnam. "The Distance" is not only the real distance between "here" and "over there" but the distance betwen the temporary discomfort of the protesters and the heart-rending suffering of the Vietnam victims. The impressions are fresh; the memories of "what it was like" sharply delineated.

The poem begins with the resistance of the protesters of whom the speaker is one. "While *we* lie in the road to block traffic from the air-force base, / *over there* the dead are strewn in the roads." [Emphasis mine.] The entire poem turns on the contrast between two kinds of violation, "here" and "there"; the violence in war that leads to death and dismemberment; and the demeaning of protesters who—by acts of civil disobedience—"obstruct" the progress of the war: blocking traffic, being hauled off to jail, singing in their cells, and refusing to eat.

"Over there"—the North Vietnamese prisoners eat their meager rice meal and smile. There is no communion between the two for there is "the distance" that can never be bridged.

The success of the poem depends upon the contrasts created, on the one hand, by the suffering of the Vietnamese who can still "sing and fight" in mutual comradeship, and on the other, the protesters, humiliated in other ways, who also enjoy their communal efforts: singing and rejoicing. The poem is a construct of repetitions: "While we lie . . .," "While we are carried . . .," "While we wait . . .," "While we refuse . . .," and "While we fear . . ." that emphasizes the drama of the events taking place "while." Compared to the suffering of the fighters, the protesters are treated rather gently, *while* the "men and women contorted, blinded, caged, are biting their tongues / to stifle, for each other's sake, their cries of agony." There is irony here in the contrasts and something almost too terrible to be named: the crown of thorns suggest the crucifixion, as the agony of inhumanity rises above politics and "enemies." The ending poses a sombre question, as the poet views her own actions, "like the first tottering of infant feet":

Could we,
    if life lasts
        find in ourselves
that steady courage, win
such flame crowns?

"The Distance," because of the contrasts, does not trivialize the sincere emotions of the protesters (who know they'll get "decent food in a matter of hours"), but it makes more palpably real the suffering of those involved in the fighting and their capacity to endure. I do not believe Levertov is making "heroes" of the captured North Vietnamese soldiers; she abhorred violence whatever the source, but that men could "sing and fight" was a staggering thought. "I see their spirits / visible . . ." she writes.

The form of the poem is a counterpart of the theme: the point-counterpoint of "while" with the actual events of war reinforce the contrast. The lines are lengthened, as the narrative grows. But at the end, the regularity of the lines breaks down. Her use of Williams's three-stepped line increases the tentative nature of the question as one is forced to pause, to hesitate, to reflect. As she had written, "There is a poetry in thought and in feeling and in perception seeks the forms peculiar to these experiences."[18]

"The Distance" is a poem not only about the horrors of what the poet sees, but about the courage and persistence suffering engenders. It does not slight the courage of the singing demonstrators being hauled off to jail, but places that experience in its proper perspective. That the actions bore fruit is proven by the fact that the war came to a close largely because of public disillusion and student protest.

Cary Nelson, writing of *The Freeing of the Dust* noted: "The flat narration establishes Levertov's respect for the suffering that is, finally, not her own."[19] "Weeping Woman" is such a poem. The language is spare as the facts speak for themselves.

She is weeping for her lost right arm.
She cannot write the alphabet anymore
on the kindergarten blackboard.

She is weeping for her lost right arm.
She cannot hold her baby and caress it at the same time
ever again.

She is weeping for her lost right arm.
The stump aches, and her side.

She is weeping for her lost right arm.
The left alone cannot use a rifle
to help shoot down the attacking plane.

In the wide skies over the Delta
her right hand that is not there
writes indelibly,
        'Cruel America,
when you mutilate our land and bodies,
it is your own soul you destroy,
not ours.'

The irony in the poem turns on the "normal" uses for a woman's arms: to write on blackboards and to caress a child, but now those arms would raise a rifle to shoot down enemy planes. The refrain, "She is weeping for her lost right arm," haunts the poem, and the images of dismemberment make a stern moral comment—a judgment that, in the years since Vietnam, has come to weigh on American minds. But in 1972, as Americans were fighting and dying in Vietnam, one can imagine that these words were not well received. Atrocities, history has proved, were perpetrated on both sides of the conflict, but in this poem, the victim is a woman—perhaps one of many Levertov saw in Vietnam. Thus Levertov's sympathy is understandable. The final images carry sufficient weight to stand without the last lines. Levertov saw and transmuted into poetry what she saw in Hanoi, and the awesome image of the dismembered woman is, in itself, enough to bruise us with its horror.

While "Weeping Woman" conveys a Vietnam that haunts us with the tragedy of innocence, "The Pilots" rests on an entirely different rhetorical structure. "Because" becomes the key term in the poem. *Because* of a host of reasons, the poet hesitates to "awaken" the pilot-prisoners or "meet the eyes of Mrs. Brown" (a prisoner's mother). The pilots, seemingly "ignorant" of the suffering they had engendered and unseeing *because* they dropped their bombs from great heights, were polite, friendly, lonesome, and homesick. The poet, drinking tea with the POWs, loses her hostility, "*because* I hope / they were truly ignorant, / as unawakened, / as they seemed." [Emphasis mine.] The irony in this poem rests on the question of whether the pilots *truly* knew what they had committed. If they *did* understand, the speaker "must learn to distrust / my own preference for trusting people." The poem is an argument and thus does not rely on sensuous images or lyrical rhythms. Its strategy lies in the logic of language and the repetitions that recur to emphasize the argument. The poem speaks; it does not sing. The persona is speculative, curious, tentative—one who inquires into the difficult matter of placing "blame," and the poem ends enigmatically. Meeting the pilots was a part of Levertov's experience in Vietnam, and the story had to be told. But it raises eternal questions of responsibility. Who is to blame? In its form, the repetitions "Because," "then," "understand," and "I hope" emphasize the question that can have no satisfying resolution. "The Pilots" is important in terms of its theme, controlled and unified in form, but it will never satisfy those critics who expect from Levertov a lyrical grace, a delicate sensitivity, and a collage of striking images. Nonetheless, it is part of the total design of the whole fabric we think of as Levertov's "poems of engagement" and is completely consistent with her unified vision of form and experience. As Levertov herself would insist, the nature of this experience in Vietnam would have called for a speculative, searching poem as she drank tea with the POWs and fought for the kind of objectivity that the very rhetoric of the poem expresses.

"May Our Right Hands Lose Their Cunning" is a bitterly *ironic* poem that piles image on image of violence and mutilation, and then moves to the narrative of the primitive who knows not bombs but summer and silence and the stillness of trees. The poem turns on the juxtaposition of "smart" and "dumb"—first as it relates to bombs, the personified "killers."

> Smart bombs replace
> dumb bombs. 'Now we can aim
> straight into someone's kitchen.'
>
> Hard rice
> sprays out of the cooking pot
> straight into the delicate jelly of eyes.

Levertov shocks the reader to attention as the "invisible pellets / . . . . bite through smooth, pale-brown skin / into perfect bodies." This is "smart" in military lingo—the accuracy of bombs. As the tone shifts, we encounter the "dumb fellow"—the natural man—whose poem celebrates life and beauty and the luminous presence of nature at peace. The theme is, figuratively, the rape of the innocent, the "uncherished idiots," the "targets" of the "smart boys" who learned their war lessons well—"obedient to all the rules." Here, Levertov is categoric. If American soldiers in Vietnam were appalled by the killings in such places as Ke San or Hue, there is no mention here. Yet the subsequent history of the Vietnam War has revealed many psychologically traumatized individuals—many still in veterans hospitals. The picture given us is that of the perfecting of death and mutilation, but we must remember that *this* is what Levertov saw in that war-torn country, in Hanoi. The emphasis here is on victims: those "living targets" that cannot be eradicated from the memory. The poem ends with the awesome knowledge engendered by the experience, shifting the anger of the narrative to the stasis of reflection:

> We who
>   know this
> tremble
> at our own comprehension.
> Are we infected,
> viciously, being smart enough
> to write down these matters,
>   scribes of the unspeakable?
> We pray to retain
> something round, blunt, soft, slow,
> dull in us,
> not to sharpen, not to be smart.

What Levertov feels at this moment is the fear—in the act of "reporting" atrocity after atrocity—of losing one's own humanity. Her journey in Vietnam would only reinforce her strong sense of conscience and her repulsion at man's inhumanity to other men. The final prayer to retain something "round, blunt, soft, slow, / dull . . ." succeeds in *softening* the bitter tone of the poem, a prayer Levertov will make often after the catharsis of anger.

"In Thai Binh (Peace) Province," dedicated to her two companions in North Vietnam, Muriel Rukeyser and Jane Hart, is from the pen of the actual observer surfeited with the horror she has seen and heard. There is a sense of exhaustion here, as the war continues to take its toll of lives; she writes of "having seen today / yet another child with its feet blown off, / a girl, this one, eleven years old." *She* is "used up" emotionally as is her film on bombed hospitals, bombed village schools, bombed silk factories. Her tears are "used up" and her eyes are dry and burning. Turning her back on the war, the poet dreams, creating within a better time, a time of peace.

Humbly, the poet makes a vow. She will bring the war home, but with the honesty that is Levertov's hallmark, she also will bring back "Child, river, light." The poem ends, not in celebration, but almost in prayer:

Here the future, fabled bird
that has migrated away from America,
nests, and breeds, and sings,

common as any sparrow.

In the poem "In Thai Binh (Peace) Province," moving in its journey from the outer world of experience (captured in photographs) to the photographs of the inner self, Levertov has struggled toward and achieved a luminous quality. The images move from violence to the haunting beauty of the bird's song—a bird common as any sparrow. The use of harsh plosives in the first series of alliterations—bombed, blown, bewildered, and burning—give way to the almost whispered sibilants of sails, slant, swift, small, sure, sings, and sparrow in the dream of peace in Peace Province.

In January 1973, Levertov takes us again to Vietnam. The poem recalls Christmas 1972, but instead of the season of peace it is during the bombing of North Vietnam. The poem is one of Levertov's most immediate poems about Vietnam, a result, no doubt, of her own experience in Vietnam where one could still capture moments of "Peace within the / long war."

As the title suggests, "Fragrance of Life, Odor of Death" juxtaposes two conditions in Denise Levertov's world in 1972. Ironically, the "fragrance of life" emanates from Vietnam, while the "odor of death" fills the air in America, "where no bombs ever / have screamed down smashing / the buildings, shredding the people's bodies, / tossing the fields of Kansas or Vermont or Maryland into the air . . ." The poem plays on the indivisibility of life and death. In Vietnam, amid the rubble, the wounded, the land "a gash of earth-guts," life stubbornly persists. Amid the realities of war, there is a "fragrance"— of flowers, of incense, of earth-mist: the "good smell of life."

Conversely, the poet writes, where there are *no* bombs, no ravished land or people, there is "everywhere, a faint seepage, / I smell death." The poem is not as convincing as "In Thai Binh (Peace) Province," for while the opening lines are dramatic and intense in their contrast between the "rubble" and the fragrance of new life, the image of a peaceful America revealing a "seepage of death" is difficult to envision. The aroma of death rests on a nightmare of what war on American soil *might* be like, but this is an unfamiliar vision for an insulated American public to conceive. The form of the poem is extremely loose, the lines fragmented. The enjambed lines convey the smooth flow of the fragrant lakes, while the images of desecration and violence crowd in upon us. The language is harsh and bitter: screaming bombs, smashed buildings, shredded bodies, and "a gash of earth-guts." The final line, nonetheless, echoes the synthesis of the poem: in America "I smell death." Levertov wrote this poem in Hanoi-Boston-Maine in November 1972, and the poem documents the duality of her experience. We are both there and here, as surely she must have felt at that time. "Fragrance of Life" is built on irony and unexpected reversals, while the odor of death in a country supposedly "whole and undefiled" haunts the modern Cassandra.

At Christmas in 1972, Levertov again wrote of the war in probably the most passionate and searing poem in *The Freeing of the Dust*. The scene is set in the title: "A Poem at Christmas, 1972, during the Terror-Bombing of North Vietnam." Instead of a hush of religious feeling, the speaker begins: "Now I have lain awake imagining murder." The poem ends:

> *O, to kill*
> *the killers!*
>
> It is
> to this extremity
>
> the infection of their evil
>
> thrusts us . . .

The poem is a daydream of retribution. The speaker *becomes* the instrument of vengeance: punishing those responsible for the bombing of North Vietnam, but here all of the violence remains in the imagination, driven by primal impulses of revenge. Although few would admit it, many Americans dreamed or daydreamed about retribution, but here Levertov has given free expression to those desires. As one would expect, the daydream is one of unleashed, primitive anger, as she lies awake "imagining murder." The objects constitute what the sixties called "the Establishment"—those in charge of perpetrating the horrors in Vietnam. The "murderer" is a near-genius of ingenuity: she has knives, napalm, and "small bombs," and her imagination provides other weapons, "All night imagining murder."

The closing lines are more characteristically Levertov as she laments the forces that have infected her with evil in this nightmarish dream—while awake. The question could be asked, Does Levertov really demand an eye for an eye? I think not. The poem is an exorcism of bitterness for the destruction of life in the sacred season of Christ's birth. The "Terror-Bombing" was a sacrilege, and the poem almost a ritualistic reenactment of punishment, but it *is* a daydream when the imagination gives reign to one's deepest—and most destructive—desires. That Levertov views "murder" as an infection—a disease unnatural to sane human beings—testifies to the basic "sanity" of the poet.

It must be noted that the poem's "anger" obliterates its ability to move us. Levertov's considerable gift in creating an aura of empathy for the suffering, her own human sense of "caritas," and her poetic power to build her poem around images of delicacy and beauty endow her with the capacity for greater subtlety, indirection, and song as opposed to stridency.

The Levertov we will remember is the voice of "Dragon of Revolutionary Love." After an account of the "grievous wounds" inflicted on the innocent, the poet turns to the land and its people—a land still brimming with life, a people enduring with courage down to the youngest children.

ii

> From the Red River's many mouths
> uprises
> > a spirit song.
> Glittering drops that fall free from the nets
> as fisherman take their catch
> are the bright scales of the spirit-dragon.

iii

> To live
> beyond survival.
> When a whole child
> hurries to school with a legless child
> on his back,
> both of them flushed with pride,
>
>
> the spirit-dragon
> flies alongside them.

The beauty of these final images is reinforced by the lyrical quality of the lines: the alliteration in from, fall free, fisherman, flushed, and flies; the flow of the rhythms like the river itself; and the magical associations of uprises, glittering, bright scales, and the children "flushed with pride." The spirit-song of the mystical spirit-dragon protecting the land and its young is triumphant proof that one *can* live "beyond survival."

At the close of "Modes of Being" (interspersed with painful "pictures" of prisoners in Saigon in animal cages), Levertov would write:

                              Joy
          is real, torture
          is real, we strain to hold
          a bridge between them open,
          and fail,
          or all but fail.
                  .   .   .   .   .
          What wings, what mighty arch
          of feathered hollow bones, beyond
          span of albatross or eagle,
          mind and heart must grow
                              to touch, trembling,
          with outermost pinion tips,
          not in alternation but both at once,
          in one
          violent eternal instant
          that which is and
          that which is . . .

Here, in 1974, in the "new landscape of knowledge," intense love and intense pain, joy and torture, mind and heart are indivisible. "Both at once, / in one / violent eternal instant / that which is and / that which is . . ." exist in the simultaneity of being exactly like the "delight of sparrows / ruffling in inchdeep lake of rain / in the jailhouse yard." Denise Levertov's own response (apart from her continuing public commitment to social issues) was manifested in two arenas of concern: the role of the poet and her spiritual quest. Both had been major preoccupations for over twenty-five years, but now they find their way more *explicitly* into her poetry.

In *The Freeing of the Dust*, there are many references to the poets—sometimes as "the scribes of the unspeakable," sometimes contemptuously as ". . . pink-faced / earnest wits— / you have given the world / some choice morsels," sometimes as the "keeper" of the writer's paraphernalia: "Typewriter, telephone, ugly names / of things we use, I use . . ."

But the heart-stopping poems come, unexpectedly, after the cynicism, the pain of war, the sense of omnipresent death. The poet's sensitivity to nature, to man's place in the scheme of the world, to the poet's "mission," lead us to a poem like "Cancion." In one way, the poem—a "Song"—celebrates the mythical identity of woman and nature: she is the sky, the "glittering bird," the sea, and finally the earth. But when a woman, she is the maker of song—the poem that emerges as if with a will of its own. The images in the poem are stunning and evocative as they merge into symbols relating nature to her own reality as woman.

When I am the sky
a glittering bird
slashes at me with the knives of song.

When I am the sea
fiery clouds plunge into my mirrors,
fracture my smooth breath with crimson sobbing.

When I am the earth
I feel my flesh of rock wearing down:
pebbles, grits, finest dust, nothing.

When I am a woman—O, when I am
a woman,
my wells of salt brim and brim,
poems force the lock of my throat.

This poem is, of course, concerned with more than the process of writing poetry. It is the act of poetic *creation* out of pain, violence, and overpowering emotion. The poem grows in tension until the final stanza when Levertov—a woman—reaches the climax of an experience from which the poem is born. The repetitions, the verbs of violence and erosion dissolve into the "wells of salt" and "poems force the lock of my throat." Brief, terse, and powerful, "Cancion" is a song one would not expect from the title.

Other poets have written about the struggle to write. Levertov has behind her in modern American poetry echoes from Williams's *Paterson:* "The language, the language / fails them / They do not know the words / or have not / the courage to use them."[20] Later, he writes, "There is no direction. Whither? I / cannot say. I cannot say / more than how. The how (the howl) only / is at my disposal (proposal): watching— / colder than a stone."[21] It is natural that Denise Levertov would seek out in poetry a source of regeneration after the experience of war and death in Vietnam. Such a poem is "Growth of a Poet" which adds luster to a volume that is suffused not only with the haunting memories of war but with the facts of divorce, living alone, and the impulse to deny. This is a work of affirmation, as each image mirrors what for most of us is the mystical, inexplicable creative process.

He picks up crystal buttons from the ocean floor
Gills of the mind pulse in unfathomed water.

In the infinite dictionary he discovers
gold grains of sand. . . .

In images of sound, blindness, and finally of touch, the poet makes his journey toward his creation. The final lines are a climax of revelation:

> When he opens his eyes he gives to what he gazes at
> the recognition no look ever before granted it.
> It becomes a word. Shuddering it takes wing.

Elsewhere, Levertov has written about the writing of a poem—in clear, concise prose. But here, the magic of that creation is imparted in a way that the reader can experience, if not "comprehend." In another part of the poem, Levertov speaks of writing poetry as a "birth": "each poem's passion / ends in an Easter, / a new life." But on a more prosaic level, she speaks of how poems begin: "To make poems is to find / an old chair in the gutter / and bring it home / into the upstairs cave; / a stray horse from the pound, / a stray boat on the weedy shore, / phosphorescent." The artifacts are reality, but the transformation takes place in the imagination.

> Only when feet begin
> to dance, when the chair
> creaks and gallops,
> do the gates open
> and we
>   discover ourselves
> inside
> the kingless kingdom.

In the concluding lines of "Growth of a Poet," we learn that the "songs" and the "experience" are one, whether of pain, or joy, or violence, or separation—dark or light."

> And now the sounds
> are green, a snowdrop's quiet
> defiant insignia:
>
> And now the sounds
> crackle with mica glitterings,
> rasp with cinder,
> call with the oboe calm of rose quartz:
>
> and now the sounds
> are bone flutes, echo
> from deepest canyon, sounds
> only the earliest, palest stars may hear:

and now the sounds
are black. Are black sounds.
Black. The deep song
delves.

Levertov's artistic "source"—as she talks with a poet in "Conversation in Moscow"—is experience as we find it both in the mystery of
life and in the mystery of the self. "Poems," the Russian poet intones, "are of two kinds: those with mystery, / those without mystery," the first preferable even if those "without mystery" are "well-
made." We read great writers, like Dostoyevsky, the poet says, because "—in him we know / our own darknesses and illuminations, /
tortures and ecstasies: our human reality." This is the source Denise
Levertov perceives to be the essence of poetry, and so at the conclusion of "Conversation in Moscow" she reaffirms the quest of the poet.

we mustn't, any of us, lose touch with the source,
pretend it's not there, cover over
the mineshaft of passion
                              despair somberly tolls its bell
                                 from the depths of,
and wildest joy,
sings out of too,
        flashing
        the scales of its laughing, improbable
                                        music,
grief and delight entwined in the dark down there.

In no other place has Denise Levertov more eloquently defended
the role of poetry to capture experience and embody it in the permanence of art, as in the poem.

The Freeing of the Dust comes full circle with "Voyage," although it
is not the last poem in the volume. But the metaphor of the journey
opens this collection, and it is fitting to return to it toward the close.
A sea voyage is underway as the poem begins, but soon the experience takes on metaphoric overtones. And, as if in anticipation of the
volumes that follow, prayers of celebration initiate the sailing. "These
are prayers. / To celebrate, / not to beseech. / Among them, leaning /
toward the water, we voyage, / are voyaged, seeing. / We share among

us / the depth of day, are borne / through it / swiftly as arcs of spray."
The poem closes with an almost ritual thanksgiving:

> Silent, smiling, receiving
> joyfully what we are given,
> we utter
> each to each
> our absolute presence.

With the final "freeing of dust" to the river and the air, the poet is
ready to say, "I am tired of the fine art of unhappiness."

Life in the Forest (1978)

> . . . currents of doubt and praise
> "Human Being"

The epigraph to Denise Levertov's next published volume, *Life in
the Forest,* is a touchstone for the substance and tone of the collection:

> We work in the dark. We do what we can. We give what we
> have. Our doubt is our passion. Our passion is our task. The rest
> is the madness of art.
>
> (Henry James)

Life in the Forest is a major step in Levertov's journey, yet as the
epigraph suggests, her recurrent concerns persist. She will work in
the inscrutable "dark woods"—she will live in the forest; she will not
slacken in her concern for social justice and the poetry of "engagement." Although Vietnam may be a raw scar, it is over, but much
remains to fight for *and* against. She will bring together from her twin
worlds, inner and outer, the material that will lead to the "madness
of art." We cannot forget the words by which she still lives as artist:
"there is a form in all things (and in our experience) which the poet
can discover and reveal."[22]
Notably, *Life in the Forest* is about death and life, doubt and faith;
and it is here that Levertov's pilgrimage points to the religious preoccupations of her next three volumes of poetry.
As she explains in the "Introductory Note," she, like Cesare
Pavese, was moving toward poetry less autobiographical, less lyrical.
She was looking toward more narrative, "expansive" forms, and trying to "avoid overuse of . . . the dominant first-person singular," with

the result that the canvas is widened and poems may be read as "sequences." Yet, it is clear from her own statement that Levertov had not repudiated the lyric mode nor had she completely turned aside from the autobiographical. Her poetry still bore the stamp of her experiences, but it is true that *Life in the Forest* includes more. Harry Marten put it well when he wrote, "She gives her attention not so much to the quality of the object perceived, or alternately to the interior of the perceiver's mindscape, as to the relationships between the world 'out there' and its apprehension by a receptive sensibility."[23]

The breadth of her subjects moves from a Jewish cabdriver to a woman meeting an old lover to fellow travellers on a jet plane to the mysterious world of Mexico to the experiences of the blind to the poet Li Po. But many sequences, like "Continuum," reveal the gripping pain of her mother's dying and death in Mexico; "Modulations for Solo Voice" ("written in the winter and spring of 1974–75 . . . might be subtitled from the cheerful distance of 1978, *Histoire de un amor*")[24] traces a long and painful love story—closing with the speaker's tongue-in-cheek epilogue, "I thought I was wounded to the core / but I was only bruised."

And among these sequences there is always the poet of social conscience in "The Long Way Round," "On the 32nd Anniversary of the Bombings of Hiroshima and Nagasaki," "For Chile, 1977," and "Greeting to the Vietnamese Delegates to the U.N." Interspersed are Levertov's poems on the condition of human life and death and her own spiritual conviction. This is a rich volume that opens new ground, new forms, and yet retains the essential Levertov—always journeying, always discovering.

One may also add: always doubting. Marten quotes Levertov's observation: "My religious faith is at best fragile."[25] "Human Being" is a religious poem that introduces the poet's existential dilemma— its theme is doubt, but its resolution is renewed faith. Here in "Human Being" the voice is speculative, humble, *asking questions*.

> Human being walking
> in doubt from childhood on: walking
>
> a ledge of slippery stone in the world's woods
> deep-layered with wet leaves—rich or sad: on one
> side of the path, ecstasy, on the other
> dull grief.   Walking
>
> the mind's imperial cities, roofed-over alleys,
>   thoroughfares, wide boulevards

that hold evening primrose of sky in steady calipers.

Always the mind
walking, working, stopping, sometimes to kneel

in awe of beauty, sometimes leaping, filled with the energy
of delight, but never able to pass
the wall, the wall
of brick that crumbles, and is replaced,
of twisted iron,
of rock,
that wall that speaks. . . .

Human beings are always searching, walking "the mind's imperial cities," working—sometimes awed by beauty, sometimes "filled with energy of delight," but "never able to pass / the wall, the wall" of suffering, of children who "suffer, are tortured, die / in incomprehension." The human condition—joy and sorrow, incomprehension and doubt—are anatomized here in the almost painful images of the soul in search of understanding. There is a faint hint of Williams's "Faitoute" in *Paterson:* "Outside / outside myself / there is a world," and he walks in that world on Sunday in the Park in Paterson searching for answers and finding only multiplicity, complexity, and deformity.[26] Levertov finds, instead, both reason to "kneel / in awe of beauty" as well as suffering, and the poem ends with thanksgiving—this human being, each night,

silently utters,
impelled as if by a need to cup the palms
and drink from a river,
the words, 'Thanks.
Thanks for this day, a day of my life.'
And wonders.
Pulls up the blankets, looking
into nowhere, always in doubt.

Denise Levertov explained that "Human Being" is a theological poem about stumbling blocks to belief. She said, "The wall is the wall that speaks, saying anonymously: children and animals cannot learn anything from suffering and thus 'die / in incomprehension.'" The innocent suffer, and not necessarily at the hands of human beings. "Suffering in those who can learn something from suffering is explicable because it can be looked upon as a painful but necessary part of growth, but the suffering of those who, as far as one can see, cannot learn from their suffering is a profound mystery and serves as

a stumbling block to many people, not just to me."[27] The problem
turns on a belief in God and a belief in the goodness of God.

So it is, at the close of the poem, the poet, after thanksgiving,
"drifts to sleep, downstream / on murmuring currents of doubt and
praise, / the wall shadowy, that tomorrow / will cast its own familiar,
chill, clear-cut shadow / into the day's brilliance." A footnote to Levertov's gloss of the poem is that her theological position had moved
on since the writing of "Human Being," and the doubts and uncer-
tainties about her faith have been laid to rest.

In many ways, "Human Being" *appears* formless, but beneath the
broken lines, the hestitations, the lack of regular meter, there is a
carefully designed order that governs the whole. Although they are
not immediately perceivable, the four stanzas that compose the poem
share recurrent rhythms and sounds. As we move through the poem,
we are conscious of the presence of the participles that emphasize
the continuum of action: walking, working, stopping, leaping, saying,
suffering, summoning, and murmuring. A closer look reveals the
alliterative w's that begin in a lyrical mode: the "world's woods," wet
leaves, wide boulevards, walking, working—and then the *wall* with
its contrasting "monotony," ominousness: "never to pass the wall."
At the end of the poem, the wall is shadowy, "that tomorrow / will cast
its own familiar, chill, clear-cut shadow / into the day's brilliance."
Levertov knows we live with the shadows, but she will find her way
to confront the "darkness." In the very next poem in the volume,
"Writing to Aaron," she closes with a note of sadness and praise.

> I know you know
> about partings, tears, eyedrops, revisions, dwellings,
>   discoveries,
> mine or yours; those are the glosses,
> Talmudic tractates, a lifetime's study. The Word itself
> is what we heard, and shall always hear, each leaf
> imprinted, syllables in our lives.

Although the poems of *Candles in Babylon* bring to a climax Levertov's theological position, these final lines testify to the strong roots
of her faith in God. There is no sense of doubt here; there is conviction: "The Word itself / is what we heard . . ."

In another poem, "The Long Way Round," Levertov deals with
what she believes to be an unsuccessful approach to racism. She
reflects upon another American enigma: what to do and say to black
people, convinced that the answer does not lie in assimilation (as
the years following demonstrated) but in the establishment of one's

identity. Only by trying to understand the struggle for self-determination in Vietnam can the homogenized poet, the "indistinguishable mixture / of Kelt and Semite, grown under glass / in a British greenhouse," begin to comprehend the Black awakening in America and "took lessons / from distant Asia; and only then / from near-as-my-hand-persons, Black sisters." She would push open her mind's door ". . . to let in the smell of / pain, of destroyed / flesh, to know,"

> for one instant's agony,
> insisted on for the sake of knowing
> anything, anything at all
> in truth,
> that the flesh belonged
> to one's own most dear,
> child, or lover, or mother—
>
> pushing open my door I began
> to know who I was and
> who I was not.

In the image of swimming through life, the activity of pain as our eyes sting and breath falters, swimming with bodies of every color, she concludes,

> While we
> swim for dear life, all of us—'not'
> as it has been said, '*not* waving,
> but drowning.'

Although all may not agree with Levertov's position on assimilation (still a hotly debated topic in this country), the poem reveals that Levertov has never lost her consciousness and concern for the disenfranchised in America, made more poignant by her increased sensitivity to the suffering in Vietnam.

Anniversaries are normally happy, evoking past joys and accomplishment, but in "On the 32nd Anniversary of the Bombing of Hiroshima and Nagasaki," Levertov brings home with recurrent guilt and terror what unimaginable destruction these bombs had wrought. America lost its innocence after the destruction of these cities, though *"with this / the war is over."* In our youth, the poet observes, the magic words that the war was over came with cries of joy and relief, and "summer was springtime." The irony of that relief came to Americans when they learned the magnitude of the bombs and all the "improved" bombs that followed. Ignorance, Levertov emphasizes, was

America's failing, but as the statistics poured in ("eighty-seven thousand / killed outright by a single bomb,") the country began to sense the birth of a new age of terror: "war had ended our childhood." "Anniversary" recounts the journey of America from innocence to knowledge. The images of horror, contrary to what we might expect, emanate from the false sense of relief: gasping mouths and widened eyes and "vague wonder"—not yet understanding the cost of that peace. Hiroshima had a death, but no resurrection, in Levertov's oblique reference to the Christian story. There is no light; there is only shadow. Yet the final lines, repeating "shadow" in a litany of sorrow, close with "urging":

> The shadow's voice
> cries out to us to cry out.
> Its nails dig
>   into our souls
>   to wake them:
> 'Something,' it ceaselessly
> repeats, its silence
> a whisper, its whisper
> a shriek,
>   while the 'radiant gist'
> is lost, and the moral labyrinths of
> humankind convulse as if made
> of snakes clustered and intertwined and stirring
> from long sleep—
> '. . . something can yet
> be salvaged upon the earth:
> try, try to survive,
> try to redeem
> the human vision
> from cesspits where human hands
> have thrown it, as I was thrown
> from life into shadow. . . .'

The voice of the shadow—that which once was Hiroshima and Nagasaki—still haunts America. Levertov's citation of the "radiant gist" carries a double irony. It is a reference from *Paterson* to Madame Curie's discovery of radium—a triumph of human ingenuity, but it is an oblique reference to the uses science is put in making instruments of destruction. Here, the "radiant gist" has been lost and the "moral labyrinths of humankind convulse . . ." Levertov, who would march again, this time for nuclear disarmament, could never forget—as too many human beings, worldwide, have forgotten—the "shadow" of Hiroshima crying out "to us to cry out." As in many of her poems on war and violence, Denise Levertov dwells not merely on the physical manifestations of horror, but on the attitudes, reactions, responses, and the lack of response of mankind in the aggregate. It is for this reason that Levertov—through the voice of the shadow—implores the world to "try, try to survive, try to redeem / the human vision . . ." which men are heir to and which still is possible. Denise Levertov is a humanitarian facing the facts of inhumanity with prayers of beseechment, and though she will turn ultimately to a higher power for support, she never loses her belief, as she told me with a puckish grin, that "God helps those who help themselves."[28] The success of the poem rests upon the symbolism of the shadow with its multiple associations, as well as the hammerstroke repetitions of future, cry, whisper, try, thrown, and humankind, human hands, human vision.

Again, in "For Chile, 1977," as in the Vietnam poems, Levertov juxtaposes beauty and the violation of the innocent. The poem begins with the magical Andean light and plays upon light and clarity against the smoke of "scorched hopes."

> It was a land where the wingéd mind
> could alight.
> Andean silver dazzling the Southern Cross;
> the long shore of gold beaten by the Pacific
> into translucency, vanishing
> into Antarctica—

The natural beauty of the land frames the tragic account of Chile's homeless, its executioners, its victims, and "The throats of singers / . . . punched into silence" and "dancers herded / into the pens." The phoenix, symbol for rebirth and our hope for renewal, "fly affrighted" from Chile, and the poem concludes on a tentative note with a litany of questions:

> When will the cheerful hammers sound again?
> When will the wretched begin to dance again?
> When will the guitars again
> give forth at the resurrected touch
> of broken fingers
> a song of revolution reborn?

In Levertov's "Introductory Note" to *Life in the Forest*, she declares her intention to continue a direction she had already taken: less autobiographic, but her social conscience is an ever-present part of Denise

Levertov as a "poet in the world" and thus will continue to be a hallmark of her poetry in the future.

The last poem in this volume that makes direct reference to Vietnam is "Greeting to the Vietnamese Delegates to the U.N." The poem, in couplets, presents antitheses: "our" and "your." These are phrases, juxtaposed for the irony implicit in the central theme that small is successful and large is powerless power. The poem is sparse; the images, flat; the repetitions penetrate our minds as we think of Levertov's view that Vietnam has wrenched with "small hands" what America could not accomplish with large ones. Levertov reminds us of a harsh reality we choose to forget: that America lost its first war in Vietnam. The most moving lines are the final ones:

> Our longing for new life
> Your building of new life
>
> Our large hands
> Your small hands

One final observation need to be made about the Vietnam poems written after Levertov's visit to Hanoi. Although there are still moments of anger, horror, and frustration that America was, according to Levertov, indifferent to the suffering in that war, there is an added dimension that enhances the aesthetic quality of these poems. Amid the tragic events she witnessed, events that were destructive of the land and innocent victims, there is always an acute awareness that can come only with "being there": the natural beauty of the still untouched countryside, the courage of a people both fighting and hoping, the insistence to "live beyond survival," and, finally, the hesitation in placing blame upon the American soldiers who were not wholly cognizant of the long-range effects of their acts: bombing from planes, napalming forests, spraying Agent Orange upon both ally and enemy. The emphasis, rather, on the pain and anguish of war contributes to the elegiac tone, enhanced by Levertov's considerable ability to find the words to voice those experiences. Many of these poems stand with the very best of the Vietnam poetry written by observers like John Balaban and others.

The final poem that merits special attention is "Life in the Forest," which gives the volume its title. The theme of "Life in the Forest" is change and prepares us for the next three volumes in which the poet seeks to find the immutable, the transcendent, the hidden continuity that refutes change. The woman in the poem living in a hut, "mumbled by termites," shrugs off change. Surrounded by the creatures of nature, "her desire / fixed on a chrysalis," awaiting the birth of the butterfly. Encircled by the erosion that is death, she fixes on life:

> How Eternity's
> silver blade filed itself fine
> on the whetstone of her life!

The butterfly metamorphoses into a man, a lover, who—like Eternity—leaves to "go wandering." Time, keeping its course unalterably, is refused entrance. Life and death co-exist.

Life in the forest is desire, joy, knowledge of death and loss. This might well be a summing up of Denise Levertov's experiences. The smile is her defiance against inexorable time, her weapon against bereavement. This is a beautiful poem, replete with images of change, life, desire, and biting loss. The rhythms are soft and fluid, achieved by the sibilants that create the music of the poem and the uneven flow of the broken lines. The ending is *not* an end, but a moment of stasis before we hear "the clang of the bell of the / deep world, unshaken . . ." in "Magic" which is "one note, / continuous, / gong / of the universe, neither beginning nor ending." "Magic" will herald the miracle of the "cup" which will remind us that the clang of the bell only seems "to cease when we cease / to listen . . ." The spiritual overtones suggest the rituals of religious life, and move us on to the next stage of Levertov's journey where she will reaffirm what she always knew.

6

Recent Poetry: Lighting Candles in Babylon

> As a poet who is also, at least sporadically, a political activist in a minor way, I feel strongly that internal and external work, the self-directed or introspective and publicly-directed or extroverted, must be concurrent, or at least rhythmically alternating. They are complementary, and neither can be substituted for the other. . . . in our own time and place those who turn away from concern for the commonweal to cultivate their own gardens are found to have lost touch with a nourishing energy. Better a bitter spring than no irrigation at all. Ivory towers look out over desert landscapes.

> The great power of art is to transform, renovate, activate.
>
> —*Cave*

Although the convictions expressed here date back to the mid-seventies, Denise Levertov continues to be faithful to these complementary aspects in her work into the eighties; her latest poetry reflects the poet in both the constantly enlarging world and the realm of the "inscape" whose depths cannot be fathomed, yet provides a wellspring for the imagination. But she never "lost touch with the nourishing energy."

Her poetic journey—at times, on a rocky road of "wavering" or suffering the injustices she perceived in the world, or witnessing the polarities of good and evil; at times, walking, dancing, moving inexorably toward God while never relinquishing the beauties of the universe—continues in the last four published volumes: *Candles in Babylon* (1982), *Oblique Prayers* (1984), *Breathing the Water* (1987), and *A Door in the Hive* (1988).

All the familiar landmarks are here: the sense of quest; the absorption with nature—both saddening and restorative; the anger at injustices round the world though Vietnam was long over—but not forgotten; the duality of grief and joy that are the unavoidable "givens" of human life; the haunting echoes of memory; the need to renew ourselves; and the poet's chosen destiny to bring the language alive on the tongue—to awaken sleepers, to free the "imprisoned." Especially notable are the poet's wide swings between hope and despair; at the very moment when one would think her faith would have left her in a stasis of tranquillity, as in "The Many Mansions" of *Candles in Babylon*, the world catapults her again into a cycle of confusion, despair, struggle, and, intermittently, stillness and an ephemeral peace. Celebration and prayer are the concomitant outcome. Thus, one part of Denise Levertov's poetic experience will be to "dance to a measure / contrapuntally, / Satyrically, the tragic foot,"[1] as Williams had written at the end of *Paterson*, but with a difference. Her quest, in the eighties, is "this need to dance," but it is also "this need to kneel."

Herein lies the expanded horizon in these latest volumes of poetry: Denise Levertov's spiritual journey toward her God, her religious quest—although she suggested that "acknowledgement, and celebration, of mystery constitute the most consistent theme in my poetry from its very beginning . . ."[2] Certainly, as Harry Marten notes, "Religious power radiates through and unites experiences"[3] and comes to fruition in these volumes.

Thus we must take care not to gloss over the poems of social conscience, for it is here her tenuous faith in *man* falters *and* revives. It is here she confesses herself unable to understand man's inhumanity to man, or his unwillingness or inability to make wiser choices. If he is to survive, Levertov believes, man *can* and *must* make those choices! This theme is a thread woven into all of her political poetry and is visible in these last volumes. The tough moral fiber characteristic of Denise Levertov as a "poet *in* the world" is a hallmark of her poetry from the very beginning, even as her increased religious absorption is revealed in these recent collections. She would still write in *Candles in Babylon*:

> I send my messages ahead of me,
> You read them, they speak to you
> in siren tongues, ears of flame
> spring from your heads to take them.

She had also written of the poet in 1968:

> The poet . . . is a priest; the poem is a temple; epiphanies and communion take place within it. The communion is triple: between the maker and the needer within the poet; between the maker and the needers outside him—those who need but cannot make their own poems . . .; and between the human and the divine in both poet and reader. By divine

I mean something beyond both the making and the needing elements, vast, irreducible, a spirit summoned by the exercise of needing and making. When the poet converses with this god he has summoned into manifestation, he reveals to others the possibility of their own dialogue with the gods in themselves. Writing poetry is the poet's means of summoning the divine. . . .[4]

By the eighties Levertov's poetic muse was transformed by the God of her religious faith, whose inscrutable power was related to the creative power of the inner self, but who could offer, as Christian orthodoxy assures, a source of hope, guidance, solace, and joy. These motifs recur in the final section of *Candles in Babylon* and *Oblique Prayers, Breathing the Water,* and *A Door in the Hive.* They are the driving energy Denise Levertov has channeled to fight the doubt, darkness, and despair of both our age and our existential condition. If, as she wrote, writing poetry was her means of summoning the divine, at this point in her life, Levertov also quested for God through prayer, rite, and Christian humility—the immemorial modes of spiritual sustenance. But Denise Levertov was a poet; her own offering was that made by the artist—the poem. As we shall see in many of the poems in these three volumes, these experiences were often coexistent.

She said, "I have definitely moved back towards my beginnings in Christian faith since I completed writing that poem [the "Mass"]. Writing the poem was a kind of reconversion experience."[5] In this same interview, she compared religious ritual with poetic ritual: "The object of ritual," she reflected, "is to transform the profane into the sacred, so actually, there is an inherent dynamic in religious ritual and therefore in poetic ritual too, because it deals with transformation. It's metamorphic, literally."[6]

In the four volumes, there is the awe of the imagination, the mystery and magic of dream, and the spiritual urging to "breathe life into the dust." And there is more: there is the personal struggle of conscience against the chaos she finds in different parts of the world; there is also love and friendship and courage, and remembrance and joy and praise and the sense of a numinous nature. Finally, there is— in moments of crisis—the "possibility: to permeate, to quicken, all of our life and the works we make."[7]

Candles in Babylon

Denise Levertov, more than most twentieth-century poets, drew her images and symbols, from Scriptures. She smiled when she said that her poetry was "shot through with Biblical references. . . . y'know, a parson's daughter."[8]

Monroe Spears had written in *Dionysus and the City: Modernism in Twentieth-Century Poetry* that most modern poets chose their major symbols from the images of the modern city—as either Dionysian or Apollonian.[9] This is not to say that Eliot and Pound did not choose images from the Old and New Testaments, but most often their "wasteland" was the contemporary city—London or Boston or, in the case of William Carlos Williams, Paterson, New Jersey. Only Robert Frost rarely found the city to be an apt symbol to convey his "lover's quarrel with the world," choosing instead the woods, the town, and the "clearing"—this last *his* private space. Denise Levertov drew her images and symbols from the world at large, as well, but frequently she dipped into the Bible as her most familiar imagistic inspiration from earliest childhood.

So it is that the title poem of this thirteenth volume evokes the vision of Babylon. Liana Sakelliou has noted that "the volume focuses on transformations of self-destructive tendencies into humanistic values."[10] The themes in *Candles in Babylon* cover a wide spectrum of Levertov's experience. Some are familiar to us—the themes of the "wanderer," the poetic rite of singing, the grief that lives within us at the loss or death of friends, the numinous beauty of the world, "staying alive," and the other world of the inscape: dream, mystery, and what Emily Dickinson had called "the undiscovered continent" within. But the poems of "engagement"—emanating from Levertov's ever-alert social consciousness—are replete with the continuing injustices in the world: the tragedy of Karen Silkwood, the horrors of El Salvador, the "age of terror" that hovers over us with the threat of nuclear annihilation. There are backward glances brought on by "anniversaries": World War II, Black Emphasis Week.

And amidst the drama and terror and nostalgia, there is the wonderful fantasy of Sylvia in "Pig Dreams"—the life and times of a pig, more human than animal, more **humane** than many people. "Pig Dreams" is a testament, not only to Levertov's understanding of human nature and of "woman" as she travels through the rituals and hurdles of her life, but also to her wit and ability to delight; we find ourselves thoroughly captivated by Sylvia, her courageous and sensitive "heroine." Marten's comment that "'Pig Dreams' ends with a grand vision of harmony and promise" is interesting for the light it casts upon the close of "The Many Mansions."[11] In 1981, *Pig Dreams: Scenes from the Life of Sylvia* was published separately with delightful illustrations. As an artistic work, it is a unique combination of beautiful sketches and a moving and humane story.

Finally, as I have already indicated, *Candles in Babylon* traces Denise Levertov's "clearest view of the force of her new beliefs."[12] If writing the "Mass for the Day of St. Thomas Didymus" was—in her words—a kind of "reconversion experience,"[13] the entire volume points the way to the humility and radiance of the final poem where she can say, "For that the vision / was given me: to know and share, / passing from hand to hand . . ."

The poem, "Candles in Babylon," serves as a fitting epigraph to the volume, because it embodies three major motifs of Levertov's poetry: her social conscience, her religious experience in the context of the Scriptures, and her sense of herself as poet. The poem demands a knowledge of the biblical account of Babylon as it appears in the Book of Jeremiah. Apart from the obvious allusions to the iniquitous city visited upon by God's wrath, the account deepens and enriches our appreciation of Levertov's dream vision.

According to 25 Jeremiah, in the first year of Nebuchadnezzar's reign over Babylon, the Lord spoke to the prophet: "Turn ye now everyone from his evil way, and from the evil of your doing. . . . I will utterly destroy them." Moreover, the Lord promised:

> I will take from them the voice of mirth, and the voice of gladness, the voice of the bridegroom and the voice of the bride, the sound of the millstones, and the light of the candle.

God's punishment was then loosed upon the wicked city for its divisiveness, its worship of false idols, its warring activities, and its trust in work and treasure rather than in God. Later, a forgiving God made a covenant with His people in Babylon, "I will not turn away from them." In the judgment of Babylon, God cried out that the children of Israel were "lost sheep." Their shepherds had caused them to go astray. So the Lord sent an assembly of great nations to destroy Babylon because Nebuchadnezzar had destroyed his covenant with God, had "sinned against the Lord." The Lord described Babylon as a "heifer at grass," which "bellows like a bull." Israel was a scattered sheep and "Israel has been forsaken." This passage in Jeremiah ends with the ominous note: "A sound of battle is in the land and of great destruction."

The lamentations of Jeremiah that follow also have significance for the poem that calls up this tragic biblical story. "Arise, cry out in the night," Jeremiah urges, "in the beginning of the watches pour out thine heart like water before the face of the Lord. . . . He hath brought me into darkness, but not into light." The sins of Babylon, the wrath of a vengeful God, and the overall tone of darkness and despair co-exist with Jeremiah's celebration of a **benevolent** and **for-giving** God, ready to make a covenant with the wayward children of Israel. ("I will not turn away from them.") That Babylon has, since biblical times, been associated with the worship of false idols, the disorder of war, and the emotions of alienation and terror serves to create the tension in the poem. For Levertov, the biblical contrasts of darkness and light, hopelessness and hope, terror and calmness would emphasize the cosmic proportions of the crises of our own times.

Thus, the title of the poem immediately carries us back to the doomed city, site of God's wrath. It also reminds us of the epithet given the modern city by F. Scott Fitzgerald and others, where in our twentieth-century Babylon, "Beauty is sold in the marketplace," (Ezra Pound's indictment in "Hugh Selwyn Mauberly"); where violence prevails; where wickedness abounds. In the poetry of Eliot and William Carlos Williams, the city becomes the symbol for divisiveness in the world. Modern Babylon is chaotic, fated, fallen away from spiritual and humanistic values, and intent upon destroying itself. So it is that Jeremiah's burning city and the contemporary "urban wasteland" merge in the imagination of the poet.

> Through the midnight streets of Babylon
> between the steel towers of their arsenals,
> between the torture castles with no windows,
> we race by barefoot, holding tight
> our candles, trying to shield
> the shivering flames, crying
> "Sleepers Awake!"
>   hoping
> the rhyme's promise was true,
> that we may return
> from this place of terror
> home to a calm dawn and
> the work we had just begun.

All of the images in the first seven lines evoke the conditions of war and destruction: the steel towers of the arsenals, the torture castles, the black night threatening the "shivering flames." The voice is desperate; the action urgent; the modern Jeremiah's vulnerable. The break in line eight with "hoping" produces a dramatic shift in tone, now quieter, more positive, directed toward "the calm dawn" of the new day. Juxtaposed to the "place of terror" is the promise of poetry that itself is a labor of truth; and "home" suggests normalcy, calmness, and commitment.

"Candles in Babylon" balances the contrasting conditions of impending destruction and a future of hope and work and sanity. Those contrasts are dramatized by the intensity of the poem's language, images, compression, enjambment, and the fast-paced rhythm of the verse suggesting urgency followed by calmness and the hope for a new beginning. The balance between terror and calm, between what is and what might be, is the result of the poem's form as well. The vision of the speaker, culminating in "Sleepers Awake!" and the last lines with the return home to a "calm dawn" are linked by one word—"hoping," which stands alone—a fragile bridge but a significant one. When we recall Levertov's own reading of her poetry, pausing momentarily at the end of the enjambed lines (". . . a kind of half-comma" she explains), we realize the dramatic function of "hoping"—alone yet linking, as the focus of the poem's unity. There is yet another gloss to be added here. Denise Levertov has commented that the phrase, "Sleepers Awake!" refers to the first of Bach's Six Cantatas (titled "Sleepers Awake!"), originally part of Bach's Cantata #140.[14]

In many ways, "Candles in Babylon" reminds us, in form, of earlier poems in its brevity, condensation, and urgency—an impressionistic vision of Babylon. It is a lyrical poem in its emotional intensity, but it is **not** a song. The charged effect is produced in the first three lines with their repetitive rhythm. The image of war is omnipresent, both literally and symbolically. Although the poem is not about nature, it focuses on **place:** that which mirrors the tragic crisis and that "other" place where calmness prevails. The speaker is more than an observer; she is a judge, a modern prophet warning the world to awaken to impending dangers. She *acts:* lighting the candles, waking the sleepers, writing the poem. By evoking the ancient myth, the sense of crisis is heightened; divine chastisement echoes in the poem as the lighting of the candles reminds us of God's threat: "I will take from them . . . the light of the candle." The repetitions, the alliteration, the oxymoron, "the shivering flames," and the suggested union of hope and despair help create the poem's tension.

"Candles in Babylon" emphasizes a theme that absorbed Levertov throughout her career as a "poet in the world": the moral dilemma of the creative artist in contemporary society who must be a modern Jeremiah and still write poetry in the calmness and quiet of home. She often asserted that the poet has a mission in the world, and that good poetry deals with crises in the world that well might bring about its end. She said, in speaking about the past, her reactions to the Vietnam War, the country's movement into the horrors of nuclear holocaust, and the arms race, "I am not a fatalist. But I'm . . . very much aware daily and constantly of terror. I don't mean that I go around being 'terrified' but this is a major terror." She continued, "The **power** [nuclear power] that is in the hands of human beings for the first time—that is our precedent. . . . But I haven't lost hope.[15] It is such hope upon which "Candles in Babylon" turns—fragile but ever-present.

Two poems in Part I: "Wanderer's Daysong" are particularly important in our consideration of Denise Levertov as a poet in the world: "Poet and Person" and the title poem of the section. As she has done in the past, Levertov brings together her "messages" to the world and her sense of herself as a prophet, a poet speaking of "what is right." In "Poet and Person," she begins, "I send my messages ahead of me," and those "messages" are well received—they are "household gifts" because they *please:* "You hear / yourselves in them, / self after self. Your solitudes / utter their runes, your own / voices begin to rise in your throats." This is the "universal" poet— the one who sings and celebrates, who writes of women and men and nature and children, of "being alive." She continues, "But soon you love me less. / I brought with me / too much." She brings the sorrow of the world, her own broken dreams and her "crutches": She brings her desire to please, "and worse— / my desire to judge what is right." Upon this line Levertov shifts her focus to a recurrent preoccupation in her poetry: her social conscience, her sense of "engagement" with the victims of injustice, and her right to proclaim what is right.

Thus, since the sixties, Levertov has not relinquished her tendency to speak out. At the end of the poem, she seems to echo her critics' complaint that she takes up so much space, and the guest who sent ahead her messages as housegifts becomes the unwanted "lingering guest," and leaves: "When I leave, I leave / alone, as I came."

The metaphor of the unwanted guest who speaks truth echoes the fables of the past: the embarrassing prophet whom one wishes would leave. The poem is replete with images of pleasure and images of impropriety—all from the vantage point of the "visited." The messages of joy are siren tongues, ears of flame, housegifts, while the unwanted truths are improper—carried by a threatening angel, a Cassandra swathed in silks and furs, but crippled and "insupportable." There is wit here and yet a poignant wish that the messages of "what is right" would fall on more sympathetic ears. As Levertov knows, human beings have resisted prophets from time immemorial. They await only messages of hope that can rise in their throats.

"Wanderer's Daysong" combines two motifs that have been recurrent in much of Levertov's poetry: the poet as wanderer, a theme she was familiar with for decades in the poetry of William Carlos Williams, and the poet as singer. The poet's voyage is internal. The "daysong" is ironically a dream vision as we "plunge into swansdown billows of / dustgold fathomless happenstance—." The lines that follow come as a shock, for the mystical, billowing rush of air would seem to prefigure a epiphanic moment, an experience both spiritual and revelatory. Instead, the lines that follow reveal an inner world of "eclipse," of vertigo, a world where "no one / has known us always." The line "We leap—" is an echo from Williams's *Paterson* when— viewing the desolate world—he cries out, "We leap awake and what we see / fells us."[16] She sees what Williams had seen "When green / loses its green spirit": the knowledge of "before": "That no-light blunted us," and the knowledge ahead: oncoming age and death. The images are penetrating: "parchment skins stretched upon crutches," pendulous breasts / hung themselves on our torsos like bundles / of parched herbs, . . ." The entire dream is shadowed in darkness and "pebbles of rain," and suddenly the "sun / gnaws its way out of its cage again," and the "skylark / tears itself out of our throats," and the song *is* the daysong. The dream ends, as it so often does in Levertov's poetry, with a new day and the hope it brings, though we are ever aware of our destiny.

> we do leap, we do
> plunge into skylake's
> haze of promise. But we feel
>
> along with the air rushing, our own breath
> rushing
> out of us.
>   See
> for an instant the arc of
> our vanishing.

This beautiful final vision, marked by the images of motions— leaping, plunging, rushing, and vanishing—bringing together life and death, is neither tragic nor regretful. Coming out of the darkness into the light does not obviate man's ultimate fate. There is a quiet acceptance as the poet perceives "the arc of / our vanishing."

After an account of the life of Sylvia in "Pig Dreams," part III of *Candles in Babylon* takes us along on Levertov's journey through "places, people, visions." As I have suggested, the range is wide as the poet touches upon the themes of motherhood, the condition of being an orphan, aging, and artists and poets Levertov had the good fortune to know—a poet like William Carlos Williams and painters

Rosalie Gascoigne and Memphis Wood. But there are poems of **place:** England, Tonga, and Brazil. The richness, the fullness of these experiences include poems of the inscape—dream and reflection—such as the poem to her son, "For Nikolai, Many Thousand Miles Away" in which she writes, "The great world and its wars / are a long way off, news wavers over / the radio and goes out, you and your life / are half a world distant, and in daylight. . . . / Above the dark ocean, over coral, over continents / the riders move, their power / felt but not understood, their will / remote."

The four poems that make up Part IV: "The Acolyte" recount a love "story" with the exception of the poem that gives its title to this brief interlude. It is interesting that "The Acolyte" comes before "Age of Terror" which reminds us of the tenuous future of our planet, the dangers that befall us, the need to awaken and save ourselves. The acolyte is a holy woman baking bread. The simplicity of the image that unifies this poem becomes complex in the final line, that the "bread that is more than bread." Bread *is* life, and the making of the bread is a painstaking art. The acolyte thinks not of the baked bread, but of the process: "the way / the dough rises and has a life of its own." In this poem, the simple act of making bread is transformed by the woman's desire to release "transformed heroes into their selves; / she wants to make / bread that is more than bread."

"The Acolyte" is a fitting transition to Part V: "Age of Terror": in one way this final part **anatomizes** an age of terror; in another it offers an age of faith. These last poems in *Candles in Babylon* turn on these two themes. The age of terror continually demands our unflagging awareness and activity, while the age of faith is the driving force that moves the poet in her pilgrimage toward her hopes and dreams for peace and humaneness in our chaotic modern world.

Always thematic is Levertov's dedication to the word—language—containing a power of its own as a bulwark against the "darkness." "Writing in the Dark" offers a fitting epigraph to the poems of this final section as the pinnacle of Levertov's artistic aspiration in a world of "age of terror."

> Keep writing in the dark:
> a record of the night, or
> words that pulled you from depths of unknowing,
> words that flew through your mind, strange birds
> crying their urgency with human voices,
>
> or opened
> as flowers of a tree that blooms
> only once in a lifetime:

words that may have the power
to make the sun rise again.

But there is the "darkness" in "Age of Terror" that hovers over an indifferent or impotent world as the poet struggles toward the light. Isolated phrases give us a dramatic sense of the condition of this contemporary "wasteland": a "Governor" adoring the grandchild playing at his feet, at the same moment is "crushing / the report on nuclear hazards into a ball and / tossing it across the room, ignoring / the wastebasket and plutonium and the idea / that he could be wrong . . ." Yet "Her death / is in his hands." The final lines reveal the "split mind"—holding both life and death in his hands. In "The Vron Woods," the poet returns to her ancestral North Wales to learn that the woods had been "felled / seven years before I was born, / levelled, / to feed a war." In "Desolate Light," "We turn to history looking / for vicious certainties through which / voices edged into song / engorged fringes of anemone swaying / dreamily, through deluge." Gazing into "the open / well of centuries," the poet sees "gleaming, / deep in the black broth at the bottom, / chains of hope by which our forebears / hoisted themselves / hand over hand toward light." But in contrast, we "stand at the edge looking back in and knowing / too much to reasonably hope. Their desired light / burns us." The speaker, in despair, invokes the drought and the wind to return her to the past—to no avail!

> *O dread*
> *drought that dries*
> *the ground of joy till it cracks and*
> *caves in,*
>
> *O dread,*
> *wind that sweeps up the offal of lies,*
> *sweep my knowledge, too, into oblivion,*
> *drop me back in the well.*
>
> *No avail.*

The use of alliteration (in the repetition, especially, of the d's that fall on our ears like a tolling bell) contributes to the tone of hopelessness in this poem; deluge, dread, deep, drought, dries, and drop emphasize the slow, deliberate rhythms and echo the "desolation" as we gaze and "see gleaming" the hopes of our forebears.

Other images that serve as touchstones for contemporary lassitude and despair are the English field "in the Nuclear Age" and the "great storm coming" in "Sound of the Axe." But the poet who still engaged in "teach-in's" and still hoped for what **could** be, articulates these moments—ephemeral as they are—in a strong and spirited voice. In an interview in 1971, she had been asked whether she felt differently than she had in 1966. Her response offers a gloss on the tone in *Candles:* "Now, most people feel mere demonstrations, mere massing of people, is no longer enough. . . . What I personally am trying to do at this point is very very mild. . . . I'm trying to organize a teach-in."[17] Nonetheless, she still transformed her "activism" into poetry and memorialized the activities of those who played a role in combating injustice and exploitation.

In three poems in *Babylon,* "Beginners," "Psalm: People Power in the Die-in," and "A Speech: For Antidraft Rally, D.C., March 22, 1980," Levertov recounts the heroic efforts of ordinary people. "Beginners" is a tribute to Karen Silkwood and Eliot Gralla. The poem opens with the poignant lines from Swinburne's "The Garden of Proserpine" (Levertov notes that the lines are "slightly misquoted." In Swinburne's poem, the lines are as follows: "From too much love of living, / From hope and fear set free, / We thank with brief thanksgiving / Whatever gods may be. / That no life lives forever; / That dead men rise up never; That even the weariest river / Winds somewhere safe to sea.") It is interesting that the "emendation" results in a tone that suits Levertov's purpose: omitted are the fear, the thanksgiving to the gods, and the "safe" voyage to the sea of inexorable death. Instead there is a new spirit of hope, despite the despair that comes when "hope and desire set free" seem thwarted, and our dreams "fail."

"Beginners" is a fitting tribute to two who fought and braved their hostile opposition and lost. They were the **beginners** and the poem "celebrates" that beginning. Each couplet of this poem that poses important questions is alive with hope: "But we have only begun / to love the earth. / We have only begun / to imagine the fulness of life," and the poet refuses to accept the fatalistic note in Swinburne's poem. The poem ends on the positive note that "So much is unfolding that must / complete its gesture, / so much is in bud." In my interview with Levertov on October 9, 1982, she vehemently denied that her poems end in "Pollyanna" optimism. But she emphasized that the need to go on hoping, acting, seeking is innate in human beings, and the courage to maintain this balance in an "age of terror," in which "too much hurt we have done to each other / that cannot yet be forgiven," requires our constant articulation. Unlike many Levertov poems, "Beginners" is sparse in its imagery and lyrical quality. The power of the poem lies in the form of its rhetoric, the questions and the answers, and the final revelation of a new beginning, and of our power "in the communion of struggle."

In the summer of 1978, two hundred demonstrators went to Washington (Levertov among them) to protest the building of a nuclear plant at Seabrook, New Hampshire. A full account of the event appeared first in *The Literary Review* (Edinburgh, 1978) and was reprinted in *Light Up the Cave*. The action was successful, and construction at Seabrook was halted. In the essay, Levertov wrote: "What happened on H Street was ignored by the press; yet it may well have revealed, much more intensely than the Seabrook June 1978 weekend's science-fair atmosphere and large crowds, what the spirit of the 80s has the potential to be."[18] What "happened on H Street" was demonstration, arrest, long "hours on the excruciating steel cots in the holding cells," and the sharing of food, the "die-in," and the final ecstatic joy upon hearing of the Seabrook suspension.

"Psalm: People Power at the Die-in," is a condensed poem that conveys the courage, the sense of communal action, the triumph of "people's power." There is a strong sense of spiritual destiny as God's wrath is evoked in the "lightning and thunder," as if echoing their own indignation. "Fierce rain blessed us, / catholic, all-encompassing." The "die-in" resembles a ritual reenactment of "the death by which all / shall perish unless we act." The language carries the spirit of a divine providence in their act: psalm, communion, luminous power, and "harvest of our striving."

The poem is comprised of couplets, a form Levertov used often in *Candles*, that underscore the basic simplicity of the actions themselves: walking in the rain and in the sun; sharing the work and the companionship; savoring the power emanating from communal effort: "great energy flowed from solitude, / and great power from communion."

The poem that follows immediately, "About Political Action in Which Each Individual Acts from the Heart," echoes the second part of "People Power" with a few significant changes. The important addition is "when"; *when* solitaries draw close, . . ." "*when* we give to each other, . . ." "*when* we taste in small victories sometimes / the small ephemeral yet joyful / harvest of our striving. . . . Then / great energy flows from solitude, / and great power from communion." [Emphasis mine.] The argument is a familiar one in Levertov's poetry; the power to change our world lies in communal action, in "people power"—a phrase Martin Luther King used effectively. Both poems focus on action, cooperation, and power.

The third poem—openly didactic—that also concerns itself with unified action is "A Speech: For Antidraft Rally, D.C., March 22, 1980." Levertov insists this speech **is** a speech, but in its rhythmic cadences, its often violent imagery, its use of repetition, assonance, consonance, alliteration, and the pattern of recurrent motifs, "A Speech" *is* a poem, though too long, the tone too often hortatory. In many ways, the poem does not approach the terse, dramatic effectiveness of some of Levertov's more condensed poems, but it has a power of its own. It juxtaposes the "ignorance" of the young—the high school kids—who are glib in their use of words like war, bombing, "Commies," and the draft; who have no sense of the events of history ("Which came first, Vietnam or Korea?"); who know only TV "violence" while truth eludes them. Levertov then proceeds to call forth all the horrors of our "age of terror," past and present: war and genocide, death by radiation and by killing, lasers and the cancerous hormones fed to caged chickens. The poem is a "teach-in" and is most successful at the close, when the poet gives way to a softer utterance, more persuasive and challenging. Dreams and acts conjoin to unite human purpose.

> Let us different dream,
> and more than dream, our acts
> of constructive refusal generate
> struggle. And love. We must dare to win
> not wars, but a future
> in which to live.

Ever conscious of the nuclear threat, Denise Levertov speculates what this immense power—harnessed for destruction—might be if "left to lie." Few Americans—scientists among them—have escaped their nightmares of nuclear disaster should this power be unleashed upon our planet. Thus, "What It Could Be" is a poignant plea to leave nature's power within nature's sanctum. Levertov struggles toward the nearly insurmountable proposal, never losing hope. The poem begins, "Uranium, with which we know / only how to destroy, / lies always under / the most sacred lands—" and the poet continues to relate the long history of the "great power," until now untouched. The final stanzas are mystical and enigmatic, for we never know how the great power will communicate its benevolence. Yet the poet clings to the idea of the power having **larger** powers to save us.

> But left to lie, its metaphysical weight
> might in a million years have proved
> benign, its true force being to be
> a clue to righteousness—

showing forth
the human power
not to kill, to choose
not to kill, to transcend
the dull force of our weight and will;

that known profound presence, *un*touched,
the sign
providing witness
        occasion,
         ritual
for the continuing act of
*non*violence, of passionate
reverence, active love.

Through its language, the poem suggests the spiritual aura of uranium—to disturb its carefully guarded secret were to disturb the sacral: it lies under "sacred" lands. Wresting it from the earth is to "ravage" the earth; gouging lumps of its power is to torture the "planet the ancients / say is our mother." Untouched, it is a "profound presence"; and it is a "sign, witness, ritual" for continuing nonviolence. Poetically, these final lines are memorable, despite the absence of images, because of the cadenced rhythm of the lines, the alliteration, repetition, the "true force," borne out in the emphatic negatives that are imperious: "*not* to kill, . . . / *not* to kill . . ." and the contrasting supplicatory appeal to man "to transcend / the dull force of our weight and will." Levertov is at her best poetically when inspired by powers beyond us that can lift us to "passionate / reverence, active love."

There is little doubt that Levertov's religious and moral conscience perpetuated a journey that called for struggle and progression in a world bent on self-annihilation. The images that dramatize humanity set against nature are striking. Nature is personified and human power confronts nature's "great power." There seems little doubt that only with "passionate reverence" and "active love" can man prevail. All of these poems reinforce Levertov's strong stand against the nuclear threat—one that concerns her into the present. She said in an interview in 1982:

The worst thing is the nuclear threat. That is greater than all the massacres in the world because it is total massacre. It's not just a question of the war [the Vietnam War] being over. When a war is over, that's just one of many wars. The nuclear threat is the central priority question . . .

the nuclear clock is ticking. We are getting closer and closer with the arms race to the virtual inevitability of a nuclear war. . . . The freeze movement in this country has activated many people who were previously inactive. Whether there is still a chance of success is something we don't really know. We feel that we must go on trying, but whether we can actually succeed is another question.[19]

But Levertov's sensitivity, not only to an impending nuclear disaster and injustice around the world but also to examples of indifference to them, still motivates her choice of themes, as we find in her tribute to her friend and fellow activist, "In Memory of Muriel Rukeyser." Watching a film during Black Emphasis Week, the speaker—stirred by the graphic depiction of the horrors of a southern lynching—is appalled by the indifference (the audience composed of only five people) of the "thousand students who chose / not to attend." Her despair shakes her in the darkness of the night; but the world at large remembers neither "Asia or Alabama." In a moment of deep discouragement, the speaker thinks, *"Perhaps / we deserve / no more, we humans, / cruel and dull. / No more time. / We've made / our cathedrals, / had our chance, / blown it."*

She then turns her thoughts to her old friend, poet Muriel Rukeyser, who had died the week before, and who was an inspiration of hope, "passion for life, the vision / of love and work . . ."; who abhorred the terror and hatred of racism: the *"sense of shame"*; who did not despair, but kept working and moving "beyond shame." In Levertov's own dark moment, Muriel Rukeyser, artist and fighter for human rights, offers a model of courage and hope. "Now. Stop shaking. Imagine her. / She was a cathedral." The poem is a melange of the shock that comes from the awareness of human persecution and human apathy, of indignation and discouragement, of memory and the strength memory offers up to continue the struggle. The poem is a reminder to us of the many who have spent a lifetime fighting racism, inhumanity, and "terror"—sometimes faltering momentarily as the poet reveals in this poem, but always renewing oneself by remembering those, like Rukeyser, who call "the unawakened" to account.

In the same way, Neruda, summoning man to "See the blood in the Streets," is another model. His words serve as an epigraph to "Unresolved," and again Levertov reveals another horror—the genocide in El Salvador. The poem, in five parts, traces human aspiration and human atrocity. Again it is "Revolution or Death," written on the wall in blood. What is unresolved, unsynthesized, is the disparity

between belief and doubt, as she witnesses the catastrophes wrought
on earth, both by man and nature:

> When one has begun to believe
> the grip of doubt tightens.

The physical maiming is given with stunning accuracy as the camera records bodies dismembered, babies murdered, and the screams
of mothers rending the air. We hear it, see it, feel it in disbelief, so
we play the scene over and over again, "for verisimilitude." In the
final part, Levertov turns to nature and to all men are capable of in
saner times.

> We know so much of daily bread,
> of every thread of lovingly knit compassion;
>
> garments of love clothe us, we rest
> our heads upon darkness; when we wake
>
> sapphire transparency calls forth our song.
> And this is the very world, the same, the world
>
> of vicious power, of massacre.
> Our song is a bird that wants
> to sing as it flies, to be
> the wings of praise, but doubt
>
> binds tight its wire to hold down
> flightbones, choke back breath.
> We know no synthesis.

In this poignant ending, Levertov seems to reach the nadir of
despair. How can one reconcile man's limitless destructive capacity
with the love, compassion, and humankindness of which he is equally
capable? "We know no synthesis," she confesses. In speaking of the
poem, "Unresolved," she noted the

> enigma of the coexistence of good and evil. It ends with a section that
> speculates on what might be, but one would have to touch those polarities
> at the same time rather than alternating between them. El Salvador talks
> about the strangeness, the bafflingness of the simultaneous existence of
> good and evil, and beauty and horror. It is unresolved.[20]

"For the New Year, 1981" invites others to share Levertov's hope—
in this new year—for renewal. The poem is spare, simple, conversa-

tional. The invitation is moving, because it is offered in the spirit of
humility, selflessness, and communion:

> I have a small grain of hope—
> one small crystal that gleams
> clear colors out of transparency.
>
> I need more.
> I break off a fragment
> to send you.
>
> Please take
> this grain of a grain of hope
> so that mine won't shrink.
>
> Please share your fragment
> so that yours will grow.
>
> Only so, by division,
> we hope to increase,
>
> like a clump of irises, which will cease to flower
> unless you distribute
> the clustered roots, unlikely source—
> clumsy and earth-covered—
> of grace.

These images are fragile, fragmentary—until "clustered"—and
delicate, creating an aura of tentativeness and guarded hope. The
opening metaphor of hope's gleaming transparency sets the tone of
the poem: moving, inviting, eager to share. The couplets and triplets
add to the simplicity of the speaker's offering, yet the line, "I need
more," stands alone, emphasizing the unity of hope that lies in communion. The climax in the poem comes in the bestowal of grace,
after the work of sharing is consummated. The metaphor of re-rooting, central to Levertov's fundamental beliefs, appears again in another poem, "Re-Rooting," for only when we return the roots to the
soil can we create new life. But in this second poem, the re-rooting
"has not yet begun." As we have seen in this one section, "Age of
Terror," Levertov has made the wide swing from despair to hope
several times, always initiated by tragic events in the world, yet unre-
mittingly in search of new beginnings.

It is at this point that Levertov chose to place the poem, "Age of
Terror," in *Candles in Babylon*, and that placement is significant, as
the poet herself has often reminded us in her notes to previous vol-

umes. In a way, the poem is a summing up of the world as Levertov perceives it in this moment. The poem takes the form of a dream, for it is in dream that we recreate our worst fears and gravest foreboding. For all humans, the "horror of Afterwards / and the despair / in the thought of no Afterwards," is chilling enough, but in the poet's dream, after experiencing a violent nuclear explosion, she materializes in the "Afterwards," a surreal vision in which the afterlife is a confused imitation of the modern, industrial world. She awakens there to find with joy her long-dead family but, fearful of possible "devastation," she begins to take roll call of those who "survived." Suddenly a disastrous thought overcomes her as she speculates about the explosion and the destruction, terror, fire and dust, radioactivity, and pain. In her dream, she is "safe" in the "Afterwards" but in the *world* of her dream, she thinks: what of the others, "others, others in agony, / and as in waking daylight, / the broken dead?"

"Age of Terror" is indeed **that**; even in our dreams of escape, in our vision of a transcendent "Beyond," there is *no* escape. "Age of Terror" is not a dream but a nightmare! That we cannot evade our responsibility to the living, "at risk," lies at the core of Levertov's moral conscience. Thus, in the advanced stage of Denise Levertov's poetic and spiritual journey, the persistent concern for injustice and the possible destruction of the world that threatens us is an unbroken continuum.

Yet, since Levertov wrote "Age of Terror," the civilized nations of the world community have made important advances to make the world safe from nuclear holocaust. Although we are not today on the brink of disaster, there is much work to be done and many voices still to be heard. An enlightened public, through its universal outcry, has put its government on notice not only on the issue of nuclear war, but on nuclear waste disposal, the changing environment, the danger of toxic wastes, and a host of other threats to the earth. Whether the efforts have been successful will be measured by future generations, but Denise Levertov was an early voice attempting to awaken sleepers.

As we shall see in *Candles in Babylon*, her poetry becomes more religious and *would seem* to remove her from worldly considerations, as had been true of poets in the past, but this is not the turn Levertov will take in her journey. As "Age of Terror" reveals, even in our imagined death there is no escape.

The two poems that conclude *Candles in Babylon* are thematically, imagistically, and spiritually in keeping with the opening poem, "Candles in Babylon." The language is predominantly liturgical or Biblical; the theme is the pilgrimage of the soul in search of a reassuring faith, growing out of doubt; the experience is a renewal, a "reconversion" (in Levertov's words), a clarity from confusion—a supernal radiance out of darkness and despair. In these final poems there is celebration and joy and a love for God's "many mansions," one of which is the tempting and undefiled beauty of Earth. As Harry Marten has noted, "Levertov affirms struggle, hope, a capacity for imaginative vision—the mortal capacities that enable us to grasp and reach toward the immortal."[21] In an interview in 1977, Levertov was asked: "What does the word 'religion' mean to you?" Her response goes far toward our understanding of Denise Levertov's lifelong struggle toward a faith when her spirit faltered as the world did not offer much hope of its own salvation. This was her reply:

> The impulse to kneel in wonder. . . . The impulse to kiss the ground. . . . The sense of awe. The felt presence of some mysterious force, whether it be what one calls beauty, or perhaps just the sense of the unknown—I don't mean 'unknown' in the sense of we don't know what the future will bring. I mean the sense of the numinous whether it's a small stone or a large mountain. I think at this particular point, that sense of joy which you've mentioned in my poems, and which I think is very real to me, and has been, is at a very low ebb. . . . My feeling this winter . . . is so doom-filled, the sense of time running out . . .[22]

Since that time, eighteen years ago, religion has come to mean all this and more for Denise Levertov. As she has said, "My theological position has moved on,"[23] and that progress in her journey is revealed in the final two poems of *Babylon*.

The "Mass for the Day of St. Thomas Didymus" represents the struggle mirrored in the biblical account of Christ's disciple, and for those who recall this important crisis of faith, Levertov's poem takes on deepened significance. In the Gospel according to John, chapter 20, verse 20, Jesus, speaking through Mary Magdalene, informs his disciples that he had not yet ascended to God but "say unto them, I ascend unto my Father, and your Father; and to *my* God and your God." On the same day, Jesus appears to the gathered disciples, proves his existence by showing them his hands and his side, and they were glad "when they saw the Lord." Jesus blesses the disciples and speaks to them: "Receive ye the Holy Ghost: / Whose soever sins ye remit, they are remitted unto them; *and* whose soever *sins* ye retain, they are retained." The biblical account then continues:

> 24. But Thomas, one of the twelve, called Did-y-mus, was not with them when Jesus came.
> 25. The other disciples therefore said unto him, We have seen the

Lord. But he said unto them, Except I shall see in his hands the print of the nails, and put my finger into the print of the nails, and thrust my hand into his side, I will not believe.

26. And after eight days again, his disciples were within, and Thomas with them: *then* came Jesus, the doors being shut, and stood in the midst, and said. Peace *be* unto you.

27. Then he said unto Thomas, Reach hither thy finger, and behold my hands; and reach hither thy hand, and thrust *it* into my side: and be not faithless, but believing.

28. And Thomas answered and said unto him, My Lord and my God.

29. Jesus saith unto him, Thomas, because thou hast seen me, thou hast believed: blessed *are* they that have not seen, and *yet* believed.

Thus, the "doubting Thomas" who needed to see to believe is rebuked by Jesus, even though forgiven. But Jesus' words here are of great significance: "blessed are they that have not seen, and yet believed." The story of Thomas Didymus frames the "Mass" because it emphasizes man's perennial search for the proof of God's existence. In form the poem is a ritual mass in six parts, each of which traces the pilgrimage from doubt to belief.

It is not my intent to follow Levertov through the rites or stages of her own "reconversion." It is sufficient to note, however, that her doubt arises from the condition of the world itself which has been dramatically portrayed in "Part IV: Age of Terror." Thus, the "Kyrie," a brief prayer, is traditionally part of the Mass (*Kyrie eleison*, Greek for "Lord have mercy [upon us]," is the response of the communicants in the Anglican service of the Holy Communion). The invocation for mercy is woven into Levertov's incantatory verse, but the motif that recurs throughout is that we live in terror of both what we know and what we *do not* know. At the same time, hope "lies / in the unknown, / in our unknowing." There is the traditional ritual of terror of the unknown here, but surely Levertov was echoing as well the uncertain future of a dying Earth. The hope in the *unknown* is her search for the inscrutable God—in her moment of personal doubt—who would "have mercy on us."

The passages that follow are variations of the ritual of the Mass: the "Gloria," praising God for the beauties of the world and "the dream still / of goodwill, of peace on earth"; "Credo," the belief in the earth and in the Creator, interrupted by doubt: "I believe and / interrupt my belief with / doubt. I doubt and / interrupt my doubt with belief"; the "Sanctus," the acceptance of the "known. / Unknown, unknowable," ending with "sanctus, hosanna, sanctus" (Holy, Save, Holy); the "Benedictus," the blessing of everything that comes in the "name of the spirit, / that which bears / the spirit within it." It is this passage in which Levertov achieves great lyrical power. For it is the *earth* which she celebrates. For a moment, she can cast off the "emptiness, / the destructive vortex that whirls / no word with it" and reach toward the power and beauty of God's creatures in which his spirit inheres. The "Sanctus" would seem to be the turning point in this search for faith, but in the final lines the speaker struggles toward her belief: "The word / chose to become / flesh. In the blur of flesh / we bow, baffled."

The poem concludes with the "Agnus Dei" (Lamb of God) in which Christ is represented in the form of the lamb. The entire passage is in sharp contrast to the previous passages. The litany of the Mass seems to disappear into colloquial speech; the rhythms of the liturgy are supplanted by a persistently questioning voice that juxtaposes innocent lambs with fearful and foolish sheep. Each sentence is, indeed, a question that leads to further bafflement. The lamb is presented at first in a sensuous, lyrical, humorous way— awkward, young, vigorous, and playful. Is this the same lamb of God *"that taketh away / the Sins of the world"?* If the Lamb is defenseless, innocent, in need of protection, then Man has been chosen by God to "protect" the Lamb. The conclusion of the "Mass" rests upon this enigma.

> And we,
>   frightened, bored, wanting
> only to sleep till catastrophe
> has raged, clashed, seethed and gone by without us,
>   wanting then
> to awaken in quietude without remembrance of agony,
>
>   we who in shamefaced private hope
>   had looked to be plucked from fire and given
>   a bliss we deserved for having imagined it,
>   is it implied that *we*
>   must protect this perversely weak
>   animal, whose muzzle's nudgings
>   suppose there is milk to be found in us?
>   Must hold to our icy hearts
>   a shivering God?
>
> So be it.
>   Come, rag of pungent
>   quiverings,
>   dim star.
>   Let's try
>   if something human still

　　　　　　　can shield you,
　　　　　　　　　　　　　spark
　　　　　　　of remote light.

　　　These final lines signal not only Denise Levertov's ultimate faith—
borne out of terror, doubt, believing and not believing, and finally
concluding with the irresistible invitation—but also a moment of
great artistic achievement. The image of the lamb—"rag of pungent /
quiverings, / dim star" as well as the significant "spark" of God's
radiance—are not only stirring but nostalgic. We are made to think
of Blake, as he addresses the tyger: "Did he who made the Lamb
make thee?" But Levertov's Lamb of God needs Man, as Man needs
God, and in this communion there is hope. The "Mass" ends with
such hope and reminds us again of the lines in scripture: "Blessed
are those who have not seen me and yet believe." The "Mass" is
followed by the final poem "The Many Mansions" that reinforces
Levertov's spiritual stasis.

　　　The poem is extremely simple, quiet, succinct; images of earthly
beauty appear, but there are no lyrical heights, only a renewed appreciation of *this world*, enhanced by "a single radiance, multiform." She
"must not forget" the beauty of an undefiled world; she must not
forget the "knowledge that vision gave me / that it was not a fragile,
only, other world . . ." Levertov's final words in *Candles in Babylon*
are that the vision was given her "to know and share, / passing from
hand to hand, although / its clarity dwindles in our confusion, / the
amulet of mercy."

　　　What emerges from this final poem is an image of *wholeness*, coherence, harmony. Often *man* is confused, and the outcome is not always
sure. Denise Levertov is not an ascetic, and her concern with confused man in a confused world continues, but there is hope here and
a quiet kind of resolution. To save ourselves from annihilation, she
told me, will take not only the actions of human beings, but "God
or providence—the X factor—to pull us through. . . . It's only if we
make the effort that maybe we'll be helped!"[24]

　　　It should be noted that since the composition of these poems,
countless efforts have been made by responsible sources to create
safety in a world that seemed on the brink of nuclear disaster. Such
work is never finished, but public outcry resulting from growing
awareness has been a critical element. Responsible governments have
initiated international agreements, and one can only hope that such
responsibility becomes more widespread. "Mass for the Day of St.
Thomas Didymus" speaks to the experience of religious renewal,
but for Denise Levertov that renewal had to be united with a renewal

of faith in man. Her own efforts, as well as those of countless artists and people of conscience, have gone a long way toward affecting the progress made to date. To repeat her hope: "It's only if we make the effort that maybe we'll be helped!"

Oblique Prayers

Characteristic of Denise Levertov's often-stated aesthetic, *Oblique Prayers* presents concurrently the "self-directed or introspective and publicly-directed or extroverted" experiences; she does not turn away from the "commonweal to cultivate [her] own garden." Those who mistake her for an ascetic might well remember her words, "Ivory towers look out over desert landscapes." Accordingly, the wide swings from despair and doubt to cautious hope and faith alternate in this volume as well.

As Levertov explains in the "Author's Note," *Oblique Prayers* is divided into four parts, governed by the thematic threads that bind the poems.

Part I is "Decipherings," and, indeed, each poem is a puzzle, a mystery that needs "decoding," or as Harry Marten suggests: "to fathom—to make out the meanings."[25]

"Decipherings" are largely poems of the "inscape," and while the world of outer experience is present, the aim of this first part centers upon the realm of the imagination as it seeks the order that Levertov has always affirmed lies beneath the world of visible things. Yet the themes of "Decipherings" seem frequently to focus on fragmentation, lack of coherence, severance, rupture, the wasteland of urban life, the foretelling of doom, loss, oncoming death, dead friends, and the taste of "bitter herbs" (with their oblique reference to the ritual reenactment at the Passover Feast, reminding those congregated of the suffering of the Exodus). There *are* poems of love and poems of hope, such as "Presence" and "Another Revenant," but on the whole the tone is one of disjunction and anguish. Nonetheless almost every poem holds out a wisp of hope, a tenuous possibility as the search continues for a more substantial affirmation. Denise Levertov is always the poet *in* the world, and it is natural that events would lead her to doubt and falter. It is not her personal faith at stake here, but her faith in society and in her own ability to hold her "center of gravity," as she expresses it in the poem, "Decipherings."

Part II, "Prisoners," documents the reasons why she falters, as she persists in reminding us of the desecration of the natural world, the atrocities in El Salvador, the polluting of our environment, the con-

tinuation of nuclear testing, and our own role as "prisoners" who
must "eat our ration."

Part III contains a translation of fourteen poems by Jean Joubert,
many of whose themes echo Levertov's own, such as "The Sentence"
which begins, "All of you are condemned to death." Thus the metaphor of man in a prison of his own making is a familiar one in Levertov's work, but Joubert also confirms her own conviction of design.
As Marten observed, like Levertov, "Joubert discovers the light of
harmony and coherence in the darkest moment."[26]

In Part IV, "Of God And Of The Gods," Levertov again, through
great struggle and moments of transcendence, turns to the themes of
joy and celebration for all of Earth's bounty, for the awareness of
God's blessedness in all things, for the ability to find her voice and
sing, even as she concludes "this happiness / is provisional." *Oblique
Prayers* concludes much as *Candles in Babylon* closes—in praise and
celebration and a renewal of hope. As usual, this volume, like those
that precede it, is characterized by Levertov's ability both to soar
with lyric grace and to ebb into darkness and despair when "events"
threaten to suffocate her, stilling her pen and leaving her incomplete.
But the journey does not cease and the poetry *is* written; and that
record of her dreams and hopes as well as her fears and foreboding
is a profoundly rich artistic achievement. In other respects, *Oblique
Prayers* presents an interesting light upon Denise Levertov's poetic.
There is great variety of forms, language, imagery, and rhetorical
structure in these poems. Some are extremely condensed—the language spare, the imagery simple, the lines short and enjambed as in
"The Avowal," yet the emotion behind the utterance is suggestive
and powerful. Other poems, like "This Day" and "Decipherings,"
are made up of several parts, replete with metaphors that echo similar
analogies. At times, stanzas are of equal line length; at other times,
order breaks down as it might reflect the disorder in the world or the
speaker's confusion. In "The Cry" Levertov chooses William Carlos
Williams's three-stepped line, achieving a kind of litany effect in
which the voice never pauses but moves from beginning to end without "conclusion"—the last lines are "eternity: / being: / milk:" In
each rhythmic form she chooses, Levertov reveals the indivisible
nature of form and content, and her repeated use of enjambed lines
frequently evokes the flow and harmony of nature or, contrastingly,
the **unfinished, inconclusive** aspect of what lies ahead for man:
tentative, inscrutable, unsure.

The poem "Decipherings" opens this volume and "Passage" closes
it; they are important as milestones in Levertov's journey in *Oblique
Prayers*, because "Decipherings" is a **process** that moves from disori-

entation and fragmentation to a transformation that begins with life in the mind and is completed in the soul. This, in many respects, is the progress of the entire volume, for "Passage" is an expression of harmony and unity as the "spirit" makes its way on the earth, transforming, regenerating the world of springtime—the spirit that is "a needle's eye / space and time are passing through like a swathe of silk." "Passage" is a poem of transcendence, here in the transformation of the world as we know it in all its beauty to a world beyond space and time.

As we examine "Decipherings," that transcendence is hinted from the opening lines—"When I lose my center / of gravity / I cannot fly:"—to image upon image of fragmentation and separation, to the final lines: "what one aches for / is the mosaic, music / makes in one's ears / transformed." The "felt life" of the mind and the music in one's ears echo in all of the poems in "Decipherings." In "Seeing for a Moment," faced with "Last Things," she concludes: "I see for a moment / that's not it: it is / the First Things. / Word after word / floats through the glass. / Toward me."

"Prisoners" brings us back pointedly to Levertov's "poems of engagement." Here there is little hope, as we, "prisoners" of our acts, face the fruits of our folly. In "Thinking about El Salvador," Levertov again (see "Unresolved" in *Candles in Babylon*) experiences shock, disbelief, and speechlessness at the atrocities occurring day-by-day in El Salvador. The poem is graphic in its depiction of violence, dismemberment, cruelty, and amorality.

> No blade of *machete*
> threatens my neck,
> but its muscles
> cringe and tighten,
> my voice
> hides in its throat-cave
> ashamed to sound
>   into that silence,
> the silence
>
> of raped women,
> of priests and peasants,
> teachers and children,
> of all whose heads every day
> float down the river
> and rot
> and sink,
> not Orpheus heads

> still singing, bound for the sea,
> but mute.

The anger at this inhumanity, the shock that renders her silent, the pathos that too large a part of the world seems untouched by the death squads, leads her finally—in "Perhaps No Poem But All I Can Say And I Cannot Be Silent"—**out** of silence to **protest!** The poem reviews a history of pogroms, concentration camps, the tragedy of Lebanon, El Salvador itself, concluding that "tragic History" weighs its guilt upon all of us.

"Silent Spring," recalling Rachel Carson's devastating account of the death of the land, **appears** in the beginning to be quiet and tranquil in its "sleep," but this is the sleep of death.

Destroyed by the spraytruck, all we hear is "your own steps / in violent silence." Similarly, "Deathly Diversions," "Rocky Flats," "Watching *Dark Circle*" and "Gathered at the River" share Levertov's concern with the desecration of the environment and the indifference of an America planning "vaster catastrophes." Because of our polluting the atmosphere, persisting in the experimentation with nuclear devices, and conducting laboratory tests on animals for the effects of plutonium, the natural world seems to have lost its health. The images of "dark slick as / plastic garbage bags," charred bones, and the evocation of Hiroshima and Nagasaki are set against those who gather to protest "the human war with ourselves"—*contra naturam*. In a familiar image, we see those gathered by the river, intoning, "*Never again. . . .* We are holding candles: we kneel to set them / afloat on the dark river / as they do / in Hiroshima." The words are not spoken in anger, but in the ritual of "singing, speaking, making vows," and the congregation appeals to whatever sanity may still prevail.

> . . . . . . We are invoking

> saints and prophets,
> heroes and heroines of justice and peace,
> to be with us, to help us
> stop the torment of our evil dreams. . . .

Those evil dreams are dramatically evoked in perhaps the most successful of these four poems, "Rocky Flats." The poem is succinct, controlled, bitingly ironic, and unmarred by emotional excess:

> As if they had tamed the wholesome undomesticated puffball,
> men self-deceived are busily cultivating,
> in nuclear mushroom sheds, amanita buttons,

embryonic gills undisclosed—rank buds of death.
Men shield their minds from horror, shield their hands
with rubber, work behind glass partitions,
yet breathe in, breathe out, that dust,
spreading throughout themselves, throughout the world,
spores of the Destroying Angel.

The poem achieves its effect from such oxymorons as "wholesome puffball," cultivating nuclear mushrooms, "buds of death," and "the Destroying Angel." The ponderous and ominous rhythm of the poem arises from the repetitions: "shield their minds" and "shield their hands," "breathe in, breathe out," and "throughout themselves, throughout the world." And finally, the language plays on the indivisible life and death of nuclear testing. The notion of bud, suggesting life, and spore, suggesting disease and death, is the enigma of this complex and powerful poem.

It is precisely because of such conditions that we are prisoners, as the title poem of this section reveals.

> Though the road turn at last
> to death's ordinary door,
> and we knock there, ready
> to enter and it opens
> easily for us.
>   yet
> all the long journey
> we shall have gone in chains,
> fed on knowledge-apples
> acrid and riddled with grubs.
>
> We taste other food that life,
> like a charitable farm-girl,
> holds out to us as we pass—
> but our mouths are puckered,
> a taint of ash on the tongue.
>
> It's not joy that we've lost—
> wildfire, it flares
> in dark or shine as it will.
> What's gone
> is common happiness,
> plain bread we could eat
> with the old apple of knowledge.
>
> That old one—it griped us sometimes,
> but it was firm, tart,

sometimes delectable . . .

The ashen apple of these days
grew from poisoned soil. We are prisoners
and must eat
our ration. All the long road
in chains, even if, after all,
we come to
death's ordinary door, with time
smiling its ordinary
long-ago smile.

The poem turns upon the contrast of the "old apple of knowledge" and the poisoned apple we eat as prisoners. The metaphors of the apples are strong reminders of Levertov's earlier use of "tasting" in *O Taste and See*. Here, in the apples, the sensuousness of "acrid and riddled with grubs," puckered mouth, ash on the tongue, griped, tart, and tasting, eating, and feeding dramatically concretizes the abstract theme. The image of the prisoners who "must eat / our ration" is a poignant reminder that man is the prisoner of his own acts. "What's gone / is common happiness." The structure of the poem that begins with the road to death's door closes with a reminder that we travel to "death's ordinary door" in chains, under the smiling gaze of indifferent time—the ultimate irony.

That we have created our own prisons by defiling the Earth is borne out in "The Cry" where we wander stammering, parched, groping in a lifeless world. Yet, there is a hardly discernible note of hope here as the poet speculates that "by luck / chance / grace perhaps" we might save ourselves.

The fragmented lines reveal the tentativeness of this possibility in the "cry" for rebirth. Thus the section, "Prisoners," concludes with the whisper of hope we search for in Levertov's most despairing moments. The poet in the world cannot relinquish either the world or man—though "unmerited."

The translations of fourteen poems by Jean Joubert are a tribute to Denise Levertov's remarkable ability to capture the spirit of Joubert in these translations. Without sacrificing the beauty of the images, the rhythms of Joubert's lines, or the tone of individual poems, Levertov has succeeded in making Joubert's gifts available to the English-speaking world. This results from her sense of poetics which must meet the challenge of another language, here French, and the unique contribution made by that language. Yet, as I have already noted, Joubert is important to Levertov for other reasons. They share fears, hopes, doubts, aspirations. Poetically, they share metaphors and images and the philosophic problems of their age and their metier. In

"Wind Script," the poet is preoccupied with language and the challenge of words themselves in expressing his experience. He writes, "Words are vulnerable: / rain, fire, the errant hand, / confusion—all can assail them. / This marks our limits, guards us / from an excess of pride . . . / Then there are left only splinters of language, / fallen letters, gray tatters / like voices far across the valley, / which echoes fracture. And sometimes nothing: / sand, silence, calligraphy of the wind." Levertov's translation here is faithful to the original, "Ecriture du vent," but through the poem, we hear her own voice as well that equates the experience with her own. How often—faced with the "terrors" of the world—she too finds, not a voice, but "sand, silence, calligraphy of the wind." Levertov's translations are a tribute to Joubert, and she deserves much credit in introducing him to popular American audiences.

Part IV of *Oblique Prayers:* "Of God And Of The Gods" is an exploration of the spiritual that ends in the stasis of peace. The eternal order has been affirmed. Levertov described herself as "writing poetry that articulates engaged emotion and belief,"[27] and this final section can be no better described. There is mystery here as well as the immanence of divine providence. *All* of the poems are set against nature; often God and the earth-gods are juxtaposed as the unknowable and the *supposed* all-knowing. There is an aura of ambiguity surrounding the "gods" who seem to cherish the earth, but it is only the "unknown God of the gods" who "watches and smiles."

All of the poems that appear in the final part are lyrical, sensuous in their imagery, and give off—in most instances—a sense of calm and harmony. There are exceptions, and they are significant. In "Of Rivers," nature, personified, recalls its origins in God, as the "gods" themselves have not:

Rivers remember
. . . . .
a touch
shuddering them forth,
a voice
intoning them into

their ebbing and flood:
. . . .
      That remembrance
      gives them their way
to know, in unknowing flowing,
the God of the gods, whom the gods
themselves have not imagined.

In "Of Gods," we are told, "God gave the earth-gods / adamantine ignorance. / They think themselves / the spontaneous shimmering of fact—" Clearly the "earth-gods" are an oblique reference to men who see themselves as gods. To add to their sin of pride, they imagine God in "The Task" as "an old man / always upstairs," not knowing that "God's in the wilderness . . . absorbed in work" and hears "the spacious hum of bees, not the din, / and hears far-off / our screams." Yet "our voices, clear under the familiar / blocked-out clamor of the task, / can't stop their / terrible beseeching."

In another poem, "This Day," we are reminded again of the profane world and its insubstantial "communion" for "God's in the dust, / not sifted / out from confusion." Yet in his struggle for salvation, ignorant, wayward man still yearns for that communion.

> Dry wafer,
> sour wine:
>
> this day I see
>
> the world, the word
> intricately incarnate, offers—
>   ravelled, honeycombed, veined, stained—
>   what hunger craves,

Levertov's own humanity permits her to communicate the pathos of man's struggle toward belief, but ignorant of the way. Other poems are hymns of praise, joy in the beauties of the world, as one of the most memorable poems in this volume, "The Avowal":

> As swimmers dare
> to lie face to the sky
> and water bears them,
> as hawks rest upon air
> and air sustains them,
> so would I learn to attain
> freefall, and float
> into Creator Spirit's deep embrace,
> knowing no effort earns
> that all-surrounding grace.

But the simile reinforces Levertov's dream that this is not for humans. Although she never articulates the need to struggle and search for her God on countless journeys, the hope that she can "float / into Creator Spirit's deep embrace" is a luxuriant, if impossible, dream.

The key word in the poem is "so would I," but "would" is wishful thinking, more fit for dream than reality.

The title poem of the volume, "Oblique Prayer," is an interior dialogue as Levertov searches for God in the arena of her soul. The question posed is "Have you been here?" What is the nature of the experience that will lead this pilgrim to God? The poet begins by citing more celebrated experiences of epiphany: St. John of the Cross' "dark night of the soul," Christ's own test in the desert—to "scorch the heart at noon, / grip the mind / in teeth of ice at evening." Hers will be another kind of experience.

The journey begins in "a place / without clear outlines, / the air / heavy and thick / the soft ground clogging / my feet if I walk, / sucking them downwards / if I stand." This is hardly a place congenial to the transcendent experience of a vision of God! Thus, the source of the seeker's questions is made evident.

> Have you been here?
> Is it
>
> a part of human-ness
> to enter
> no man's land?

Yet, she answers, "I can remember / (is it asking you / that / makes me remember?)":

> even here
> the blesséd light that caressed the world
> before I stumbled into
> this place of mere
> not-darkness.

Although there is the echo that God has left the world "to darkness and to me," recalling Gray's "Elegy in a Country Churchyard," there is **memory** recalling "the blessed light that caressed the world." "Oblique Prayer" answers the question, "Have you been here?" and for the poet, that memory will suffice. The poem is moving in its simplicity and in the need to ask and answer one's own questions. But there again is the ray of hope that validates God's concern with man in "this place of mere / not-darkness."

". . . That Passeth All Understanding" is a poem suffused with harmony, quiet, awe, and a gratitude for the "Peace that passeth understanding," a translation of the prayer "Shantih" from the Hindu

Upanishads. Again, the form of the poem is a series of questions after "A gratitude / had begun / to sing in me."

The poet asks, "Was there / some moment / dividing / song from no song? / When does dewfall begin? / When does night / fold its arms over our hearts / to cherish them? / When is daybreak?" The simplicity of these invocations is prefigured by a confidence in God's providence. It is a poem of expectancy, not doubt, of affirmation, not uncertainty. Perhaps the most eloquent testimony of faith in this final part of *Oblique Prayers* is "Of Being," for the speaker—her pilgrimage here nearing conclusion—is fully aware of the unfathomable enigma of being: the knowledge that we can relish the beauties of the earth and the joy of "being alive" at the same time we are faced with our unknowable destiny:

> I know this happiness
> is provisional:
>
>> the looming presences—
>> great suffering, great fear—
>>
>> withdraw only
>> into peripheral vision:
>
> but ineluctable this shimmering
> of wind in the blue leaves:
>
> this flood of stillness
> widening the lake of sky:
>
> this need to dance,
> this need to kneel:
>>> this mystery:

In the presence of the sensuousness, the beauty, the mystery of life—the need to dance and the need to kneel coexist in the twin worlds of Denise Levertov's experience. She would celebrate—often through the creation of poems, and often through prayer. Yet these worlds merge in that inscape from which the poem is born.

As we shall see in the final volumes to be examined, Denise Levertov will again reach that stasis of faith and re-dedication to her art and her need for "being alive," but here in "Of Being" she achieves a tranquillity of spirit and a statement of purpose not so emphatically voiced elsewhere. The last two lines of the poem focus on the word "need," and it is this need that propels her on the next stage of her journey. Her resiliency of spirit and her sense of herself as a poet have never been so succinctly expressed.

Breathing the Water

Breathing the Water was published in 1984 and republished yearly until 1987. These are poems of both the world of the poet's experience and the experience of the "inscape" as well as the subtle ways in which those experiences interact. In many ways, it is a collection that comprises Levertov's most comprehensive work, for it includes *all* of her major themes, variations in tone and imagery, and personal reminiscences only hinted at in former poems. Significantly, *Breathing the Water* is the culmination of Levertov's artistic response to a wide range of experiences over many decades. While the two preceding volumes centered on two major motifs—the "age of terror" that is the modern world and Levertov's struggle toward the transcendent experiences that would reinforce her religious faith—this later collection of poems reminds us of the very broad scope of her interests.

Now, in *Breathing the Water,* Denise Levertov offers poems on the writing of poetry, on corruption, on death and the death of close friends, on her parents, her son, and her sister, on nature, on injustice round the globe, on pain as well as joy, and on the landscape of the soul. The volume is replete with myths, religious symbols, biblical references, fairy tales, and the sense of the micro-macrocosm. Ever present is the theme of bringing peace to what Levertov perceived to be a chaotic universe. She writes of resurrection and honor, of dreams, of a complex world that she still seeks to awaken. The voice is varied: at times nostalgic, meditative; at times humble as she praises God; at times faltering, mystical, dreamy, while at other times, richly sensuous.

As I have intimated, there is great variation in the *form* of the poems. Some are short, enigmatic, abbreviated to the point of terseness. Other poems are longer, more reflective, the images more elusive, the cadences lengthened to give an "unhurried" quality to the line. Many poems move away from the intellectual, rhetorical mode to a more intuitive, "spontaneous" response when the poem treats inexplicable sensations, the world of the inscape where "meanings" are ambiguous, more elusive, more mysterious. In her use of myths and archetypal patterns, Levertov takes us to that private region of the soul where "understanding" is felt along the bone rather than the brain. In *Breathing the Water* Levertov is deep in her spiritual voyage as the final lines seem to echo throughout the entire volume: "What we desire travels with us. / We must breathe time as fishes breathe water. / God's flight circles us."

I should like to focus on what Levertov always refers to as her "poetry of engagement," for though the Vietnam War was over, too many Americans were untouched by the threats posed by the murders in El Salvador, apartheid, "profit and power," the "dark times" we live in, the fevered Earth "waiting the next blow." But of equal importance is the response Levertov makes—consistent with her former practice—of finding answers: in "being alive," in loving, in celebration, in singing (writing the poem), and always in the achievement of spiritual stasis. Although Denise Levertov knew the value of group protest and public outcry, she also found her way to be, like Dame Julian Norwich (whom she celebrates in this volume) hoping that "all shall be well."[28]

Enclosing the entire volume *Breathing the Water* is Rainer Maria Rilke's *The Book of Hours, Book I.* Rilke was Denise Levertov's most eminent "master," and substantial references to Rilke recur in her earliest work—both poetry and prose. In *Light Up the Cave,* Levertov pays homage to Rilke in "Rilke as Mentor," stressing both his reverence for his art and his innate sense of joy. At the close of this essay, Levertov quotes this significant passage.

> To keep our inward conscience clear and to know whether we can take responsibility for our creative experiences just as they stand in all their truthfulness and absoluteness: that is the basis of every work of art. . . ."[29]

Levertov had written to Bill Burford that Rilke was preoccupied with the tragedy of war "deeply, deeply concerned and involved in the 14–18 war—in the very first weeks, caught up in it, in the collective furor—quickly disillusioned, sickened . . . and becoming more and more deeply opposed to it as it dragged on."[30] She refers to Rilke's comments in his letters about "*looking,* about the humble yet passionate looking that woos a Thing to reveal itself, and which proves to reveal also far more about individual feeling and 'voice' than any introspective abstraction."[31] She believed Rilke to be "the most devoted of poets, the one who gave himself most wholly to the service of his art."[32] And she refers to a letter in which Rilke expressed the belief that "—we shall only be wholly in the right when we understand that even this most urgent realization of a higher reality appears, from some last and extreme vantage point, only a means to win something once more invisible, something inward and unspectacular—a saner state in the midst of our being."[33]

Rilke had said that verses are not "simply feelings . . . they are experiences."[34] Finally, in Levertov's most often quoted line from Rilke: "—unlived life, of which one can die," we find the quintessential appeal this German poet had for a modern American poet to whom inertia was anathema. In a world that was often an "age of terror" Rilke offered the hope of "being alive."

It is not surprising, therefore, that three poems in *Breathing the Water*, the first, last, and a third, dominate the central motif of the volume: "Thus the Infinite / plays, and in grace / gives us clues to His mystery." Levertov is careful to note that many of the ideas and images are her own, revealed by a comparison of Rilke's *Book of Hours* with her own poems.

The opening poem, "Variations on a Theme by Rilke," sets the tone for the entire volume—which is reinforced by the other "Variation" poems.

> A certain day became a presence to me;
> there it was, confronting me—a sky, air, light:
> a being. And before it started to descend
> from the height of noon, it leaned over
> and struck my shoulder as if with
> the flat of a sword, granting me
> honor and a task. The day's blow
> rang out, metallic—or it was I, a bell awakened,
> and what I heard was my whole self
> saying and singing what it knew: *I can*.

The poem begins with a simple awakening, what for all of us is the beginning awareness of day, but quietly the experience is transformed into an act of "knighting" as the poet is granted both "an honor and a task." The resounding metaphors that follow are characteristic of Levertov's poetry: the blow, the bell, the awakening. The coming to awareness recalls "Sleepers Awake!" in "Candles in Babylon," and the language is urgent.

The poem is a coming to life, the poet arising from sleep to the challenges of the new day, but impelled by the mysterious "presence" that **smites** her into action. The day is a numinous presence, and though never stated, the hand of God bestows the honor and the task.

The "poems of engagement" in this volume differ in several respects from Denise Levertov's earlier activist poetry. One notes instantly a difference in tone. There is no anger here; no *overt* summons to action—"Revolution or Death!"—no violent images; no "age of terror." But we would misread these poems if we missed the subtle

yet insistent assertion that, as humans, we must be responsible for
our Earth and ourselves and, most significantly, that we do not remain
blind to the inhumanity all around our globe. There is a great deal
of reflection in these poems, an insistence on "witnessing," and a
tone that is frequently elegiac—not only for the innocence of childhood, the memories of loved ones, but for the Earth we have ren-
dered lifeless and whose urgent whisperings continue to haunt us.

Thus in "Window-Blind," Levertov begins with a sentence preg-
nant with meaning: "Much happens when we are not there."

> Many trees, not only that famous one, over and over,
> fall in the forest. We don't see, but something sees,
> or someone, a different kind of someone,
> a different molecular model, or entities
> not made of molecules anyway; or nothing, no one:
> but something has taken place, taken space,
> been present, absent,
> returned. Much moves in and out of open windows
> when our attention is somewhere else.

This theme of "blindness" and the need to *see* is thematic in all of
Levertov's poetry, but especially crucial here, for we seem to **will**
ourselves not to see. "We are animals and plants that are not well. /
We are not well but while we look away," much happens. It is Lev-
ertov's way of saying, "Attention must be paid." In the final lines of
"Window-Blind" Levertov touches on "possibility":

> . . . . one or two leaves
> fall, and when we read them we can perceive,
> if we are truthful, that we are not dreaming,
> not dreaming but once more witnessing.

In other poems, this failure of vision is reflected in such words as
"uninterpreted" and "abandoned" in "The Absentee"; "trapped" and
"scarred" in "Captive Flower"; the "dry lips" of "To One Steeped in
Bitterness"; and the poisoned well in "The Stricken Children."

"Carapace" is an ironic and bitter poem of the ways we harden
ourselves to tragedy that *seems* to lie beyond our ability to erase it—in
this instance, the desecrations in El Salvador. Men are compared to
turtles, who sink into their shells that guard them from injustice in
the world: "I am growing mine / though I have regretted yours."

The poem goes on to describe the acts of horror perpetrated by
the Guardia Civil—the militant arm of the government—that shoots
civilians without trials, that leaves families destitute as the men "dis-

appear," the survivors numbed to the point of death by these inhu-
manities. The speaker, trying to hide in the shadow to protect herself
in her "carapace," finds "That burning, blistering glare / off the
world's desert / still pushes in." In a world of terror, it is impossible
to hide, since conscience, a life dedicated to non-violence, and the
plea for human dignity have no armor strong enough to shut out the
world.

Similarly, "From the Image-Flow—South Africa 1986," portrays
South Africa as a living hell, a slave ship, in which the sea itself lives
the torment of the enchained. The poem is a strong outcry against
apartheid, which for Levertov—as for most of the western world—
is a crime against the sane principles of civil liberties and humane
treatment. The images in the poem are more violent than any in this
volume and the brevity, the metaphor of the slave ship, and the heavy
beats produced by the alliterative technique communicate Levertov's
indignation and horror.

> Africa, gigantic slave-ship, not anchored yet not moving,
> all hatches battened down, living tormented cargo
> visible through dark but transparent sides. The sea
> writhing too, but slowly, serpentine. In the vast hold,
> vinelike hands reach out from crowded souls, strike sparks
> from chains,
> light fires in what space they make between their bodies:
> not the ship only begins to burn,
> the viscous depths it rides on
> already smoulder.

The smouldering deep is an echo of her phrase in other poems: *contra
naturam*.

"Urgent Whisper" reiterates a motif Levertov has explored in other
poems in her protests against nuclear testing. This poem is an elegiac
backward glance over the shoulder. Here, it is the betrayed physical
Earth, like a patient dying of pneumonia.

There is little question that Levertov's love for nature, her sense
of the death of the land at the hand of men, will always haunt her.
The possibility of the dying land is still a vital public issue three
years after the publication of *Breathing the Water*, as ecologists and
other scientists, concerned citizens, legislators, and artists address
themselves to the problems and solutions before it is too late.

"Urgent Whisper" is a poem moving in its understatement, its
pathos of a Earth "trembling" silently and the "urgent whisper" of
the listener herself, in its simplicity reinforced by the repetitions that
remain in our consciousness: "beneath me, / beneath this house,

beneath / the road and the trees"; the trembling "comes from the Earth itself, I tell you, / Earth herself."

"Wavering" opens with a wellspring of images—the sounds, sights, touch of earth's riches in its micro forms: "scintillations, junebugs, / rain of fireflies low in the rippling fog, / motes abundant, random, pinpoints of intelligence / floating like bright snow . . ."; then the tone shifts dramatically as we envision "A world, the world, where *live shell* / can explode on impact or, curled elaborate bone, / be an architecture, domicile / of wincing leisurely flesh." The shock comes when the poet reminds us of how rapidly in the technological age in which we live, we can accomplish our own destruction. The luminous presence of vision and rite and the faith in the journey "toward a river forever"—"palm upraised"—is the only response one can make in an "age of terror." But the attention "wavers" and the "shimmering curtain" permits only an "intermittent gleaming" of a "different river." "Wavering" is a poem of the world and the inscape and of the difficulty of holding what Wordsworth called the "visionary gleam," but however ephemeral, Levertov affirms the gleam, however intermittent over pools and marshes.

It would be a grave omission to end this study of *Breathing the Water* without including those poems that offer a whisper of hope amid the visions of destruction, loss, and inhumanity. One such poem is "A Blessing," which reaffirms for the poet the faith in her artistic journey to find life in a world of shadows. A friend tells her, "Your river is in full flood," and indeed, this volume is fitting proof that the poet has reached a high level of poetic achievement through the many decades of her imaginative journey. A friend tells the poet, "'You give me / my life,' she said to the just-written poems, / long-legged foals surprised to be standing." Not completely convinced, the friend's words "work in the poet."

"A Blessing" is lyrical and abounds in nature's gifts. The poet's gifts are imaged in the river as it gives life to the land. So the imagination gives life to the poem, and the flow of the river is reinforced by the rhythmic flow of the enjambed lines which carry the reader to the vision of the river itself at the close:

> The river swiftly
> goes on braiding its heavy tresses,
> brown and flashing,
> as far as the eye can see.

But the "pain" is ever present, as she reveals in "Zeroing In."

Here, we are privy to that "undiscovered continent" Emily Dickinson wrote of, but in this poem the landscape within is a source of danger: a companion warns of "'sinkholes, places / or sudden terror, of small circumference / and malevolent depths.'" And the second speaker confirms the "'quagmires there that can pull you / down, and sink you in bubbling mud.'" These are the terrors of the inner self, but as the first speaker concludes,

> 'Yes, we learn that.
> It's not terror, it's pain we're talking about:
> those places in us, like your dog's bruised head,
> that are bruised forever, that time
> never assuages, never.'

Levertov had talked with me about this kind of pain, observing, "suffering in those who can learn something from suffering is explicable, because it can be looked upon as a painful but necessary part of growth . . ."[35] As she so movingly expressed in "To Olga,"

> I felt the veil
> of sadness descend
>
> but I was never afraid for us,
> we were benighted but not lost, and I trusted
> utterly that at last,
> however late, we'd get home.
> No owl, no lights, the dun ridges
> of ploughland fading. No matter.
> I trusted you.
>
> But you? Irritably you'd ask me
> why I was silent. Was it because
> you felt untrusted, or had no trust
> in yourself? Could it,
> could it have been that
> you, you were afraid,
> my brave, my lost
> sister?

The presence in *Breathing the Water* of this poem of childhood is significant if one can penetrate the symbolic overtones of the two children heading home in the dark. We cannot presume to answer Levertov's question, for we know too little of Olga whom the poet saw as "my brave, my lost / sister," but surely we can perceive Denise Levertov's own strength and sense that they were "benighted but not lost." Despite the language of this volume—wavering, sink holes, quagmires, stricken children or bruising pain—Denise Levertov is not lost. The evidence of her faith, her belief in "being alive," her tenacity in continuing to hope lead us to "Making Peace" and the poems "Variations on a Theme by Rilke" that come at the close of the collection. "Making Peace" is, in a significant way, Levertov's response to her critics who have censured her for imagining "disaster" and making violence, war, and protest a subject matter for poetry.

In her note to this poem, Levertov wrote:

> The "imagination of disaster" is Henry James's phrase. He said Americans had it—but do they still? Imagination is what makes reality real to the mind (which is why it's so hard to imagine peace, for it has not been experienced in the reality of our life in history except as the absence of war). Yet not only peace but the disastrous realities of our time go unimagined, even when "known about," when "psychic numbing" veils them; and thus the energy to act constructively, which *imaginative* knowledge could generate, is repressed.[36]

The tone of the poem is reasoned—no anger, no moralizing, no peremptory voice calling for action. The entire poem turns on the ironic observation that poets cannot "give us imagination of peace"; indeed, poets can only imagine, know peace "in the words of its making." The poem begins with a voice from the dark, calling out:

> "The poets must give us
> imagination of peace, to oust the intense, familiar
> *imagination of disaster*. Peace, not only
> the absence of war."

But, as the poet argues, "peace, like a poem, / is not there ahead of itself, / can't be imagined before it is made, / can't be known except / in the words of its making, / grammar of justice, / syntax of mutual aid." Using the terms of "language"—rhythm, metaphor, pause and cadence, stanza and line—Levertov relates "peace," a creation that can only be possible if we "restructure" our lives, to the poets' need to restructure poems. *People* make peace; *poets* make poems that articulate what man has created. These complementary acts of creation are equally important and interdependent. The poem concludes,

> A cadence of peace might balance its weight
> on that different fulcrum; peace, a presence,
> an energy field more intense than war,

might pulse then,
stanza by stanza into the world,
each act of living
one of its words, each word
a vibration of light—facets
of the forming crystal.

The "vibration of light" that is Levertov's final vision is an immanence of supernal power. "Man is man," she told me, "because he
has choices."[37] The success of this poem depends on the primary
metaphor—an identification between what man and the poet can
create. But the tone of the poem—the logic by which it makes its
way toward conclusion—is equally memorable.

The second "Variations on a Theme by Rilke" follows a group
of poems, "spinoffs," randomly inspired by myths, fables, religious
meditation, dreams, and paintings. The poem opens with depictions
of Christ interpreted by the great masters of art: Giotto, Van Eyck,
Rembrandt, Roualt—all of whom painted the "truth" as they envisioned it, according to the old monk revealing the book of paintings.
What emanates from these varied portraits is not fiction but God's
"manifold countenance."

In this starkly simple poem, the revelation is that man contains the
"clue" to God's mystery. Against the embellished, richly ornamented
church is the "art" of the painter, revealing the clue that brings with
it the rebirth implied by the blossoming morning. All this is given
through God's grace.

The faith that guides this poem leads us to a series of poems on the
fifteenth-century mystic "Juliana of Norwich" (known more widely as
"Julian"). Levertov feels a kinship with the ancient mystic because,
as she writes, "She lived in dark times, as we do." But Julian's
message was the great love of God for men and the consequently
detestable nature of human sin. This is the enigma Levertov wrestles
with throughout her work, but Julian "clung to joy" with the knowledge that "Love was his meaning."

Thus in the final poem, "Variation and Reflection on a Theme by
Rilke," Denise Levertov resolves that mystery for herself, but not
until she has dismissed "logic" and transcended the world of "cause
and effect," events, machines, and her own "bustling senses." The
poem, in one respect, is an echo of Emerson's "Goodbye, proud
world. I'm going home," but this poet of the world knows, in her
own wisdom, that the "pulse of the flesh" and the "dust of our being"
are not to be denied. The poem begins almost colloquially and rises
to spiritual longing in the final utterance:

If just for once the swing of cause and effect,
                              cause and effect,
would come to rest; if casual events would halt,
and the machine that supplies meaningless laughter
ran down and my bustling senses, taking a deep breath
fell silent
and left my attention free at last . . .

If we are to suppose the "you" to be a numinous "presence," the mind freed of prosaic distractions could both possess and relinquish the force to "flow back into all creation." In the last part of the poem, the poet admits, "There will never be that stillness," and the image of the voyaging pilgrim in search of God, hungry to fill her thought "to the very brim, / bounding the whole flood of your boundlessness," knows that what "we desire travels with us." The final lines are a way to be.

We must breathe time as fishes breathe water.
God's flight circles us.

This beautiful image that closes the volume perfectly reflects Denise Levertov's worldly **and** spiritual convictions over decades. As a poet **in** the world, she is too much aware of its hold upon us, and as a spiritual pilgrim in search of her God, she recognizes His presence circling over us. The metaphor of breathing the water **is** "staying alive," even as we know that "What we desire travels with us." This is a source of comfort and a source for celebration. Levertov has reinforced a faith she has had since her youth: "there is a form in all things (and in our experience) which the poet can discover and reveal . . ." At this point in her many journeys, she has validated her quest that affirms her world—whatever her fears for its future may be—affirms her role as a poet, and affirms her religious faith.

A Door in the Hive

There is only one thing that all poetry must do; it must praise all it can for being as for happening.
                                        —W. H. Auden[38]

In 1988, Denise Levertov brought forth her latest volume of poetry, an event that not only has drawn the admiration of the literary world, but also has re-affirmed her place as one of America's leading poets. *A Door in the Hive* is an important book, not only because at its very heart it is a work of praise "for being as for happening," but because it is a work of superior craftsmanship. It follows from Levertov's lifelong interests and concerns.

Among familiar motifs and experiences, there is the ever-present voice of social conscience, so that *Hive* is part of a larger continuity: the "poetry of engagement." But there are new voyages and new revelations that emanate from fresh experiences and a perspective shaped by the passage of time and the necessity of looking ahead. There *are* moments in the abyss.

The poet forces us to look at the inhumanity in the world— changed place names but the same violence and violation, and again the betrayal of the land itself as the environment becomes more fragile with each assault upon its natural state. And, as in the past, she speculates about death, about friends and mentors, and about her own faltering efforts to secure her faith and renew herself in "staying alive." Nature is a cause for celebration. The past is always with us. Poetry, painting, and music reflect both the joys and despair of life. Dreams and voyaging are familiar means for exploring the inscape. Biblical myths, rituals, and parables, intrinsic to Levertov's vision from the beginning, are explored here in "On the Mystery of the Incarnation," "On the Parables of the Mustard Seeds," "Annunciation," "Nativity: An Altarpiece," "A Calvary Path," "St. Thomas Didymus," and "Ikon: The Harrowing of Hell." Thus, the wide range of themes and the shifts in tone and vision combine to form a complex and rich artistic work—at times mystical, at times celebratory, at times speculative, at times dreamy, often heightened with the incandescent gleam of language perfectly matched with Levertov's continuing search for the world Rilke opened for her, as she suggests in the first poem, "a shimmering destination."

Since the years of the Vietnam War and its aftermath, as we have seen, Levertov has weathered the censure of her critics; as each new volume appeared in the seventies and eighties, critical acclaim has grown, and a recognition of her achievement has crystallized into an international reputation.

A Door in the Hive is not, I suspect, Levertov's last book, but surely it is a culmination of her finest talents: her energetic spirit of confrontation, her lyric power, her joy in nature, her anxiety for a world at risk, and her hope—however cautious—for the future. There is doubt here and affirmation; wit and struggle—"wrestling with the angel"—; the world outside and the "continent" within. The experiences themselves call up a sharpened sensibility. Words like strength, courage, invincibility, and endurance come to mind as we read even those poems in which the poet confesses to have lost

her direction or her enthusiasm, although these losses—if recurrent—
are not permanent.

She still adheres to the assumption that "Poetry is necessary to a
whole man, and that poetry be not divided from the rest of life is
necessary to *it*. Both life and poetry fade, wilt, shrink, when they
are divorced."[39] Denise Levertov, like Rilke, believes the basis for
art is "To keep our inward conscience clear and to know whether we
can take responsibility for our creative experiences just as they stand
in all their truthfulness and absoluteness . . ."[40]

A Door in the Hive reveals a poet renewing herself intellectually and
spiritually against the fragility of the future—both her own and the
earth's, revealing a mind as rich in scope and complexity as the voice
summoning our better selves in the sixties but ripened with time. It
is a book of praise, as Auden might have prophesied, where, in the
midst of the "vast enigma" with "no instructions," the prayer rings
out in "Two Threnodies and a Psalm."

> Lift us to seize the present,
> wrench it
> out of its downspin.

As we begin to examine *Hive* in detail, we are immediately struck
by the great variations of form. Levertov has always been sensitive
to line length, stanzaic variety, and the rhythmic structure of both
the line and the whole poem as an inherent part of her theme and
tone. This collection seems particularly experimental. Most striking
is her collaboration with the composer, Newell Hendricks, in the
creation of a libretto for the oratorio, "El Salvador: Requiem and
Invocation," performed by Back Bay Chorale and the Pro Arte Cham-
ber Orchestra at Harvard in 1983. The poem is a long, ambitious
"drama" that, as Levertov tells in her notes, "moves from pre-Colom-
bian times through a condensed history of the intervening centuries
. . . to very recent events."[41] The work is not only striking for its
length but for the complexity of its narrative structure.

Other poems are stanzaic in pattern, though the stanzas are often
uneven in length and line. In other instances, Levertov evokes her
earlier lyric poetry—here frequently in her response to the awesome
beauty of nature—but at times with a brevity that reflects the ineffable moment of a passing thought or emotion. Still other poems are
reflective, deliberate speculations of the mind, borne out by long
lines and no stanza breaks. "St Thomas Didymus" is unique in its
form. There is a faint evocation of William Carlos Williams's "stepped
line"; the poem is characterized by long enjambed lines followed by

brief one or two stressed lines, giving a "flowing" quality to the poem, suggestive of its narrative motif, the spiritual tone, and the "vast unfolding design" that closes the poem.

"To Rilke," the first poem in *A Door in the Hive*, evokes already familiar associations: the presence of the poet's mentor, the dream form of the experience, and the "voyage"—here on a boat. The poem is made complex by paradox, for Rilke at the prow is "all voice, though silent," as the *needful* journey moves toward some veiled, unknown shore. The physical effort of rowing is "transcended," for the gaze of the man at the prow silently promises "a shimmering destination." Like many dreams, there is mystery, and the communion of souls is transmitted wordlessly. The final lines reveal the poet's awareness of Rilke's real journey on the Nile, "the enabling voice / drawing that boat upstream in your parable." The last two lines unite the dream with the real experience: "Strange that I knew / your silence was just such a song." The entire poem is symbolic of a theme Levertov has often returned to: the need to journey to plumb the "imperative mystery." She sets herself against the impenetrable, the difficult, but not impossible task of finding her "shimmering destination." The poem sets the tone for the volume where conflict is an ever-present reality and the transcendence of the forces "running against us" is an equally ever-present possibility. The poem closes with Rilke's silent "song"—intimations of hope and realization. As we have seen, the journey metaphor is a recurrent image of questing in much of Levertov's poetry: here in "A Traveler," the speaker wants to go a long way, slowly.

> If it's chariot or sandals,
> I'll take sandals.
> I like the high prow of the chariot,
> the daredevil speed, the wind
> a quick tune you can't
> quite catch
>   but I want to go
> a long way
> and I want to follow
> paths where wheels deadlock.
>   And I don't want always
> to be among gear and horses,
>   blood, foam, dust. I'd like
> to wean myself from their strange allure.
> I'll chance
> the pilgrim sandals.

Much of the poem's charm comes from the conversational tone—

unexpected in a poem of the high seriousness of the pilgrimage. One is hardly aware of the metaphors, though they inform the poem in concretizing the poet's mode of voyage. She chooses the means of humility, of a slow cadence, of immediacy unobscured by chariots or charging horses. Yet the poem is energized by the traveler's courage, confidence, and will. Like Frost she will choose her own road. The poem ends on the colloquialism of a gamble: "I'll chance / the pilgrim sandals."

In yet another instance, "Entering Another Chapter," she travels by ship, while in "For Instance" she finds herself on a "train rattling not fast or slow . . ." Yet all this motion leads to "The Blind Man at the Edge of the Cliff" whom she envies, because he lives "at the jutting rim of the land," and has chosen "a life / pitched at the brink." The poem reveals Levertov's often-stated desire for a place where "nothing intrudes, palpable shade, / between his eager / inward gaze / and the vast enigma." Part of her is the poet committed to a world that cries out in protest; part of her is the poet of the "inward gaze" where the "vast enigma" draws her inexorably toward the "elusive deep horizon." This same impulse, it appears to me, is present in the poem that gives the volume its title.

"Dream 'Cello," as the title reveals, takes us again into that inner world of Levertov's experience. The subject is the musician whose music conjures up all the exotica of palaces, Arabian serpents, and "sleek rats plus as / young seals." The poet finds herself near a granary, golden with its harvest. Notably, the entire poem is a series of questions, first about the musician: "from what / unpremeditated congeries of wisdoms / did the sounds appear, woven / like laser tracings on the screen of air?" and then, inevitably, about her own role as a poet. Sounds take her to words—the "real ones"—present in the mystical "nowhere" of the granary. At this moment, the poet turns to ask questions that anticipate the yearnings of the artist.

> Could we live there? Is it dark?
> Could the grain shoals
> not light us with their golden sheen?
> Invisible hive, has it no small door
> we could find if we stood
> quite still and listened?

These final questions stress the urgency of the poet's quest. The repetitions, the brevity of the lines, the parallel constructions—all serve to intensify the mood which began as speculation and becomes transformed into a desire to summon up the magic words. The metaphors of the granary and the hive both suggest plenitude, the golden gleam of harvest, and the activity that the hive evokes—regeneration, life. The final lines are plaintive, as the poet dreams of finding a small door, not only to the life of the spirit but to the life of the artist as well—standing still and listening for the words. Levertov has touched upon silence as part of the creative act; here the images of the granary and the invisible hive are beautiful additions to her lexicon of the human experience seeking renewal. The delicacy of such images as "the laser tracings on the screen of air" and the golden sheen of the "grain shoals" enhance the impalpable mystery of the visionary dream world. It is significant that the poem ends as it began, with unanswered questions. The life of the hive evokes another echo of the bees in *Oblique Prayers*. In "The Task," we are reminded of God's presence in the "wilderness next door" where "absorbed in work" He "hears the spacious hum of bees, . . ." Clearly, the poet's own quest has not attained its "shimmering destination" as she seeks the small door to the invisible hive.

Denise Levertov's "poems of engagement" take us to those parts of the world where violence, inhumanity, and fear still hold hostage an otherwise peace-loving people. But compounding the crimes of murder and violation is the indifference of a "safer" world blinded by its own inclination for self-survival. In "Distanced," "Shepherds in summer pastures / watched the invaders . . ." but although "They marvelled, they sorrowed," they "distanced" themselves from the river of fleeing people. The concluding lines, "But they could see no faces, / and no blood," testifies to their blanket indifference. Levertov believes that human beings have become inured to human suffering, which is an appalling truth of this poem, and—in its own way—is as painful as the actions of the "invaders." She still seeks to awaken sleepers.

The poem is a prelude to "Land of Death-Squads," a poem whose theme is the "disparatos" (the "disappeared") of El Salvador (victims of the "death squads") who are found buried in shallow graves by the vultures and the hungry searching for food and "dreading / what else may be found." This brief poem is powerful in its understatement, for without the title, the theme might be more obscure, but for those of us who read daily of the unending murders, the poem's meaning is crystalline:

> The vultures thrive,
> clustered in loft blue above
> refuse-dumps where humans too
> search for food, dreading

what else may be found.
Noble their wingspread,
Hideous their descent
to those who know
what they may feast on:
sons, daughters.
And meanwhile,
the quetzal, bird of life, gleaming
green, glittering red, is driven
always further, higher,
into remote
ever-dwindling forests.

The juxtaposition of opposites—death with receding life, imaged in the gleaming quetzal; the nobility of the vultures' wingspread with their "hideous" intent; the green of life and the red of death—reinforces the ironic tone. The poem concludes with the vision of the "ever-dwindling" forests, dying even as the humans which people them. This intense, brief poem appears before the longer libretto that tells the story of El Salvador's tragedy, *El Salvador: Requiem and Invocation*.

In her introduction to *El Salvador: Requiem and Invocation*, Levertov explains that the work was begun after the murders of Archbishop Oscar Romero and the three American nuns and a lay sister in El Salvador. Asked by composer Newell Hendricks to compose a libretto, Levertov suggested the focus upon El Salvador and its tragic history as well as the murders, and as she explains at length in her notes, she worked without knowledge of the music until the final rehearsal. Thus, she included in her text "a few stage directions": "with the opening words and phrases I included the suggestion not only that they were for chorus but also that their sounds be loud, harsh, cacophonous; or elsewhere that voices overlap and die away into silence, or perhaps be followed by an orchestral interlude."[43] So it was that Levertov created her own "music" that Newell enhanced in his own composition, which Levertov has called "a very strong and remarkable piece of music." The oratorio was first performed in 1983, and it is of special interest here that Levertov chose to make *El Salvador* the centerpiece of *A Door in the Hive*.

The work is a dramatic narrative in which the principal voices are those of the Chorus, the Voice of the Questioner, the Narrator, and individuals such as Romero, Sisters Dorothy, Maura, Ita, and Jean—all murdered in El Salvador. Interspersed with the voices are prayers and invocations. Both the Narrator and the chorus recount the long history of suffering, relieved only by brief periods of peace and plenty, while the Sisters bring us into the present with their own story of why they came to this land of rapacious violence and fear. After their deaths, the Chorus completes their story. The major role of the Questioner is to initiate the telling of the story, but in addition, the Questioner asks those questions for which one has no answers if one believes in the respect for human dignity:

> O Mayan land! El Salvador!
> what brought you to this time
> of horror? Long ago
>   it was not so—

The opening of *El Salvador* explodes with the "Terror and Violence" that the poet re-creates—the horror of the unimaginable made palpably real:

> Blood Rape Kill Mutilate Death-squad Massacre
> Torture Acid Order National Guard Thirst Pain
> Crying Screaming Bloated Naked Helicopter
> Slaughter Shoot Machine-gunned Beaten Vomit
> Slash Burning Slit Bullhorns Sprayed Blinded
> Bullets Machete Wounds Smash

The Chorus continues this catalog of terrors, closing with the words: "No one is safe." At the urging of the Questioner, the Chorus begins to recount the story of El Salvador's past when "Long ago / it was not so, / the land was generous, / the people lived at peace. / The land and people / were one, and lived / at peace." From this point both the Narrator and the Chorus look back with nostalgia and pride on the Mayan past. They "knew the cycle, the rituals: / earth & sky, / fruits, animals, / humans." The Mayans obeyed their gods, lived in harmony, and flourished. The narrative continues to relate the invasions and plundering of the land and its people for gold and slavery. With the passage of time, recurring over centuries, the slaves were dominated by one invader or another, reduced to hunger, suicide, and the deaths of their children. The twentieth century "made / the whole world into a marketplace!" Uprisings were quelled by machine guns and more death and destruction followed. In the "present" the conquerors came in the name of God—so they professed—but they too crushed the people. Yet among them were "new voices / voices of mercy / voices of pity / voices of love for the poor." Such was Archbishop Oscar Romero who came to the salvation of the people, while the "junta's anger / smouldered." Strengthened by Romero, the people renewed their faith in their own dignity and the life of the land. The holy Sisters declared that they came to "a land that / is writhing in pain. . . . We came in answer / to a call." The Narrator continues the story of the gunning down of Romero and the rape and murder of the Sisters, and once more the poor of El Salvador were vanquished. The ironic voice of the Chorus responds: *"but in martyrdom / is a seed of power!"* Near the close of the poem, the Chorus reiterates:

> Their deaths
> enjoin upon us, the living,
> not to give up the vision
> of lives freed from the lead weight
> of centuries.

The disembodied voices of Romero and the Sisters offer the final invocation, echoed by the masses:

> Let us unite
> in faith and hope
> as we pray:
> as we pray for the dead
> in faith and hope:
> in faith and hope
> as we pray:
>
> as we pray for ourselves
> for faith
> as we pray
> for hope.

Levertov has noted that the "basic models of my listening experience were the Bach Passions and various Handel and Haydn oratorios. The Narrator, then, plays a role equivalent to that of the Evangelist in the St. Matthew or St. John Passion music." The words of several historical figures were taken from actual accounts, and the list of names which are intoned by the Archbishop were real victims of "right-wing death-squads."[44]

Taken as a whole, the dramatic narrative is a powerful and moving poem, reminiscent of a Greek tragedy as both the Chorus and the Narrator recount and comment upon the events. There is a wide range of emotions here: pathos, anger, a cry to God for succor, despair, false hope that culminates in a glowing hope as Romero assumes a voice of power. The poem is often incantatory, often nostalgic, moving—in the people's patient ability to wait and hope for deliverance. The key phrase that illuminates the whole is "And life continued." Life always continues, as human beings endure, even as the land endures, to pray for hope.

Levertov's deep commitment to the people of El Salvador speaks out in every line. Yet it is a controlled voice, one that understands the dignity of the oppressed and hopes with them for a redemption of their suffering. *El Salvador* is a work of artistic merit, but it also is a work that emanates from an abiding belief in God and in human endurance. Aesthetically, the poem is an ambitious new form for Levertov who has worked out its structure with great care. It is not as episodic as "Staying Alive," as she adheres to her musical models and maintains the dramatic-narrative form. As for the poem's violence which appears in the Chorus' initial outcry, this dissolves as the story moves forward. The acts are violent; the language is measured. And, as always in Levertov's poetry, the end is stasis as the Chorus intones its prayer for faith and hope. It should be remembered, however, that *El Salvador* is the libretto for an oratorio, and its final achievement should be measured when heard with the music of composer Newell Hendricks, but it is significant that Levertov included the libretto in *Hive* as a poem, complete to stand on its own merits.

Other poems that reveal Levertov's concern with the desecration of the land by modern technology, with the general indifference to this exploitation, with humanity at risk, and with other environmental disasters appear here. The barrenness of a world devoid of human compassion, love, fertility is equalled by the nadir of despair in "The Book Without Words." The irony of the title sets the tone for, perhaps, the most pessimistic poem in the collection. As in early poems like "Durgan," the setting is the bleak shore: gray waves, limitless ocean, barren plain, land's end. "The sea-voyage was to begin," but ahead there is only the "void upon void." The book that was to offer directions is wordless. While the speaker has come to the shore, prepared to make a voyage, "There are no instructions." Levertov's poem reveals a *readiness* to embark on a voyage, but like Dante in the "selva oscura," humans cannot journey without guidance. It is that guidance Levertov will continue to search for in other moments.

In "Variations on a Theme by Rilke," the poet muses on the end of the century. The poem begins with questions: "Is the great scroll / being shaken, the scroll / inscribed by God and daubed with our lives' graffiti, / to raise this wind that churns / the sleep of listeners?" She speculates on the great scroll of the new century: what will be inscribed there? Even as "the powers / exchange dark looks" the sleepers merely "watch and listen." Once again Levertov would urge the sleepers to awaken, but here they are passive and watchful. The scroll may reveal "a pallid, empty field," recalling the wordless book, but the poet asks, "Where, if we discover the runes continue, / shall we seek out / their hierophant?"—the sacred priest who will unfold to us the mysteries. Even as we stand at the threshold of a new century, what awaits us? The lack of hope is not as numbing as the "void upon void," but there is a sense of trepidation that there are still "no instructions." There is a hint here of Yeats' own fears as the curtain opened on the twentieth century, and his prophetic voice is equalled here by Levertov who has experienced the fulfillment of that prophecy. Unlike Yeats, she still leaves with us the faint hope that we will find the hierophant who might be able to penetrate those mysteries.

"In California: Morning, Evening, Late January" brings together a source of celebration with the despondency of seeing the land irreparably destroyed. In early morning there is a sacred beauty illuminating the land "the dew / lingering, / scripture of / scintillas," but too soon the mowers, the pesticides, the helicopters spraying vineyards, the bulldozer, excavators impinge on nature with a "babel of destructive construction." It is indeed a "Fragile paradise." The poet asks in wonder,

> Who can utter
> the poignance of all that is constantly
> threatened, invaded, expended
>
> and constantly
> nevertheless
> persists in beauty,
> . . .

The "Fragile paradise" still prevails, though, for how long the poet cannot know, but while it lasts, the earth's delicate beauty evokes a lyrical and poignant reverence.

Again, in "Two Threnodies and a Psalm," Levertov, more forceful and dramatic than in "In California," serves witness on the destruction of both man and nature. This is, indeed, a lamentation, a cry of despair for the innumerable violations of mankind, of the land, of the threat to existence itself. "The body being savaged / is alive. / It is our own." The causes for our "unacknowledged *extremis*" is developed in the third part of the poem.

> Our clear water
> one with the infested water
> women walk miles to

each day they live.
One with the rivers tainted with detritus
                              of our ambitions,
and with the dishonored ocean.
Our unbroken skin
one with the ripped skin of the tortured,
          the shot-down, bombed, napalmed,
          the burned alive.
One with the sore and filthy skin of the destitute.

The poet calls on the transcendent Spirit to waken the sleepers from "the stasis / in which we perish." What follows is a litany of the unity of all creation: "Our flesh and theirs / one with the flesh of fruit and tree. / . . . Our being / tinder for primal light." The poem closes with the prayer that will lift man to awareness.

> Lift us, Spirit, impel
> our rising
> into that knowledge.
>
> Make truth real to us,
> flame on our lips,
>
> Lift us to seize the present,
> wrench it
> out of its downspin.

The poem is moving in its urgency, its profound concern for man to save himself and his earth, its faith that the "Spirit" can awaken sleepers. This faith is reinforced in other poems such as "The Love of Morning," in which the poet observes, "God has saved the world one more day," and we are summoned once more to the love of morning. Many of the poems that follow are indeed the poet's response to that summons as she celebrates the winter stars in the constellation, mountains, sacred bats, and Spring, as in "Envy" when the poet admits her envy of "The bare trees" that have already "made up their seed bundles." Awaiting life, the trees are superior to humans who seem to be out of touch with nature's rhythmic cycle of renewal.

> Their Spring will find them rested.
> I and my kind
> battle a wakeful way
> to ours.

Significantly, humans *will* battle their way to renewal. As always in Levertov's poems celebrating the numinous beauty of nature, as in "The Love of Morning," the images are delicate and haunting: the "sunlight's gossamer" lifting in its net "the weight of all that is solid"; and in "A Sound" the orchards of apricot, nectarine, and peach filling the valley. In spring, the "unexplained sound" . . . "drifted in ruffles / of lacy white, of lacy pink"; the seasons—pacing "in their circle-dance"; again in "Early" the magical early light "so pale a gold / it bathes in silver / the cool and still / air a single bird / stirs with tentative song." And in "Web," homage is paid to the intricacy and mystery of the spider's art:

> Intricate and untraceable
> weaving and interweaving,
> dark strand with light:
>
> designed, beyond
> all spiderly contrivance,
> to link, not to entrap:
>
> elation, grief, joy, contrition, entwined;
> shaking, changing,
> > forever
> > > forming
> > > > transforming:
> *all praise,*
> > *all praise to the*
> > > *great web.*

The praise for the spider's web—nature's way to "link" and transform—is a hint of the unity and coherence in the earth that is Levertov's praise, as well as for a power that harmonizes all, despite man's tendency to fragment and violate that unity. The image of the web and the hive are only two examples of Levertov's revelations of the earth as "God's hieroglyph," as Whitman had observed in *Leaves of Grass*.

With few exceptions, most of the poems in sections III and IV are brief, imagistic, irregular in line length, and generally undivided into stanzas. The unity of each poem rests on a single impression captured in a moment of time—sometimes an epiphany, sometimes a mystery left unexplained, sometimes an evanescent experience of joy and thanksgiving. The total effect is one of poetry as transcendent, as "intricate and intraceable," as the spider's "great web." In this sense,

Levertov's original form has few equals in contemporary American poetry.

As we have noted before in the poetry written in the eighties, Levertov's faith vibrates between doubt and affirmation even as her faith in humanity ebbs and flows. The last part of each volume from *Candles and Babylon* to *Breathing the Water* is built around Levertov's struggle toward her God. This pattern continues in *A Door in the Hive* as well. In "Flickering Mind," she confesses, "Lord, not you, / it is I who am absent."

Clearly, this is a riposte to those who through the ages have cried out: "Lord, Thou has deserted me." The poem continues in almost a colloquial vein, as the monologue with the Lord reveals the journey that began in belief and then fell into the depth of doubt: "but now / I elude your presence. / I stop / to think about you, and my mind / at once / like a minnow darts away." She upbraids her wandering self, confessing again, "Not you, / it is I am absent." In the moving close of the poem, the penitent praises the Lord's power and appeals for direction:

> You are the stream, the fish, the light,
> the pulsing shadow,
> you the unchanging presence, in whom all
> moves and changes.
> How can I focus my flickering, perceive
> at the fountain's heart
> the sapphire I know is there?

The crucial word here is *know* because, despite the absence, the wandering, the flickering, at the profoundest level of her soul, the poet believes—knows the presence of her Lord. The poems in Part V document that faith, and in "Midnight Gladness" the poet humbly accepts "Gift after gift." The final part of the volume continues the theme of the poet's religious pilgrimage, and for a moment she identifies herself with St. Thomas Didymus who needed proof of Christ's sacred identity. Again, she recalls Thomas' appeal to his God: "Lord, I believe, help thou/ mine unbelief, / and knew him / my twin." After the suffering of doubt and the invocation, echoing Thomas' own, *"Lord, / I believe, / help thou / mine unbelief,"* the Lord responds to her plea and leads her into the light. Again, as in other poems of disbelief and pain, the ending here is triumphant in the firmness of its faith:

> I witnessed
>   all things quicken to color, to form,

                        my question
                                    not answered but given
                                                    its part
                        in a vast unfolding design lit
                                            by a risen sun.

It is this "design" that Levertov has affirmed from her earliest state-
ments on the nature of poetry, nature, and man himself (who is too
often unaware of the design). Like all humankind living in a fragmented world, Levertov needs constant reassertion of that design,
and it is such a poem that permits the artist to "verify" that faith.

The final poem in *A Door in the Hive*, "Variations on a Theme by
Rilke," is a subtle interweaving of the major threads in Levertov's
poetry since the 1960s: the world on the brink of destruction coupled
with society's often appalling indifference; the presence of a transcendent Power: omnipotent, omniscient; and finally the guarded
hope that man will endure as a part of the grand design of the universe of which he once was a part. The key terms in this poem in
which Levertov's themes coalesce into an invisible whole are construct, hope, seek, conceive, hungers, and imbedded. Juxtaposed in
the opening lines are the destructive forces threatening the fragile
life of man and earth and the need to define the indefinable. Like
Job who cannot penetrate the all-powerful God to whom he pleads
as advocate, the poet reveals man's insubstantiality and God's illimit-
able dominion. The end of the poem poignantly returns to a motif
Levertov has touched upon before: man's hunger to return to the
universal design. Closing, as it does, an artistic work that balances
social awareness with the need to restore man's dignity in the "vast
mosaic," the poem is itself a design of eloquent power.

            With chips and shards, rubble of being,
            we construct
                        not You but our hope of You.
            We say—we dustmotes in the cosmos—
            'You dome, arching above us!':
            as if You were the sanctuary
            by which we seek to define You.

            Our cities pulverize, proud technologies
            spawn catastrophe. The jaws of our inventions
            snap down and lock.
                            Their purpose will be forgotten;
            Time is aeons
            and we live in minutes,
            flies on a windowpane.

Who can conceive the span of You,
great vault, ribbed cauldron slung beneath the abyss,
cage of eternity?

Metaphors shatter, mirrors of poverty.

But something in us, while the millennia
monotonously pass
                     and pass,
hungers to offer up
our specks of life as fragile tesserae
towards the vast mosaic—temple, eidolon;

to be, ourselves, imbedded in its fabric,
as if, once, it was from that we were broken off.

The images in this final poem are often shattering in their power; the ironic contrasts numbing. The view of man, awesome in his ability to both invent and destroy, is balanced by the view of man against time and the cosmos: "flies on a windowpane." *Yet*, in the end, the poet casts her lot with mankind "to be ourselves, imbedded in its fabric, / as if, once, it was from that we were broken off." It is fitting that Rilke again haunts this poem, for the duality of his vision: what man is and what he is capable of being are at the core of Levertov's own perception. *A Door in the Hive* is additional proof that Denise Levertov's sensibility, her artistic gifts, and her warm affection for a wayward modern world continue to impel her to express her experiences in this "Fragile Paradise."

Afterword

> The function of the poet is to put us into the world, not to take
> us out of it. Levertov knows that. Poetry has nothing to do with
> escape. It has to do with involvement, engagement.
> —William Slaughter
> *The Imagination's Tongue*

This study began with the assumption that a poet in the modern
world, Denise Levertov, could follow Emerson's declaration of independence: "We will walk on our own feet; we will work with our own
hands; we will speak our own minds," and could still maintain her
integrity as an artist. Some critics have viewed this goal as a balancing
act destined to ensure the inevitable fall from the high wire. Yet for
more than thirty years, since Levertov awakened to the horrors of
the Vietnam War, the social injustices perpetrated round the world,
the nuclear threat that hangs over mankind forebodingly, and the
devastation of nature, she has been able to write twelve volumes of
poetry that combine her sense of social purpose: her commitment to
speak out, to "awaken sleepers." But her poetry is more than the
fulfillment of this deeply felt task. It is also the artistic re-creation of
all of her experiences: of her joy in being alive; of her love of nature;
of people she has known and loved and lost; of writing poetry; of her
fears and doubts and "wavering"; and—ultimately—of her private
quest for her God.

We search for language to describe both her poetry and her person,
for they are difficult to view separately. We think first of resilience,
for Denise Levertov has never "given up" on man, herself, or God.
Morally, she is "tough." In a twentieth century darkened by war,
holocaust, and a public too often silent and indifferent, Denise Levertov has raised an insistent voice of protest, while maintaining her
love for life and for man. It is not accidental that she would be drawn
to Rilke and Julian of Norwich. She shares with them her right as
critic and right as a human being to have "a lover's quarrel with the
world," as Robert Frost wrote. Other words come to mind: celebrant,

singer, dancer. In the words of the sixties' song of defiance, "staying alive" resonates throughout her poetry.

Early in her poetic career, Denise Levertov wrote a delightfully disarming poem, "Overland to the Islands," comparing her poetic voyage to the seemingly haphazard cavortings of an inquisitive dog— a blithe spirit—whose feet take him wherever his curiosity leads him:

> Let's go—much as that dog goes,
> intently haphazard. The
> Mexican light on a day that
> "smells like autumn in Connecticut"
> makes iris ripples on his
> black gleaming fur—and that too
> is as one would desire—a radiance
> consorting with the dance.
>
> Under his feet
> rocks and mud, his imagination, sniffing,
> engaged in its perceptions—dancing
> edgeways, there's nothing
> the dog disdains on his way,
> nevertheless he
> keeps moving, changing
> pace and approach but
> not direction—'every step an arrival.' (1958)

The simile, humorous and serious simultaneously, will describe Levertov's own "intently haphazard" pilgrimage over the next thirty years: a wandering, but not without direction; a dance, a voyage of the imagination. That pilgrimage will be in the real world, the same world as that of the radiant, sniffing, moving, changing dog.

The final phrase of the poem has caught the imagination of the poet's critics, as we have seen. It suggests to them an arrival that is always an *achievement*, perhaps a revelation. Yet, as we have seen, in moments of loss and suffering, the poet stands still. This happens on rare occasions in Levertov's pilgrimage. She never suggests in this line that the arrival will be a joyous one—though that is to be hoped; instead the arrival may be the discoveries she makes along the way. As I view the long road of Denise Levertov's voyage, the arrival variously suggests the gaining of wisdom, an instant of hope, a epiphanic moment, a sense of the joy of living that gives her poetry the radiance "consorting with the dance."

Another aspect of this study was to examine the poetic quality of

Denise Levertov's work. Here, briefly, I have followed her growth as a lyric poet, but, more fully, I have studied the poetic power that underlies her utterances. She draws upon all the techniques of sight and sound in her use of repetition, alliteration, assonance, and consonance; and she has developed her concept of the line that often reveals a subtle ambiguity in her thought. Levertov creates her own special music that often suggests dance rhythms. Over the decades, she has experimented widely with form: succinct, almost terse poems with limited imagery to longer, more reflective poems rich with images from scripture, myth, ritual, and nature. Levertov takes her images from both the world in which she "journeys" and the world of the inscape: that inner realm of dream and imagination—mysterious, ineffable. Levertov never lost her lyric power, but many of her most memorable poems are fragmented in form, harsh in imagery, and penetrating in tone. She does not always sing; she speaks out.

Her tone changes as her experience in the world changes: she moves from despair to joy, from a deadening hopelessness to a faint, ephemeral, flicker of hope. She never capitulates to the kind of melancholy we find in so many women poets writing in the twentieth century. Yet, she writes about women, the female pride and independent spirit, the state of being alone without being lonely. And like many modern poets for whom art is craft as well as statement, she writes in poetry *and* prose about what Tillie Olsen called "the frightful task"—the task of creating art.

Denise Levertov has reached a point of stasis in her journey, for although her faith wavers and quickens, as we witness so clearly in her latest volume, *A Door in the Hive,* she affirms and reaffirms a unified, harmonious universe beneath the surface fragmentation of the visible world. She has found herself, aesthetically and spiritually, and she waits—somewhat impatiently—for the world to find *itself.* As Americans celebrate *Earth Day, 1990,* the awareness of dangers is growing, but there is much to be done to save the land. This is only one of Levertov's preoccupations.

And all the time, she continues to write, as each day reveals new insights, new sensations, new dangers, new occasions for thanksgiving. It is thus fitting to close this study with the poem "From the Image Flow—Summer of 1986," which succinctly expresses Denise Levertov's outlook *in this moment in time.*

> These days—these years—
> when powers and principalities of death
> weigh down the world, deeper, deeper
> than we ever thought it could fall and still

keep slowly spinning,
Hope, caught under the jar's rim, crawls
like a golden fly
round and round, a sentinel:
it can't get out, it can't fly free
among our heavy hearts—
but does not die, keeps up its pace,
pausing only as if to meditate
a saving strategy . . .

Notes

References to Denise Levertov are indicated by the initials "D. L."

Introduction. "Make truth real to us."

1. Ralph Waldo Emerson, "The Poet," in *Selections from Ralph Waldo Emerson*, ed. Stephen E. Whicher (Boston: Houghton-Mifflin, 1957), 239–40.
2. Emerson. "The American Scholar," *Selections*, 80.
3. D. L., Letter to author, 19 July 1988.
4. D. L., Interview with author, 9 October 1982.
5. Emerson, *Selections*, 225.
6. William Carlos Williams, "Transcriptions by John Thirlwall" in *Interviews*, ed. Linda Wagner (New York: New Directions, 1976), 40.
7. Jeffrey Walsh, "'After Our War': John Balaban's Poetic Images of Vietnam," *Vietnam Images: War and Representation*, eds. Jeffrey Walsh and James Aulich (New York: Macmillan, 1989), 45.
8. Ezra Pound, "Hugh Selwyn Mauberly," *Selected Poems of Ezra Pound* (New York: New Directions, 1957), 63.
9. D. L., Interview with author, 19 October 1982.
10. D. L., *Cave*, 131.
11. D. L., *Cave*, 60.
12. Ezra Pound, *ABC of Reading* (New York: New Directions, 1960), 66.

Chapter 1. A Portrait of the Artist in the Twentieth Century: "As never before . . ."

1. Emma Lazarus, "The New Colossus," Inscription on the Statue of Liberty, New York.
2. W. B. Yeats, "The Second Coming," in *Selected Poems and Two Plays of William Butler Yeats*, ed. M. L. Rosenthal (New York: Collier Books, 1961), 91.
3. William Carlos Williams, "To Elsie," in *The Collected Earlier Poems* (New York: New Directions, 1966), 270.
4. M. L. Rosenthal, *The New Poets: American and British Poetry since World War II* (New York and London: Oxford University Press, 1967), 80.
5. John Dos Passos, quoted in Andrew Hook, *Modern Culture and the Arts* (New York: McGraw Hill, 1967), 204.
6. Hook, *Modern Culture*, 205.
7. Ezra Pound, "Hugh Selwyn Mauberly," *Selected Poems*, 63–67.
8. Rosenthal, *The New Poets*, 111.
9. *The Humanities: Cultural Roots and Continuities*, vol. 1 (Lexington, Mass. and Toronto: D.C. Heath, 1985), Mary A. Witt, ed., 361.

10. Pablo Neruda, quoted by D. L. in *Cave*, 131.
11. Francis Fitzgerald, *Fire In The Lake* (Boston: Little, Brown, 1972), 429.
12. Albert Camus, in *Humanities*, 376.
13. Rosenthal, *The New Poets*, 184–92.
14. D. L., *Poet*, 3.
15. D. L., *Poet*, 5.
16. D. L., "Author's Preface," in *To Stay Alive*, ix.
17. John Balaban, *The Washington Post*, 12 January 1990.

Chapter 2. The Poet and the Poem: "What lies at hand"

1. D. L., *Poet*, 7–14 ff.
2. D. L., *Poet*, 14.
3. David Ossman, "An Interview with D. Levertov," *The Sullen Art* (New York: Corinth Books, 1963), 75–76.
4. D. L., *Poet*, 70.
5. Ibid., 7.
6. Ibid., 3.
7. D. L., *Poet*, 54.
8. Ibid., 63.
9. D. L., *Cave*, 127.
10. D. L., *The Bloodaxe Book of Contemporary Women Poets*, ed. Jeni Couzyn (Newcastle Upon Tyne: Bloodaxe Books, 1985), 78–79.
11. D. L., *Cave*, 241.
12. Richard Howard, "Denise Levertov." *Tri-Quarterly*, no. 7 (Fall 1966): 197.
13. Ibid., 133–43.
14. D. L., *Cave*, 241.
15. D. L., *Poet*, 80 ff.
16. D. L., Interview with author, 9 December 1988.
17. D. L., Letter to Bill Burford, Boxing Day, 1965 ff.
18. D. L., *Cave*, 60 ff.
19. D. L., *Poet*, 3.
20. Ibid., 52.
21. Ibid., 105.
22. Ibid., 106.
23. Ibid., 123–24.
24. D. L., *Cave*, 126–28.
25. William Packard, "Craft Interview with Denise Levertov," *New York Quarterly*, v. 7 (1974): 97.
26. D. L., "Author's Preface," *To Stay Alive*.
27. Thomas F. Merrill, *The Poetry of Charles Olson, A Primer* (Newark: University of Delaware Press, 1982), 44.
28. Robert Frost, "Birches," in *Robert Frost: Poetry and Prose*. ed. Edward Connery Lathem and Lawrance Thompson, (New York: Holt, Rinehart & Winston, 1952), 55.
29. D. L., *The Bloodaxe Book*, 37.
30. William Beidler, *American Literature and the Experience of Vietnam* (Athens: University of Georgia, 1982), 71.
31. Paul Breslin, "Black Mountain: A Critique of the Curriculum," *Poetry*, 136, no. 4 (1980): 219–39.

32. Cary Nelson, "Levertov's Political Poetry," in *Denise Levertov: In Her Own Province*, ed. Linda Wagner (New York: New Directions, 1979), 131–35.

33. James F. Mersmann, *Out of the Vortex: A Study of Poets and Poetry Against the War* (Lawrence: Lawrence University Press, 1974), 102–11.

34. Charles Altieri, *Enlarging the Temple* (Lewisburg: Bucknell, 1979), 225–55 ff.

35. D. L., *Cave*, 60.

36. Peter Middleton, *Revelation and Revolution in the Poetry of Denise Levertov* (London: Binnacle, 1981), 1–17.

37. D. L., *Poet*, 17.

38. Ibid., 114.

39. Middleton, *Revelation and Revolution*, 14.

40. Samuel B. Charters, "Charles Olson," in *Studies in American Underground Poetry since 1945, Some Poems/ Poets* (Berkeley: Oyez, 1971), 21–35.

41. Robert Creeley, "Charles Olson: 'The Maximus Poems, 1–10'," *A Quick Graph: Collected Notes and Essays, In the U.S.A.* (San Francisco: Four Seasons Foundation, 1970), 157–58.

42. Ann Charters, *Olson/Melville: A Study in Affinity* (Berkeley: Oyez, 1968).

43. Louis Simpson, *The New York Times Book Review*, 28 December (1969): 12, 18.

44. Ralph Mills, *Contemporary American Poetry* (New York: Random House, 1985), 176–96.

45. Todd Gitlin, "The Return of Political Poetry," *Commonweal* 3 (1971): 75–78.

46. Walter Sutton, *American Free Verse: The Modern Revolution In Poetry* (New York: New Directions, 1973), 210.

47. Julian Gitzen, "From Reverence to Attention: The Poetry of Denise Levertov," *The Midwest Review* (1975): 330, 340.

48. Susan Hoerchner, "Denise Levertov," *Contemporary Literature* 15, no. 3, (1974): 437.

49. Joan F. Hallisey, "Walt Whitman, Hart Crane, and Denise Levertov: Poets/ Prophets in the Tradition of Ralph Waldo Emerson," Dissertation, Brown University, 1978, 2–6.

50. Kenneth Rexroth, *American Poetry in the Twentieth Century* (New York: Herder & Herder, 1971), 163.

51. D. L., Letter (salutation missing). January 1961.

52. Jerome Mazzaro, "Denise Levertov's Political Poetry," in *Essays On Denise Levertov*, ed. Linda Wagner-Martin (Boston: G. K. Hall & Co., 1991), 172–87.

Chapter 3. Early Poems of "Awareness": "Westward through danger to the shores of peace."

1. C. M. Bowra, *The Romantic Imagination* (New York: Oxford University Press, 1961), 6.

2. Samuel Taylor Coleridge, *Biographia Literaria I*, ed. John Shawcross (Oxford: Oxford University Press, 1907), 95.

3. Bowra, *The Romantic Imagination*, 12.

4. Robert Frost, "The Lesson for Today," in *Robert Frost: Poetry and Prose* (New York: Holt, Rinehart & Winston, 1969), 146–50.

5. Bowra, *Romantic*, 110.

6. D. L., *Cave*, 126.

7. Robert Browning, "Songs from *Pippa Passes*," *The Victorian Age*, ed. John Wilson Bowyer and John Lee Brooks (New York: F. S. Crofts, 1941), 264.

8. D. L., Interview with author, 9 October 1982.

9. Ibid.

10. Ibid.

11. D. L., Interview with author, 10 December 1988.

12. Ibid.

13. Martin Buber, *Tales of the Hasidim: Later Masters*, tr. Olga Marx, 1948, quoted by Levertov in *The Jacob's Ladder*.

14. D. L., Interview with author, 10 December 1988.

15. Ibid.

16. D. L., Note, "The Peachtree" in *The Jacob's Ladder*, 65.

Chapter 4. Vietnam and the Sixties: "La selva oscura"

1. Edward Keynes, Quotation from Justice Grier's "Opinion," in *The Prize Cases*, 67, U.S. 635,669 (1863), *Undeclared War: Twilight Zone of Constitutional Power* (University Park: Pennsylvania State University Press, 1982), 110 ff.

2. William Eastlake, *The Bamboo Bed* (New York: Simon & Schuster, 1969).

3. Walter McDonald, in *Carrying the Darkness: American Indo-China—the Poetry of Vietnam*, ed. William Daniel Ehrhart (Lubbock: Texas Tech University, 1989).

4. William Ehrhart, *Carrying the Darkness*.

5. Oliver Stone, statement made at Academy Awards Presentation, 1990.

6. Adrienne Rich, "Three Conversations. (1974)" *Adrienne Rich's Poetry* (New York: Norton, 1974), 111.

7. William Packard, D. L. Interview, "Craft Interview with Denise Levertov," *The New York Quarterly* 7 (1974): 94.

8. Nancy Condee, "American Poetry and the Political Statement: An Overview of the Sixties and the Seventies," *Zeitschrift Fur Anglistik Und Amerikanistik* ed. Eberhart Bruning et al. Leipzig, East Germany, 30, no. 3 (1982): 232–43.

9. D. L., "Olga Poems," *The Sorrow Dance*, 60.

10. D. L., "Great Possessions," Lecture, 1970, for "Arts, Religion, and Contemporary Culture," New York, in *Poet*, 99, 106.

11. William Shakespeare, "Hamlet," *William Shakespeare: The Complete Works*, ed. by Charles Jasper Sisson (London: Odhams Press Limited, 1953), 1013.

12. D. L., "On Responsibility to the Self Versus Responsibility to the Community," in *Denise Levertov: In Her Own Province*, ed. Linda Wagner (New York: New Directions, 1979), 65.

13. James F. Mersmann, *Out of the Vietnam Vortex: A Study of Poets and Poetry Against the War* (Lawrence: University Press of Kansas, 1974), 77–79.

14. D. L., *Cave*, 96.

15. Marjorie Perloff, "Beyond the *Bell Jar:* Women Poets in Transition," *South Carolina Review*, 11, no. 2 (Spring 1979): 4–11.

16. Susan Hoerchner, "Denise Levertov," *Contemporary Literature* 3 (1974): 435–7.

17. D. L., "Statement on Poetics," in *The New American Poetry, 1945–60*, edited by Donald M. Allen (New York: Grove Press, 1960), 412.

18. D. L., "On The Edge of Darkness: What is Political Poetry?" *Cave*, 128.

19. T. S. Eliot, "The Waste-Land," *The Complete Poems and Plays, 1909–1950* (New York: Harcourt, Brace & World, 1952), 38.

20. William Packard, "Craft Interview with Denise Levertov," *The New York Quarterly*, Ed. William Packard, 96–97.

21. Packard, "Craft Interview," 98.

22. Charles Altieri, *Enlarging the Temple: New Directions in American Poetry in the '60's* (Lewisburg: Bucknell, 1979), 228–29.

23. Ibid.

24. T. S. Eliot, "East Coker, *The Complete Poems and Plays*, 127.

25. Robert Frost, "Directive," in *Robert Frost. Poetry & Prose*, edited by Edward Connery Lathem and Lawrance Thompson (New York: Holt, Rinehart & Winston, 1969), 156–57.

26. Herman Zimmer, Epigraph to "Relearning the Alphabet," 110.

27. D. L., "Writers Take Sides in Vietnam, 1966," *Poet*, 119.

28. William Carlos Williams, *Paterson*, 3 (New York: New Directions, 1963); *Spring & All* in *Selected Poems*, (New York: New Directions, 1969), 28 ff.

29. T. S. Eliot, "Little Gidding," *The Complete Poems and Plays*, 135.

30. D. L., "Preface," *Alive*, ix ff.

31. D. L., "Notes," *Alive*, 85.

32. Cary Nelson, "Levertov's Political Poetry," *Denise Levertov: In Her Own Province*, 131.

33. Hayden Carruth, Review of *The Poet in the World* and *To Stay Alive*, *The Hudson Review*, 27, 3 (Fall 1974): 475–80.

34. D. L., *Cave*, 128.

35. D. L., "Notes," *Footprints*, 58.

Chapter 5. Poems of the Seventies: Echoes and Footprints

1. D. L., *Poet*, 49.

2. T. S. Eliot, "Preludes," *The Complete Poems and Plays, 1909–1950* (New York: Harcourt, Brace & World, 1952), 13.

3. D. L., *Poet*, 106.

4. D. L., "Notes," *Footprints*, 58.

5. James Joyce, "The Dead," *Dubliners* (New York: Viking, 1962), 224.

6. D. L., "Notes," *Footprints*, 58.

7. Olga Levertoff, "The Ballad of my Father," *The Sorrow Dance*, 94.

8. W. R. Evans, *Best Sellers* 35 (February 1976): 349.

9. G. K. Harris, *Library Journal* 100 (14–21 Aug. 1976): 554.

10. David Ignatow, *The New York Times Book Review* (30 November 1975): 54–55.

11. See "Introduction," note #5.

12. Edna St. Vincent Millay, "I Being Born A Woman and Distressed," in *Collected Poems* (New York: Harper and Bros., 1956), 601.

13. Ignatow, 54–55.

14. Richard Howard, "Denise Levertov," *Alone with America: Essays on the Art of Poetry in the U.S.A. since 1950* (New York: Atheneum, 1969), 305.

15. Ibid.

16. Harry Marten, *Understanding Denise Levertov* (Columbia: University of South Carolina Press, 1988), 134.

17. Ibid., 132.

18. D. L., *Poet*, 14.

19. Cary Nelson, "Levertov's Political Poetry," in *Denise Levertov: In Her Own Province* (New York: New Directions, 1979), 133 ff.

20. William Carlos Williams, *Paterson* (New York: New Directions, 1963), 11.

21. Ibid., 18.

22. D. L., *Poet*, 7.

23. Harry Marten, Review of *Life in the Forest* in *New England Review and Breadloaf Quarterly 2* (Autumn 1979): 162–64.

24. D. L., "Note" in *Life in the Forest*, 66.

25. Marten, Review of *Life in the Forest*, 162–64.

26. Williams, *Paterson*, 53.

27. D. L., Interview with author, 9 October 1982.

28. Ibid.

Chapter 6. Recent Poetry: Lighting Candles in Babylon

1. W. C. Williams, *Paterson* (New York: New Directions, 1963), 239.

2. D. L., quoted by Harry Marten, *Understanding Denise Levertov* (Columbia: University of South Carolina Press, 1988), 161.

3. Ibid.

4. D. L., *Poet*, 47.

5. D. L., Interview with author, 10 December 1988.

6. Ibid.

7. D. L., quoted by Marten in *Understanding D. Levertov*.

8. D. L., Interview with author, 9 October 1982.

9. Monroe Spears, *Dionysus and the City: Modernism in Twentieth Century Poetry* (New York: Oxford University Press, 1970), 25–26.

10. Liana Sakelliou-Schultz, *Denise Levertov: An Annotated Primary and Secondary Bibliography* (New York: Garland, 1988), 42.

11. Marten, *Understanding D. Levertov*, 164.

12. D. L., Interview with author, 9 October 1982.

13. D. L., Interview with author, 10 December 1988.

14. D. L., Interview with author, 9 October 1982.

15. D. L., Interview with author, 10 December 1988.

16. Williams, *Paterson II: 2*.

17. William Packard, "Craft Interview with Denise Levertov," *The New York Quarterly* V. 7 (1974): 99.

18. D. L., "With the Seabrook National Guard in Washington, 1978," in *Cave*, 162 ff.

19. D. L., Interview with author, 10 October 1982.

20. Ibid.

21. Marten, *Understanding*, 162.

22. Packard, Craft Interview, 20.

23. D. L., Interview with author, 10 December 1988.

24. D. L., Interview with author, 10 October 1982.

25. Marten, *Understanding*, 167.

26. Ibid., 169.

27. D. L., Interview with author, 10 December 1988.

28. Dame Julian Norwich, quoted by T. S. Eliot in "Little Gidding," *Four Quartets*, in *The Complete Poems and Plays*.

29. D. L., *Cave*, 290.

30. D. L., Letter to Bill Burford, 1969.

31. D. L., *Poet*, 174.

32. Ibid., 112.

33. D. L., quoted in *Poet* from a letter by Rilke to Gertrude Oukama Knoop, 113.

34. D. L., *Poet*, 109.

35. D. L., Interview with author, 10 December 1988.

36. D. L., "Note 40," *Breathing the Water*, 85.

37. D. L., Interview with author, 10 October 1982.

38. W. H. Auden, "Inaugurating the Ewing Lectures at the University of California, 3 and 5 Oct. 1956," published as a pamphlet at University of California Press, Berkeley and Los Angeles, 1958.

39. D. L., *Poet*, 112.

40. Ibid., 290.

41. D. L., "Notes" to *A Door in the Hive*, 109–10.

42. Ibid., 109.

43. Ibid., 110.

44. Ibid.

Works by Denise Levertov

A Door in the Hive. New York: New Directions, 1989. *(Hive)*

"The Arena Where We Fight," *The Nation* 197, no. 21 (December 1963): 440–41.

Breathing the Water. New York: New Directions, 1987. *(Breathing)*

Candles in Babylon. New York: New Directions, 1982. *(Candles)*

Collected Earlier Poems, 1940–1960. New York: New Directions, 1979. (CEP)

"Denise Levertov Writes." *The Bloodaxe Book of Contemporary Women Poets.* Edited by Jeni Couzyn. Newcastle Upon Tyne: Bloodaxe Books, 1985.

The Double Image. London: The Cresset Press, 1946. *(Image)*

Footprints. New York: New Directions, 1972. *(Footprints)*

The Freeing of the Dust. New York: New Directions, 1975. *(Dust)*

Here and Now. The Pocket Poet Series: Number Six. San Francisco: City Lights Pocket Book Shop, 1956. *(H&N)*

The Jacob's Ladder. New York: New Directions, 1961. *(Ladder)*

Letter (no salutation), 1961. Univ. of Texas. The Humanities Research Center.

Letter to author, 19 July 1988.

Letter to William Burford, 1965. University of Texas. The Humanities Research Center.

Life in the Forest. New York: New Directions, 1978. *(Forest)*

Light Up the Cave. New York: New Directions, 1981. *(Cave)*

Modulations for Solo Voice. San Francisco: Five Tree Press, 1977.

Oblique Prayers: New Poems with 14 Translations from Jean Joubert. New York: New Directions, 1984. *(Prayers)*

O Taste and See. New York: New Directions, 1964. *(Taste)*

Overland to the Islands. Highlands: Jonathon Williams, Publisher, 1958. *(Islands)*

Pig Dreams: Scenes from the Life of Sylvia. Woodstock, Vermont: The Countryman Press, 1981. *(Pig Dreams)*

Poems 1960–1967. New York: New Directions, 1983. *(PS:60–67)*

Poems 1968–1972. New York: New Directions, 1987. *(PS:68–72)*

The Poet in the World. New York: New Directions, 1973. *(Poet)*

Relearning the Alphabet. New York: New Directions, 1970. *(Alph)*

Selected Poems (of Eugene Gullevic). Translated by D. L. New York: New Directions, 1969 *(GSP)*

The Sorrow Dance. New York: New Directions, 1967. *(Dance)*

"Statement on Poetics." *The New American Poetry 1945–1960.* Edited by Donald M. Allen. New York: Grove Press, 1960.

To Stay Alive. New York: New Directions, 1971. *(Alive)*

With Eyes at the Back of Our Heads. New York: New Directions, 1960. *(Eyes)*

Select Bibliography

Aiken, William. "Levertov, Robert Duncan, and Allen Ginsberg: Modes of the Self in Projective Poetry." *Modern Poetry Studies* 10, no. 2–3 (1981): 200–245.

Apocalypse Now. United Artists. Francis Ford Coppola, 1979.

Altieri, Charles. *Enlarging the Temple: New Directions in American Poetry During the 60's.* Lewisburg: Bucknell, 1979.

———. "From Experience to Discourse: American Poetry and Poetics in the Seventies." *Contemporary Literature* 21, no. 2 (1980): 191–224.

———. "From Symbolist Thought to Immanence: The Ground of Postmodern American Poetics." *Boundary Two*, nos. 1, 3 (Spring 1973): 605–41.

Arendt, Hannah. *Cries of the Republic.* New York: Harcourt, Brace, Jovanovich, 1922.

Auden, W. H. "Inaugurating the Ewing Lectures at the University of California, October 3 and 5, 1956." Pamphlet. Berkeley and Los Angeles: University of California Press, 1958.

Baker, Richard E. *Feast of Epiphany.* Tacoma: Rapier Press, 1981.

———. *Shell Burst Pond.* Tacoma: Rapier Press, 1980.

Balaban, John. *After Our War.* Pittsburgh: University of Pittsburgh Press, 1974.

———. *Vietnam Poems.* Oxford: Carcanet Press, 1970.

Barbusse, Henri. *Under Fire (Le Feu).* Translated by F. Wray. New York: E. P. Dutton, 1917.

Beidler, Philip D. *American Literature and the Experience of Vietnam.* Athens: University of Georgia, 1982.

Belanger, Charles A. "Once Upon a Time When It Was Night." *Angels in My Oven.* Edited by John Schulz. Chicago: Columbia College Press, 1976.

Berlandt, Herman and Neeli Cherkovski, eds. *Peace Or Perish: A Crisis Anthology.* Fort Mason Center, S.F. 94123: Poets for Peace, 1988.

Bowra, C. M. *The Romantic Imagination.* New York: Oxford University Press, 1961.

Breslin, James E. B. "Denise Levertov." In *From Modern to Contemporary.* Chicago: The University of Chicago Press, 1984.

Breslin, Paul. "Black Mountain: A Critique of the Curriculum." *Poetry* 136, no. 4 (1980): 219–39.

Brown, Corinne. *Body Shop.* New York: Stein & Day, 1973.

Brown, John Russell, ed. "Criticism and Poetry." In *American Poetry*, 175–96. New York: St. Martin's Press, 1965.

Browning, Frank and Dorothy Forman. *The Wasted Nations.* New York: Harper, Colophon Books, 1972.

Browning, Robert. "Songs from *Pippa Passes.*" In *The Victorian Age*, 264. Edited by John Wilson Bowyer and John Lee Brooks. New York: F. S. Crofts, 1941.

Buber, Martin. "The Ladder." In *Tales of the Hasidim: The Later Masters*. Translated by Olga Marx. New York: Schocken Books, 1948.

Carruth, Hayden. "Levertov." Review of *The Poet in the World and To Stay Alive*, by Denise Levertov. *The Hudson Review* 27, no. 3 (Fall 1974): 475–80.

Charters, Ann. *Olson and Melville: A Study in Affinity*. Berkeley: Oyez, 1968.

Charters, Samuel B. *Studies in American Underground Poetry Since 1945, Some Poems/ Poets*. Photos by Ann Charters. Berkeley: Oyez, 1971.

Chomsky, Noam. *At War with Asia*. New York: Pantheon, 1970.

Coleridge, Samuel Taylor. *Biographia Literaria. I*. Edited by J. Shawcross. Oxford: Oxford University Press, 1907.

———. *Princeton Encyclopedia of Poetry and Poetics*. Edited by Alex Preminger. Princeton: Princeton University Press, 1972.

Coming Home. MGM-United Artists. Hal Ashby, 1978.

Condee, Nancy. "American Poetry and the Political Statement: An Overview of the Sixties and Seventies." *Zeitschrift Fur Anglistik Und Amerikanistik*. Edited by Eberhart Bruning, et al. Leipzig, East Germany, 30, no. 3 (1982): 232–43.

Corson, William R. *Consequences of Failure*. New York: Norton, 1973.

Crane, Stephen. *The Red Badge of Courage*. New York: Holt, Rinehart & Winston, 1964.

Creeley, Robert. *American Poets in 1976*. Edited by William Heyen. Indianapolis: Bobbs-Merrill, 1976.

———. "Charles Olson: The Maximus Poems '(1–10)'." In *A Quick Graph: Collected Notes and Essays in the U.S.A.*, 157–58. San Francisco: Four Seasons Foundation, 1970

The Deer Hunter. United Artists. Oliver Stone, 1986.

Del Vecchio, John. *The Thirteenth Valley*. Toronto: Bantam, 1982.

DuPlessis, Rachel Blau. "The Critique of Consciousness and Myth in Levertov, Rich, and Rukeyser." *Feminist Studies* 3, no. 1–2 (Fall 1975): 199–221.

Eastlake, William. *The Bamboo Bed*. New York: Simon & Schuster, 1969.

Ehrhart, William Daniel. *Carrying the Darkness, the Poetry of Vietnam*. Edited by William Daniel Ehrhart. Lubbock: Texas Tech University Press, 1989.

Ehrhart, W. D. *The Awkward Silence*. Stafford, Va.: Northwood Press, 1980.

Eliot, T. S. "Four Quartets." In *T. S. Eliot: The Complete Poems and Plays, 1909–1950*, 117–38. New York: Harcourt, Brace, & World, 1952.

———. "The Metaphysical Poets." In *Selected Essays*, 241–50. New York: Harcourt, Brace & Co. 1950.

———. "The Music of Poetry." In *On Poetry and Poets*, 17–33. New York: The Noonday Press, 1961.

———. "Preludes." In *T. S. Eliot: The Complete Poems and Plays*, 12.

———. "Tradition and the Individual Talent." In *The Sacred Wood*, 47–59. London: Methuen & Co Ltd, 1920.

———. "The Waste-Land." In *Complete Poems*, 37–50.

Emerson, Ralph Waldo. "The American Scholar." In *Selections from Ralph Waldo Emerson*, edited by Stephen E. Whicher, 63–80. Boston: Houghton Mifflin, Riverside Ed., 1957.

———. "The Poet." In *Selections*, 222–41.

Evans, W. R. Review of *The Freeing of the Dust*. *Best Sellers* 35 (February 1976): 349.

Fitzgerald, F. Scott. *Tender Is The Night*. New York: Scribner, 1933.

Fitzgerald, Francis. *Fire in the Lake*. Boston: Little, Brown, 1972.

Frost, Robert. "The Figure A Poem Makes." In *Robert Frost. Poetry and Prose*, edited by Edward Connery Lathem and Lawrance Thompson, 393–96. New York: Holt, Rinehart & Winston, 1969.

———. "The Lesson for Today." In *Robert Frost. Poetry and Prose*, edited by Edward Connery Lathem and Lawrance Thompson, 471–76. New York: Holt, Rinehart & Winston, 1969.

Full Metal Jacket. Warner Bros. Stanley Kubrick, 1987.

Gelpi, Albert. "The Uses of Language." Review of *O Taste and See*. *The Southern Review* 3 (Autumn 1967): 1024–35.

Gilbert, Sandra M. "'My Name Is Darkness': The Poetry of Self-Definition." *Contemporary Literature* 18, no. 4 (1977): 443–57.

———. "Revolutionary Love: Denise Levertov and the Poetics of Politics." *Parnassus: Poetry in Review* 12, no. 2 (1985): 335–51.

Gitlin, Todd. "The Return of Political Poetry." *Commonweal: A Weekly Review of Public Affairs, Literature, and the Arts* 94, no. 16 (23 July 1971): 375–78.

Gitzen, Julian. "From Reverence to Attention: The Poetry of Denise Levertov." *Midwest Quarterly: A Journal of Contemporary Thought* 16, no. 3 (April 1975): 328–41.

Good Morning, Vietnam! Touchstone Films. Rollins, Moira, & Brezner, 1987.

Gubar, Susan. "The Blank Page and the Issues of Female Creativity." *Critical Inquiry* 8, no. 2 (Winter 1981): 243–63.

Guibert, Rita. "Interview with Denise Levertov." In *Light Up the Cave*, 131.

Halberstam, David. *One Very Hot Day*. Boston: Houghton-Mifflin, 1967.

Hallisey, Joan F. "Denise Levertov's 'Illustrious Ancestors': The Hassidic Influence." *Melus* 9, no. 4 (Winter 1982): 5–11.

———. "Walt Whitman, Hart Crane, and Denise Levertov: Poets/Prophets in the Tradition of Ralph Waldo Emerson." Diss., Brown University, 1978.

Harris, G. K. Review of *The Freeing of the Dust*, by Denise Levertov. *Library Journal* 100 (1 September 1975): 1554.

Hartke, Vance. *The American Crisis in Vietnam*. Indianapolis: Bobbs, Merrill Co., 1968.

Hemingway, Ernest. *A Farewell to Arms*. New York: Scribner, 1929.

Hersh, Seymour. *My Lai 4: Report of the Massacre and Its Aftermath*. New York: Random House, 1970.

Higgins, Marguerite. *Our Vietnam Nightmare*. New York: Harper & Row, 1965.

Hoerchner, Susan. "Denise Levertov." *Contemporary Literature* 15, no. 3 (1974): 435–47.

Hoffman, Daniel. "Schools of Dissidents." In *Harvard Guide to Contemporary American Writing*, edited by Daniel Hoffman, 533–36. Cambridge, Mass.: The Belknap Press of Harvard University Press, 1979.

Hook, Andrew. "Commitment and Reality." In *Modern Culture and the Arts*, edited by James B. Hall and Barry Ulanov, 204–9. New York: McGraw-Hill, 1967.

Howard, Richard. *Alone in America: Essays on the Art of Poetry in the United States since 1950* New York: Atheneum, 1969.

Hughes, Langston. "Lenox Avenue Mural." In *American Negro Poetry*, edited by Arna Bontemps, 67–70. New York: Hill & Wang, 1963.

Ignatow, David. Review of *The Freeing of the Dust*, by Denise Levertov. *The New York Times Book Review* 30 (November 1975): 54–55.

———. "Williams' Influence: Some Social Aspects." *Chelsea 14* (January 1964): 154–61.

Joyce, James. "The Dead." In *Dubliners*. New York: Viking, 1962.

Juhasz, Suzanne. *Naked and Fiery Forms: Modern American Poetry by Women: A New Tradition*. New York: Harper Colophon Books, 1976.

Kalb, Marvin and Elie Abel. *Roots of Involvement: The U.S. in Asia 1784–1971*. New York: Norton, 1971.

Keynes, Edward. *Undeclared War: Twilight Zone of Constitutional Power*. University Park: Pennsylvania State University Press, 1982.

Lacey, Paul A. *The Inner War: Forms and Themes in Recent American Poetry*. Philadelphia: Fortress, 1972.

———. "The Poetry of Political Anguish." *Sagetrieb* 4, no. 1 (Spring 1985): 61–71.

Lazarus, Emma. "The New Colossus." Inscription on the Statue of Liberty, New York Harbor, N.Y.

Lazer, Hank. "In Defense of American Poetry." *Ohio Review* 20, no. 3 (1980): 9–22.

Lifton, Robert Jay, Ed. *America and the Asian Revolutions*. New York: Aldine, 1970.

Lowell, Robert. "The Dead in Europe." In *Chief Modern Poets of Britain and America, II: America*, edited by Gerald De Witt Sanders, John Herbert Nelson, and M. L. Rosenthal, 412–13. 5th ed. New York: Macmillan, 1970.

Lowenfels, Walter, et al., Ed. *Where Is Vietnam?* Garden City, N.Y.: Anchor, 1967.

Luce, Don and John Sommer, Eds. *The Unheard Voices*. Ithaca: Cornell University Press, 1969.

McCarthy, Mary. *The Seventeenth Degree*. New York: Harcourt, Brace, & Jovanovich, 1974.

———. *Vietnam*. New York: Harcourt, Brace & World, 1967.

McDonald, Walter. "Lebowitz." *RE: Artes Liberales* 3, no. 1, 1976.

McKay, Claude. "If We Must Die." In *American Negro Poetry*, edited by Arna Bontemps, 31. New York: Hill & Wang, 1963.

Marten, Harry. Review of *Life in the Forest*. *New England Review and Bread Loaf Quarterly* 2 (Autumn 1970), 162–64.

———. *Understanding Denise Levertov*. Columbia: University of South Carolina Press, 1988.

Mazzaro, Jerome. "Denise Levertov's Political Poetry." In *Critical Essays on Denise Levertov*, edited by Linda Wagner-Martin, 172–87. Boston: G. K. Hall, 1991.

Merrill, Thomas F. *The Poetry of Charles Olson: A Primer*. Newark: University of Delaware Press, 1982.

Mersmann, James F. *Out of the Vietnam Vortex: A Study of Poets and Poetry Against the War*. Lawrence: University Press of Kansas, 1974.

Middleton, Peter. *Revelation and Revolution in the Poetry of Denise Levertov*. London: Binnacle, 1981.

Millay, Edna Saint Vincent. "I Being Born a Woman and Distressed." In *Collected Poems*, 601. New York: Harper & Bros. 1956.

Mills, Ralph J. Jr. *Contemporary American Poetry*. New York: Random House, 1965.

————. "Creation's Very Self: On the Personal Element in Recent American Poetry," In *Cry of the Human; Essays on Contemporary American Poetry*. Urbana: University of Illinois Press, 1975, 1–47.

Nelson, Cary. "Levertov's Political Poetry." In *Denise Levertov: In Her Own Province*, edited by Linda Wagner, 131–53. New York: New Directions, 1979.

Nelson, Rudolph Laurens. "Edge of the Transcendent: The Poetry of Levertov and Duncan." *Southwest Review* 54, no. 2 (Spring 1969): 188–202.

Nemerov, Howard. *Reflexions on Poetry and Politics*. New Brunswick, N.J.: Rutgers University Press, 1972.

Newman, John. *Vietnam War Literature: An Annotated Bibliography of Imaginative Works About Americans Fighting in Vietnam*. Metuchen and London: Scarecrow Press, 1982, 1988.

Ossman, David. "An Interview with Denise Levertov." In *The Sullen Art*, 73–76. New York: Corinth Books, 1963.

Packard, William, ed. "Craft Interview with Denise Levertov." *The New York Quarterly* 7 (1974): 79–100.

Perloff, Marjorie. "Beyond *The Bell Jar:* Women Poets in Transition." *South Carolina Review* 11, no. 2 (Spring 1979): 4–16.

Platoon. Orion Pictures. Oliver Stone, 1986.

A Poetry Reading Against the Vietnam War. Edited by Robert Bly and David Ray. Madison, Minn.: The Sixties Press, 1966.

Pound, Ezra. *ABC of Reading*. New York: New Directions, 1960.

————. "Hugh Selwyn Mauberly." In *Selected Poems of Ezra Pound*, 61–77. New York: New Directions, 1957.

————. *Make It New*. New York: New Directions, 1960.

Review of *Vietnam Poems*, by John Balaban. *New York Herald Tribune*, 12 February 1971.

Rexroth, Kenneth. *American Poetry in the Twentieth Century*. New York: Herder & Herder, 1971.

————. "Bearded Barbarians or Real Bard?" *New York Times Book Review*, 12 February 1961, 1.

Rich, Adrienne. "Three Conversations (1974)." In *Adrienne Rich's Poetry*. Selected and edited by Barbara C. Gelpi and Albert Gelpi. New York: Norton, 105–22.

Rodgers, Audrey. Interviews with Denise Levertov: 9–10 October 1982 and 10 December 1988.

Rosenfeld, Alvin H. "'The Being of Language and the Language of Being': Heidigger and Modern Poetics." *Boundary Two* 4 (Winter 1976): 535–53.

Rosenthal, Macha Louis. *The Modern Poets: A Critical Introduction*. New York: Oxford University Press, 1960.

————. *The New Poets: American and British Poetry Since World War II*. New York and London: Oxford University Press, 1967.

Sakelliou-Schultz, Liana. *Denise Levertov: An Annotated Primary and Secondary Bibliography*. New York: Garland, 1988.

Schlesinger, Arthur Jr. *The Bitter Heritage: 1914–1966*. Boston: Houghton-Mifflin, 1967.

Schoenbrun, David. *Vietnam, How We Got In, How We Got Out*. New York: Atheneum, 1968.

Shakespeare, William. *William Shakespeare: The Complete Works*. Edited by Charles Jasper Sisson. London: Odhams Press Limited, 1953.

Shaw, Robert, Ed. *American Poetry Since 1960: Some Critical Perspectives*. Cheadle, England: Carcanet Press, 1973.

Shelley, Percy Bysshe. "England in 1819." In *The Norton Anthology*, 669. New York: W. W. Norton, 1975.

Simpson, Louis. "Essay." *The New York Times Book Review* 28 (December 1959): 12–18.

Slaughter, William. *The Imagination's Tongue: Denise Levertov's Poetic*. Portree: Aquilla, 1981.

Smith, David. *Local Essays: On Contemporary American Poetry*. Urbana: University of Illinois Press, 1985.

Spears, Monroe K. *Dionysus and the City: Modernism in Twentieth Century Poetry*. New York: Oxford University Press, 1970.

Stromberg, Peter Leonard. "A Long War's Writing: American Novels About the Fighting in Vietnam while Americans Fought." Diss., University of Michigan, 1975.

Surnam, Diana. "Inside and Outside in the Poetry of Denise Levertov." *Critical Quarterly* 22, no. 1 (Spring 1980): 57–70.

Sutton, Walter. *American Free Verse: The Modern Revolution in Poetry*. New York: New Directions, 1973.

Trumbo, Dalton. *Johnny Got His Gun*. New York: Lippincott, 1959.

Valery, Paul. *The Art of Poetry*. New York: Houghton-Mifflin, 1939.

Wagner, Linda. *Denise Levertov*. New York: Twayne, 1967.

———. *Denise Levertov: In Her Own Province*. Edited by Linda W. Wagner. New York: New Directions, 1979.

———. *Critical Essays on Denise Levertov*. Edited by Linda Wagner-Martin. Boston: G. K. Hall & Co., 1991.

———. "Matters of the Here and Now." *The Nation* (22 June 1974): 795.

———. "Transcriptions by John Thirlwall of Conversations with William Carlos Williams." In *Interviews*. Edited by Linda Wagner. New York: New Directions, 1976.

Walsh, Jeffrey. "After Our War." In *Vietnam Images, War & Representation*. New York: Macmillan, 1989.

Williams, William Carlos. "Against the Weather." In *Selected Essays of William Carlos Williams*. New York: New Directions, 1939.

———. *Paterson*. New York: New Directions, 1963.

———. "To Elsie." In *Selected Poems*, 28–30. New York: New Directions, 1949.

Witt, Mary Ann Frese et al., Ed. *The Humanities: Cultural Roots and Continuities, Vol. II—the Humanities and the Modern World*. 2nd ed. Lexington, Mass. and Toronto: D. C. Heath, 1985.

Woodcock, George. "Pilgrimage of a Poet." *The New Leader* 57, no. 5 (4 March 1974), 19–20.

Wordsworth, William. "London, 1802." In *The Prelude with a Selection from the Shorter*

Poems, the Sonnets, the Recluse, and the Excursion, edited by Carlos Baker, 183. New York: Holt, Rinehart, & Winston, 1961.

Wright, James. "Gravity and Incantation." *The Minnesota Review* 2 (Spring 1962): 424–27.

Yeats, William Butler. "The Second Coming." In *Selected Poems and Two Plays of William Butler Yeats*, edited and with an introduction by M. L. Rosenthal, 91. New York: Collier Books, 1966.

Young, Philip. *Ernest Hemingway, A Reconsideration*. New York: Harbinger, 1966.

Zimmer, Heinrich. Untitled. In *Relearning the Alphabet*, 110. New York: New Directions, 1970.

Index: Poems by Denise Levertov

General Index